1999

THE ROAD TO NOWHERE

PRINCETON STUDIES IN AMERICAN POLITICS:
HISTORICAL, INTERNATIONAL, AND
COMPARATIVE PERSPECTIVES

IRA KATZNELSON, MARTIN SHEFTER, THEDA SKOCPOL, EDS.

THE ROAD TO NOWHERE

THE GENESIS OF PRESIDENT CLINTON'S
PLAN FOR HEALTH SECURITY

Jacob S. Hacker

PRINCETON UNIVERSITY PRESS   PRINCETON, NEW JERSEY

Copyright ©1997 by Princeton University Press
Published by Princeton University Press, 41 William Street,
Princeton, New Jersey 08540
In the United Kingdom: Princeton University Press,
Chichester, West Sussex
All Rights Reserved.

Library of Congress Cataloging-in-Publication Data
Hacker, Jacob S.
The road to nowhere : the genesis of President Clinton's
plan for health security / Jacob S. Hacker.
p. cm. — (Princeton studies in American politics)
Includes index.
ISBN: 0-691-04423-6 (alk. paper)
1. Health care reform—United States.
2. Managed care plans (medical care)—United States.
3. United States—Politics and government—1993–
I. Title. II. Series.
RA395.A3H33 1996
362.1'0973—dc20   96-8083

This book has been composed in Sabon

Princeton University Press books are printed
on acid-free paper and meet the guidelines
for permanence and durability of the Committee
on Production Guidelines for Book Longevity
of the Council on Library Resources
Printed in the United States of America

3 5 7 9 10 8 6 4

http://pup.princeton.edu

To the Memory of Walter, Richard, and Sarah

Contents

Preface

THE DEFEAT of President Bill Clinton's proposal for comprehensive health care reform stands out as one of the most dramatic reversals of political fortune since President Woodrow Wilson's ill-fated campaign on behalf of the League of Nations. Already, a horde of journalists and political scientists is scrambling through the historical rubble to understand why a presidential initiative with such apparent promise foundered so quickly and so completely. Although the failure of the president's reform proposal is one of the subjects of this book, the questions I address are broader and more basic—not why President Clinton's attempt to reform American medical care failed, but why he made that attempt in the first place and why it took the direction that it did. In particular, I examine how and why President Clinton came to champion the specific collection of policy ideas that was contained in the health care reform proposal he presented to Congress in 1993. This collection of ideas—a mixture of regulated competition and budgetary controls that I term the "liberal synthesis"—burst into the political spotlight during the 1992 presidential campaign and quickly became the subject of heated, if not particularly enlightening, debate. Understanding where these ideas came from, how they made their way into the Clinton campaign, and why Clinton embraced them is critical to understanding the political assumptions undergirding the president's reform effort and why they proved so disastrously wrong.

This book began as an attempt to explain a puzzling change in the terms of the health care reform debate that I observed during the 1992 presidential race. In early 1992, politicians and political commentators talked about national health care reform, but there was a sense that the prospects for reform remained uncertain and that the real debate was still years off. The reform plans that were being discussed most frequently— indeed, the only ones that seem to have been considered credible at the time—were the various employment-based plans grouped under the rubric of "play-or-pay" and supported by the Democratic leadership in both houses of Congress; the more far-reaching "single-payer" proposals for full-fledged, Canadian-style national health insurance; and the relatively incremental "tax-credit" plans supported by the Bush administration and congressional Republicans. By the end of the summer, however, as the likely outcome of the 1992 presidential election came into view, the terms of discourse shifted. Increasingly, the question among congressional Democrats was not whether reform would pass but when. More significant still, another approach to health care reform began receiving serious consideration: "managed competition." Democratic candidate Bill Clinton endorsed the approach in a special speech in September, and he and President Bush spent the last weeks of the campaign quarreling over who truly supported it. In the House of Representatives, a group of conservative Democrats led by Representative Jim Cooper of Tennessee introduced a health care reform bill entitled the "Managed Competition Act of 1992." In the Senate, a group of liberal Democrats promoted a very different version of managed competition and developed legislation of their own. Everyone, it seemed, wanted to be identified with this once-obscure reform design that the *New York Times* was lauding as "the best way to provide high-quality care to all Americans."[1]

I had thought the reasons for this shift would become clearer with the passage of time. In many ways, however, the puzzle only grew deeper. Most health policy specialists and political scientists, whatever their personal views about the political or technical feasibility of managed competition, seemed to accept the turn toward managed competition uncritically. They discussed the outstanding questions surrounding the approach and whether it had a better chance than other reform designs of being enacted. But surprisingly few explained why managed competition was suddenly the favored reform alternative, and if they did, they generally linked its emergence either to Clinton's election or to some random fluctuation in the political environment. I began to wonder if the rise of managed competition was really so self-evident or unfathomable. True, Clinton had endorsed the approach during the presidential campaign. But why had he chosen a reform alternative on the periphery of the national debate? Although there was clearly an important element of randomness governing the choice of alternatives for debate, a deeper process seemed to be at work as well. Moreover, I noticed that when politicians and policy experts spoke about managed competition, they were not all talking about the same thing. Deep disagreement about the meaning of managed competition lay just beneath the surface. What were the sources of this disagreement, and what would its consequences be?

To answer these questions, I began to delve more deeply into the scholarship on the making of American public policy. I soon discovered that many of my queries about this particular episode in American politics intersected with the concerns of a broader literature in political science. Although the body of research remains small, numerous political scientists have attempted to understand the process by which problems and policy proposals to address them become the subject of government consideration. Students of public affairs have long had a name for this process—"agenda setting"—but for many years they lacked a comprehensive theoretical framework for studying it. Then, in 1984, John Kingdon revitalized agenda-setting theory with a pathbreaking study based on extensive empirical research.[2] Kingdon's study was followed in 1993 by another ambitious work on the subject—Frank Baumgartner and Bryan Jones's *Agendas and Instability in American Politics*.[3] Both works developed novel indicators of the government agenda. Both offered broad generalizations about the process of agenda setting and the actors involved. And both explained how interactions among political leaders seeking public support, interest groups demanding favorable policy regimes, and strategic entrepreneurs hoping to incorporate their ideas into public policy can lead to the rapid redefinition of policy issues or the sudden emergence of new problems or proposals.

The literature on agenda setting confirmed what I had suspected. Far from being idiosyncratic, the sudden emergence of managed competition as a leading paradigm for health care reform reveals broader patterns in American politics—patterns that have become increasingly prominent over the last several decades but which, scattered across diverse policy areas and instances of policy innovation, rarely appear as clearly and in as close proximity to one another as they do in this particular case. Much of this book is therefore devoted to an exploration of the process by which managed competition moved onto the government agenda and became the cornerstone of President Clinton's reform proposal. I use the literature on agenda setting to develop a conceptual framework for understanding this process and to identify similar cases against which to test the conclusions I reach. A second aim of this book, however, is to move beyond previous research and examine the relationship between agenda setting and the enactment of policy proposals. As I studied the development and defeat of President Clinton's reform proposal, I realized that previous theorists had not been attentive enough to the aspects of agenda setting that might actually hurt the prospects for passing legislation or lead political actors to misperceive the political risks and opportunities they faced. This led to the argument, presented in the concluding chapters of this book, that the process by which managed competition emerged onto the government agenda and seeped into the Clinton campaign prevented President Clinton and his advisers from recognizing and preparing for the political, institutional, and cultural barriers that stood in their path. This failure, I argue, contributed to the defeat of President Clinton's proposal. It also draws our attention to a persistent and increasingly troublesome disjunction between the promise of American democracy and the limits of American government.

The possibilities for scholarly innovation, like the possibilities for policy innovation, depend upon the presence of informed and well-situated allies. I have been fortunate to have many such allies in the course of my research, and my gratitude to them is immense.

My greatest debt is to two scholars whose support and intelligence made this book possible: Theda Skocpol and Ted Marmor. Both read early versions of the manuscript, helped me clarify my thinking through countless revisions, and guided me through the seemingly interminable process of preparing the final manuscript for publication. James Morone and Mark Peterson also read and commented on the complete manuscript. Their kind words of encouragement and penetrating criticism, as well as their own distinguished work on U.S. health politics, helped me discover connections in my argument I had overlooked and weaknesses I had failed to confront. Frank Baumgartner took time out from his own research on agenda setting to critique mine and to provide me with invaluable data from his ongoing analysis (with Bryan Jones and Jeffery Talbert) of congressional hearings. David Mayhew generously shared his impressive knowledge of Congress, read and critiqued several draft chapters, and otherwise assisted in the development of my argument about congressional action in the first chapter. As the book went to press, Paul Pierson reviewed and provided timely advice on parts of the final manuscript. Finally, Andrew Martin, with energy and insight, helped get this project off the ground when it was only a jumble of ideas and observations.

I am especially grateful to the many congressional and White House staff members, policy experts, and journalists who granted interviews for this book. Of those I interviewed, Linda Bergthold, Alain Enthoven, Ira Magaziner, Jack Rosenthal, and Paul Starr deserve special thanks for reading all or part of the manuscript, checking it for accuracy, and offering excellent suggestions. Lynn Etheredge did this and rummaged through his files to find every last scrap of relevant information about the Jackson Hole Group. Without his help, or the assistance of Diana Elser and Barbara Winch of the Jackson Hole Group, I would not have had access to the rich collection of materials on the Jackson Hole Group that informs my account of the group's activities.

Other people who read the manuscript or helped me complete it include John Benson, Robert Blendon, Sherwin Chen, Tara Davies, Scott Hemphill, Mark Schlesinger, Ian Shapiro, and Peter Stern. My editors at Princeton University Press—first Malcolm DeBevoise, then Malcolm Litchfield—were consistently helpful. David Blair ably copyedited the manuscript, and Sterling Bland, Walter Lippincott, and Heidi Sheehan patiently guided me through the production process. I also received critical institutional support from the Ford Foundation and Institute of Politics—both at Harvard—and from the Robert Wood Johnson Foundation. Duke University Press allowed me to reprint portions of "National Health Care Reform: An Idea Whose Time Came and Went," which was published in the *Journal of Health Politics, Policy and Law*, vol. 21, no. 4 (winter 1996), and appears here in modified form as chapter 1.

Countless others, from instructors to friends, have contributed to this work in more indirect ways. I am particularly grateful to the participants in the health policy seminars sponsored by Yale's Institution for Social and Policy Studies. During my tenure at Yale, they have provided a sounding board for my ideas and, perhaps more important, a fertile atmosphere for discussion and thought.

Reflecting on the many debts I have accumulated over the years, I am struck by how much I owe to those closest to me: my parents, Margaret and Thomas Hacker; my two sisters, Sarah and Alice; and, most important, my wife, Oona Hathaway. Oona has done more to help me with this book than I can thank her for here. She has been my most trusted editor and my closest friend, my most honest critic and my strongest advocate. Were it not for her love, patience, and insight, this book would not have been written.

Finally, this book is dedicated to Walter Hathaway, Richard Hacker, and Sarah Hodnett—three family members who were all in their own ways devoted to the pursuit of knowledge and the improvement of the human condition. Though they died too young, coming to terms with their deaths has given me new appreciation for the lessons their lives embodied.

THE ROAD TO NOWHERE

The Puzzle

IN A SPEECH before a joint session of Congress on September 22, 1993, President Bill Clinton outlined one of the most ambitious policy initiatives in American history—his proposal for comprehensive health care reform. During the 1992 presidential campaign, Clinton had pledged to tackle the pressing problems in American medical care. Shortly after taking office, he had created a special task force to develop his reform plan, appointing his wife, Hillary Rodham Clinton, as its chair. Although the task force had completed its work, the proposal was not yet finished. Even as the President addressed the nation, his health policy advisers were scrambling to put the final touches on the mammoth proposal, which was already months behind schedule.

Although the legislation remained incomplete, the basic structure of the plan was not in doubt. Late in the presidential campaign, Clinton had firmly committed himself to a reform strategy known as "managed competition." The cornerstone of this approach was universal health insurance through competing private health plans. Under managed competition, most Americans would obtain health insurance through new regional insurance purchasing cooperatives that would contract with private health plans and monitor the competition among them.

By the time of Clinton's historic address to Congress, managed competition was among the hottest domestic policy topics in Washington. Capitol Hill was abuzz with meetings and media events devoted to exploring and promoting the approach, and the press was unleashing a torrent of articles on the potential structure of the president's plan. Yet, just a year earlier, Clinton's decision to endorse "competition within a budget" had taken many observers by surprise. Although managed competition had received some attention during the presidential campaign, it had not been considered a leading model for national health care reform. Instead, three alternative proposals had dominated the national debate: a Canadian-style "single-payer" system of national health insurance, the "tax-credit" plan supported by leading Senate Republicans and President George Bush, and the "play-or-pay" proposal embraced by the Senate Democratic leadership, which would have required employers to provide their workers with health insurance or pay into a public health plan.

This book aims to understand how and why managed competition displaced these competing policy alternatives to become the basis for

President Clinton's reform proposal. The puzzle it seeks to unravel is why Clinton and his advisers embraced a reform strategy that was on the periphery of the national political agenda. In the process of exploring this question, this book will take up many others. It will explain why health care reform became a policy issue of particular prominence in the early 1990s, and what its prominence reveals about the instability of the government agenda and the logic of congressional action. It will chronicle the conceptual twists and turns that managed competition took as it made its way onto the agenda of government and into President Clinton's reform initiative. And it will explore how the president's embrace of managed competition contributed to the defeat of his reform proposal in 1994. Nonetheless, the key question that this book sets out to answer is not why the recent legislative push for national health care reform failed, but why it took the direction that it did. The central focus is not the inability of President Clinton to forge a legislative compromise on health care reform, but the process by which he came to champion a particular policy proposal. This process—the process of "agenda setting"—helps us understand why the recent momentum toward national health care reform failed to produce legislative results. Its more enduring lessons, however, concern the forces that promote policy innovation in American politics and the obstacles that prevent it.

In 1977 Alain Enthoven, an economist and former assistant secretary of defense, authored a proposal for universal health insurance that embodied the core concepts of the managed-competition approach. Enthoven's proposal aimed to give people financial incentives to choose low-cost "managed-care" plans, such as health maintenance organizations (HMOs), by making them pay the extra cost of more expensive plans. Health plans would then compete among one another to attract enrollees within a restructured private market. Enthoven subsequently adapted the approach to include health insurance "sponsors"—collective purchasing agents that would contract with competing health plans on behalf of nonworkers and the employees of small firms. In 1990 he teamed up with a group of medical industry leaders and health policy experts known as the "Jackson Hole Group" to develop a health care reform proposal based on managed competition that was completed in the summer of 1991.

The three major reform approaches under consideration in 1991 differed in important ways from managed competition. The single-payer approach emulated the national health insurance systems found in other advanced industrial democracies, most notably Canada. This reform strategy entailed a much more direct role for government in medical financing than did managed competition, and it explicitly rejected competition among managed-care plans as a cost-containment mechanism. Instead, the single-payer model envisioned the government as the primary insurer, reimbursing physicians and hospitals directly with tax revenues collected from the citizenry.

Although the tax-credit strategy shared many of the philosophical tenets of managed competition, it focused on the financing of medical care rather than on the health plans through which care would be delivered. The defining feature of this approach was a system of refundable tax credits that would make health insurance more affordable for lower-income Americans. These credits were usually coupled with reforms in the insurance market that were designed to give high-risk individuals greater access to health insurance. Some further-reaching tax-credit plans also envisioned broader changes in the structure of the medical sector, such as an evolution away from employment-based health insurance. Nonetheless, the basic aim of the tax-credit strategy was to increase the prevalence of private insurance, not restructure the medical market to encourage competition among managed-care plans.

Finally, the play-or-pay model struck a middle ground between the single-payer and tax-credit approaches. Employers would be required by law to provide health insurance to their workers or pay a tax to fund a public health insurance plan that would finance health care for uncovered workers. To guarantee insurance coverage to all citizens, those not covered through employment would also be provided public insurance.

In contrast to these three prominent approaches, managed competition was not featured in public and political discussions of health care reform in 1991 and early 1992. The term *managed competition* had yet to appear in the pages of the popular press, and even many health policy specialists were unfamiliar with the concept. Although the debate over health care reform was gathering momentum, no legislation embodying the managed-competition approach had been introduced in Congress. The puzzle, then, is how managed competition moved so quickly from relative obscurity to the top of the national political agenda.

The emergence of managed competition as a cornerstone of President Clinton's reform proposal is an important historical and conceptual puzzle for at least three reasons. First, the rise of managed competition represents an enormously significant chapter in recent political history. We simply cannot begin to understand why President Clinton's reform effort failed, or why he launched that effort in the first place, without an appreciation of the forces that pushed health care reform to the forefront of American politics and managed competition to the top of the president's domestic agenda.

Second, and more broadly, the history chronicled in this book contains many important and telling lessons about the recent debate over national health care reform—and about debates in the United States over divisive policy issues more generally. Whenever possible, I have attempted to draw out these more general lessons, verify them against other similar cases of policy innovation in American politics, and explain their wider significance.

Finally, the movement of managed competition from the periphery to the center of national attention represents a paradigm case of political agenda setting—the process by which policy issues and proposals to address them become the subject of government consideration. Political scientists have long noted the critical importance of agenda setting.[1] Democratic theorists, for instance, endlessly debate the question of whether political elites or privileged groups in society control the agenda of government, thus allowing the broader public to influence policy only within narrowly prescribed limits. Political scientists make much of the fact that the authoritative decisions of government are influenced not only by the preferences of elected representatives and their constituents but also by the availability and ordering of policy alternatives. Yet despite a recent flowering of interest in the subject, the body of research on agenda setting is still small, and many important questions about the process remain unresolved. This book aims to provide new insights into the dynamics of agenda setting and, in the process, point out where existing theories on the subject appear to succeed or fall short. The research on agenda setting in turn supplies the theoretical framework for the book, allowing me to develop a deeper account of the genesis and politics of President Clinton's health care reform proposal than historical narratives or single-case studies generally permit.

Like other recent studies of agenda setting, this book relies heavily on interviews with individuals involved in making policy to reconstruct events and exchanges among key participants in the policy process.* The justification for this method is straightforward. Studies of agenda setting need to examine the strategies of political actors who attempt to shape the agenda of government, and, in most cases, these strategies can only be fully understood by speaking with the actors themselves. The difficulty of reconstructing strategic action is compounded in this particular case by the paucity of published accounts that examine the events described in this book. Although a large amount has been written about the political conflict surrounding President Clinton's reform proposal, surprisingly few political scientists, historians, or journalists have examined the theoretical and empirical puzzle that is at the core of this book.

Nonetheless, interviews have significant limitations as a research method. The most serious difficulty is that individuals involved in policy-

---

* The interviews are listed and the research methodology is discussed in appendix A.

making may not be the best judges of what influences their actions or of what influence their actions have. People in and around government generally do not recognize how much their actions are shaped by such diffuse influences as economic pressures, currents of public opinion, institutional constraints, cultural values, patterns of media coverage, and the gradual dissemination of ideas. Moreover, they tend to be reluctant to ascribe their actions to self-interested motives or to the pressure of narrow organized interests.

Another methodological hurdle inherent in interviews is that people involved in the making of government policy generally magnify their role in the policy process and their influence over outcomes. Reporters often take the claims of people in and around government at face value, which helps account for the highly personalistic character of journalistic analyses of politics. But political scientists, too, can succumb to the temptation to search for the powerful inner circle of participants that "really" makes government policy. As Hugh Heclo suggests, political scientists "tend to look for one group exerting dominance over another, for subgovernments strongly insulated from other outside forces in the environment, for policies that get 'produced' by a few makers. . . . Looking for the few that are powerful, we tend to overlook the many whose webs of influence provoke and guide the exercise of power."[2]

I have attempted to compensate for the shortcomings of interviews in several ways. First, I have tried to verify the claims made by my interview respondents against other interviews and other data sources. Nearly all the statements that buttress my argument or enrich my historical account were confirmed by several interview subjects as well as by published and unpublished sources. In the rare cases where the narrative relies on a very small number of respondents, I have made that clear. None of the broader empirical and theoretical conclusions of this book is based solely on the interviews.

Second, I have relied on several data sources in addition to the interviews. These include original empirical research conducted in conjunction with the interviews, recent popular and scholarly writings on the health care reform debate, and more general works on U.S. health policy and politics and the process of agenda setting. A common complaint about single-case studies is that they do not allow researchers to make broader generalizations. I have addressed this problem by situating my findings within the existing literature on agenda setting, and by making explicit where this case appears to confirm, disconfirm, or challenge existing theories.

This book is neither a work of history nor a work of theory. It is an attempt to bring both history and theory to bear on a specific intellectual puzzle. If I pay more attention to historical questions than political scientists often do, it is because I believe that my conclusions can only be evaluated against this historical backdrop. Furthermore, since this book represents the first comprehensive analysis of the development of President Clinton's reform proposal, I hope that its canvass of history will be of interest even to those who disagree with my conclusions or are uninterested in the theoretical issues I address. If I have delved deeper into theoretical issues than historians generally do, it is because this is a book about politics rather than history. Although this episode in American politics is interesting and significant in its own right, my aim is to offer a theoretically grounded *explanation* rather than an exhaustive historical account.

In keeping with this mission, I have not attempted a chronological narrative. Each chapter generally follows a chronological structure, but the book as a whole is organized thematically. It begins with an examination of the factors that moved health care reform onto the national political agenda and then moves back and forth through time exploring the separate streams of policy that fed into Clinton's reform effort. The fifth chapter, which explores the development of the proposal that President Clinton finally presented to Congress in 1993, is itself divided into smaller thematic sections, although these are largely ordered chronologically. The chapters are best viewed as pieces of a jigsaw puzzle—or, perhaps more appropriately, as clues in a murder mystery—that will be fit together into a cohesive whole after each piece is studied and understood.

Chapter 1 begins to unravel the puzzle of why Bill Clinton embraced managed competition by taking up an important prior question: Why did national health care reform move onto the agenda of the federal government in the early 1990s? Despite the extensive commentary on health care reform, this is a question that has received relatively scant attention. The general assumption has been that the increase in public and political attention to health care reform was a by-product of Clinton's election victory. Yet extensive evidence suggests that attention to health care reform preceded the 1992 election and, to some extent, even the 1991 Senate campaign of the proreform Democrat Harris Wofford. A compilation and review of this evidence makes it possible to begin sorting out the respective roles of the public, media, interest groups, election results, and national politicians in raising health care reform's stature on the government agenda.

The next two chapters examine two distinct streams of policy that carried the ideas embodied in President Clinton's proposal onto the national political agenda and into the Clinton campaign. These streams were not wholly independent from one another, but the direction that they took and the participants who were involved were very different. Chapter 2 examines the first stream, which resulted in the reform proposal of the

Jackson Hole Group and a bill introduced by a group of conservative House Democrats in 1992. Chapter 3 examines the second stream, which took the managed-competition approach in a new and quite unanticipated direction.

Chapter 4 brings us to the heart of the puzzle: Bill Clinton's decision to endorse managed competition during the 1992 presidential campaign. This decision must be understood against the backdrop of the primary and general election contests, the ideological themes and commitments of the Clinton campaign, and the specific confluence of ideas and political actors that converged during the campaign. At critical points in the presidential race, and at the behest of key policy advocates, the policy ideas explored in the previous two chapters entered the Clinton campaign and came to be seen as credible alternatives to the reform approach that Clinton had previously supported.

Chapter 5 lays to rest the common misperception that Clinton's health care task force developed the president's reform proposal from scratch. It begins by detailing how the reform framework Clinton had articulated during the campaign survived through the transition period and into the new administration, despite attempts by some advisers to move the president-elect in a different direction. The focus then shifts to the broader policy development process as it played out amid the legislative battles of the Clinton administration's first year. Finally, the discussion turns to the political strategies that grew out of this process—the expectations and assumptions embodied in the plan itself. Here some of the chief weaknesses of the president's strategy, and their link to managed competition, become unmistakably apparent.

The conclusion brings together all the historical and conceptual pieces laid out in the previous chapters and integrates them into a general explanation of the genesis of President Clinton's reform proposal. The literature on agenda setting furnishes a set of theoretical tools with which to sift back through the history presented in chapters 2 through 5. The conclusions that emerge from the history in turn form the basis for a critique of existing theories of agenda setting. The close of the book takes up the question of why health care reform failed in 1994. It shows that although the sudden emergence of managed competition does not explain why President Clinton's reform proposal was defeated, it does help us understand why the president and his advisers overestimated both the possibilities for policy change and the potential of managed competition to break the stalemate over health care reform.

CHAPTER 1

The Rise of Reform

IN EARLY AUGUST 1991, Harris Wofford's advisers gathered in a conference room in Philadelphia to discuss the future of his senatorial campaign. The special election, only three months away, promised almost certain defeat for the little-known Democratic senator—and certain victory for his seasoned Republican opponent, former Pennsylvania governor and former U.S. attorney general Richard Thornburgh. Just months earlier, Wofford had been appointed to the Senate by Governor Robert Casey following the untimely death of the Republican incumbent, John Heinz. Now, surveys of the Pennsylvania electorate showed the liberal intellectual roughly 40 percentage points behind Thornburgh, validating the prevailing consensus that Wofford's brief tenure in the Senate would soon be brought to a close.

To those meeting in Philadelphia, however, the race was far from over. In addition to Wofford, the room contained the two principal architects of the campaign, James Carville and Paul Begala; the campaign's pollster, Mike Donilon; and a number of other campaign aides. Donilon passed around the findings of a two-question survey that he had conducted to assess voter's feelings about national health insurance—an issue that Wofford had been emphasizing in his campaign. The two questions were virtually identical. Each asked respondents to choose between Wofford and Thornburgh on the basis of a brief list of each candidate's qualifications. The second question, however, included a single caveat: Wofford wanted to enact national health insurance; Thornburgh did not. By a more than 3-to-1 ratio, voters asked the first question preferred Thornburgh. When national health insurance was mentioned, however, the relative position of the two candidates dramatically reversed, with Wofford skyrocketing from more than a 40-point deficit in the polls to an almost 10-point lead. As Begala would later tell reporters, national health care reform was the policy issue that could "turn goat spit into gasoline."[1]

The significance of Donilon's poll was not lost on Carville, who argued vigorously for making national health care reform the central theme of the campaign. As one participant in the meeting recounted, Carville saw the issue as the only real vehicle for recapturing the race: "Carville said, 'I don't think we can win this election any other way. We don't have a hope in hell against [Thornburgh] with the time we have, the name recognition we have, and the money we have. [National health care reform] is what we have, and it's definitely the long bomb, the Hail Mary. But it's a pretty damn good Hail Mary.' "[2]

The others in attendance agreed. Wofford would campaign on national health care reform.

Wofford won Pennsylvania's U.S. Senate race with a startling 55 percent of the vote—a landslide by Pennsylvania standards. But it was *how* he won that was truly significant. Seemingly overnight, health care reform was an issue that won votes. Post-election polls revealed that for half of Pennsylvania's voters "national health insurance" was among the top two concerns reflected in their voting decision; for almost a quarter of voters it was the top concern.[3] Although national health insurance was expected to appeal to the low-income residents of the Rustbelt and Appalachian portions of the state, Wofford also defeated Thornburgh in Philadelphia's suburban counties, where no fewer than two-thirds of the residents were registered Republicans. Furthermore, he performed much better than expected in the overwhelmingly Republican regions of northeastern Pennsylvania and made significant inroads among the state's most loyal Republicans, the Pennsylvania Germans.[4] The message of the election seemed clear: no candidate could afford to appear indifferent to a policy issue of such broad public concern.

The Senate race in Pennsylvania was not the first time that health care reform appeared on the American political agenda. Comprehensive health care reform received widespread attention at many other points in American history: during the Progressive Era and the New Deal; under Presidents Truman, Kennedy, and Johnson; and in the 1970s. In none of these periods, however, did public pressure for reform play a critical role in spurring political leaders to action. In the Progressive Era, reformers looked not to the public for inspiration but to the social policies of Germany and Britain. During the New Deal, the Truman years, and the 1960s, the impetus for reform largely came from within the executive branch. And although attention to health care reform was more widespread in the 1970s, it was still primarily the province of national political leaders, labor unions, and public interest groups.

By and large, then, past reformers found that their cause evoked sentiments among the citizenry that were lukewarm and superficial. While polls showed that many Americans were receptive to the idea of national health insurance, public support was never strong enough to allow reformers to overcome the cultural, political, and institutional barriers that lay in their path. Most people expressed little interest in the plight of the uninsured or, for that matter, in the rising cost of health care. To the majority of Americans, the system seemed to work.

Viewed in this light, the public discontent manifested in the Pennsylvania election begs an explanation. Why was the campaign strategy chosen by Wofford and his tacticians so effective? To answer this question, we need to understand how a medical system that once muted public concerns became the source of such widespread dissatisfaction.

THINGS FALL APART

With the massive growth in private insurance coverage following World War II and the passage of Medicare and Medicaid in 1965, the task of mobilizing broad popular support for universal health insurance became deeply problematic.[5] The vast majority of Americans were now covered by private and public health insurance, and most were largely unaware of its cost because they paid for it through discreet tax increases and slower real wage growth. Beginning in the early 1970s, however, the rate of increase in real wages decelerated and inflation in the medical sector accelerated. The result was that premiums for employer-provided health insurance began to absorb a higher percentage of the growth in real wages. Indeed, from 1973 to 1989, health insurance premiums paid by employers accounted for more than half the rise in real total compensation per full-time employee.[6]

The cost of health insurance to working Americans also grew more visible. Starting in the late 1970s, many corporations attempted to shift the growing burden of medical spending onto workers. This shift first took the form of insurance deductibles: between 1979 and 1984, the percentage of large corporations requiring their employees to pay deductibles grew almost fourfold, from 14 to 52 percent.[7] Shifting costs from employers to workers provided only temporary relief, however, and business began to search for new ways to moderate medical inflation. The simplest solution, of course, was to stop offering insurance altogether, which many new entrants and small firms did, especially in the growing service and retail sectors of the economy. For larger employers, eliminating or cutting back on dependent coverage became increasingly attractive. Many larger firms also began to pay employee claims themselves, thus limiting the extent to which they subsidized the health care expenses of other firms' employees. Under the terms of the 1974 Employee Retirement Income Security Act, self-insurance held the additional attraction of exempting firms from state taxes on insurance premiums and state-mandated medical benefits.

The increasing cost-sensitivity of employers also further encouraged, sometimes inadvertently, a whole series of trends already under way in insurance marketing and claims management. First among them was the new vigor with which private insurers were seeking out employer groups with lower than average health care costs. Until the end of World War II, subscribers in a given geographic region generally paid the same "community" rate for group policies. This was the prevailing practice, for example, among the nonprofit Blue Cross/Blue Shield plans that dominated the group insurance market until the 1950s. In the early postwar period, however, smaller commercial insurers began to enter the insurance market, undercutting the Blues by offering low-risk groups less expensive policies. By matching premiums to the expected actuarial risk of subscribers, a practice known as "experience rating," commercial insurers eliminated many of the cross-subsidies—from healthy to ill and from young to old—inherent in community rating. Soon the Blues were experience rating too.

Experience rating runs counter to the goal of social insurance, which is to spread risk across the whole of society.[8] Taken to its natural extreme, the logic of experience rating would have left many high-risk individuals unable to afford insurance at all. Yet the early effect of experience rating was moderated by two factors: health insurance was for most firms still an incidental expense, and insurers were unable to predict actuarial risk with any real accuracy. Beginning in the 1970s, however, all that changed. Strapped by rising medical costs, firms began to seek out less expensive insurance policies, and, responding to their pleas, private insurers refined their methods for rating employer groups and avoiding those with the highest health risks.

As firms self-insured in growing numbers, moreover, the market for private insurance began to shrink. By 1988 most of the financial risk of insuring employees had shifted from insurance companies to employers.[9] In general, firms that failed to self-insure did not have enough employees to pool the risk of illness or injury. Compared with large employers, these firms were characterized by higher levels of employee turnover, more variable workforce health, and lower rates of insurance coverage. As the insurance market contracted and fragmented, therefore, rates of coverage among employer groups grew more uneven and the degree of uncertainty surrounding the health and tenure of employees increased. In this environment, the ability of insurers to accurately predict the risk of potential subscribers became crucial. If insurers had accepted all firms on an equal basis, firms that expected to incur higher than average health care costs would have been more likely to purchase coverage than those that did not. To prevent such "adverse selection," insurers resorted to increasingly sophisticated forms of underwriting to screen out or limit the coverage of costly, high-risk applicants.

The increasing pervasiveness and stringency of medical underwriting represented another major change in the insurance market of the 1980s. Underwriting is performed for all forms of insurance, but for health insurance it takes on a uniquely sinister cast. Health care costs are not evenly distributed across the population; in any given year, approximately 20 percent of the population incurs about 80 percent of total medical expenses.[10] As a consequence, it is very much to a health insurer's advantage to screen out subscribers who are likely members of this high-cost group. The object of medical underwriting is thus to identify and avoid insuring those who need protection most.

The first phase of underwriting generally occurs at the level of the firm. Insurers are wary of insuring firms in professions characterized by seasonal employment or a high employee turnover rate (such as restaurants and hotels) or those that present a high risk of occupational illness or injury (such as mining or logging). A firm that does not fall into such "redlined" professions may still be refused insurance if an insurer classifies one or more of its employees as high risk. In some cases, insurers will offer such firms coverage only after excluding high-risk employees. Even after enrolling in a health plan, most subscribers are denied coverage for "pre-existing conditions," usually for a period of six months to two years. When pre-existing condition exclusions expire, insurers frequently raise the premium rate charged to the employer group to offset the predictable increase in claims—a process known as "durational rating." As rates rise, many firms then switch to another insurer, which is likely to impose a new set of pre-existing condition exclusions on the group.

The interplay of pre-existing condition exclusions and durational rating generates substantial turnover in the insurance market, particularly the small group market. As firms seek out lower premiums, insurers constantly step up their underwriting efforts to protect themselves against adverse selection. Because of this churning effect, significant gaps in insurance coverage are a fact of life for employees of small firms. And for all workers, leaving a job can mean forgoing necessary coverage in the future.

A final important trend that was encouraged by employers in the 1980s was the movement by insurers away from traditional indemnity plans and toward managed care.* Before the passage of the HMO Act of 1973, the Nixon administration predicted that sixteen hundred new health maintenance organizations would be created by 1980, with 20 percent of

---

* Since the term *managed care* is often used loosely, I should make clear that I employ it to mean network health plans. These are plans that "restrict coverage in whole or part to services provided by a specified network or group of physicians, hospitals and other health care providers." Marilyn J. Field and Harold T. Shapiro, eds., *Employment and Health Benefits: A Connection at Risk* (Washington, D.C.: National Academy Press, 1993), 100. Network plans include all the plans mentioned in this chapter and several variants thereof. They do not include conventional fee-for-service insurers that exercise some oversight over physician, hospital, and patient behavior.

the public enrolled.[11] Even accounting for the contradictory design of the HMO legislation, these expectations were wildly unrealistic. Indeed, when federal start-up grants for HMOs were curtailed in 1981, the actual number of HMOs fell far short of the Nixon administration's goal.[12] If the 1970s was a decade of unrealized expectations, however, the 1980s brought unprecedented growth. By 1991 there were more than five hundred HMOs in operation in the United States with a total enrollment of nearly 40 million people.[13]

Proliferating even more rapidly were more loosely organized systems of managed care, such as preferred provider organizations (PPOs) and point-of-service (POS) plans. Members of PPOs and POS plans receive treatment through a limited network of care-givers. In contrast to tightly integrated HMOs, however, physicians and practitioners who contract with these plans are not salaried employees, and patients can seek care outside the network (although coverage is less complete). While HMOs with integrated financing and delivery systems (so-called staff-model HMOs) have been shown to deliver quality care less expensively than conventional fee-for-service insurance (primarily by reducing the hospital use of their members), there is no evidence to suggest that PPOs and POS plans have significantly reduced costs—except, perhaps, to shift them onto other payers.[14] Nonetheless, PPOs and POS plans grew from their inception in the early 1980s to cover about a quarter of American workers by 1991.[15]

With employers demanding lower premiums, even fee-for-service insurance plans rushed to adopt the cost-management mechanisms pioneered by managed care. Utilization review techniques—such as the requirement that patients receive an insurer's authorization before being admitted to a hospital—quickly became part of the standard operating procedure of claims management. Although physicians complained loudly about the growing encroachments upon their clinical autonomy, utilization review held out the promise of one-time cost savings—a prospect that few employers could pass up.[16] By 1990 only 5 percent of employees in the United States remained in plans with no utilization management, down from more than 40 percent in 1987.[17]

Partly as a result of these trends, and partly due to cutbacks in Medicaid, the number of uninsured rose steeply during the 1980s, leaving an estimated 36 million Americans without health insurance in 1991.[18] Among the poor the decline in coverage reversed somewhat in the late 1980s due to an expansion of Medicaid (which covered about half of the poor in 1991). Nonetheless, the uninsured still came predominantly from low-income families. The vast majority of these families were headed by workers, who were generally self-employed or employed by small firms. In a political sense, however, the uninsured hardly formed a group at all.

They were faceless and quiescent, without common ties or identification, and more than a quarter were children. So the growing number of uninsured could not by itself be expected to spur political leaders to action. Something more was needed to create significant public pressures for national health care reform. As it turned out, that something was the intrusion of rising health care costs into the medical security of the middle class.

THE MIDDLE CLASS AND
NATIONAL HEALTH CARE REFORM

In the summer of 1991, as Harris Wofford climbed back from his early deficit in the polls, James Carville came across an article in *Harper's* magazine that immediately caught his attention. Its author was Paul Starr, a sociologist at Princeton and author of the Pulitzer Prize–winning book, *The Social Transformation of American Medicine*. Entitled "The Middle Class and National Health Reform," the article was a reprint of a short piece that Starr had written for the *American Prospect*, the fledgling liberal quarterly he coedited.

For years Starr had lamented that reformers in the United States would never be able to overcome the formidable roadblocks to national health insurance. Now, however, he saw new possibilities. Although significant political obstacles remained, "the underlying pressures for the adoption of national health reform in the 1990s" were stronger than they had been "for decades." The reason, claimed Starr, was the "increasing jeopardy of the middle class."

In the past, Starr argued, "advocates of universal insurance, like advocates of so many other liberal policies since the 1960s, found themselves . . . appealing to middle-class voters to support change, not for their own good, but for the benefit of a minority—and a hazily defined, politically inaudible minority at that. . . . To the middle-class taxpayer, even the family of the unionized worker, or the elderly protected by Medicare, national health insurance seemed to promise too little for too much."

This was no longer the case, Starr claimed. The efforts of employers to control costs and of insurers to screen out high-risk individuals were "undoing some of the middle-class insulation from health care costs that made it so difficult to construct an alliance for health insurance reform across class lines." Thus health care reform could become the Democrats' "best campaign issue in the nineties."[19]

For obvious reasons, Carville found Starr's thesis persuasive. He called one of Wofford's legislative assistants and ordered him to "get Wofford together with this guy." In early October, Wofford and Starr met at the senator's home in Pennsylvania, and for most of the day they drifted through the house together, chatting about health care reform and its role in the campaign. According to one campaign aide, "They both saw very much eye to eye."[20]

Starr and Wofford were not mind readers of the middle class. It was no secret that public discontent with the cost of health care and the vagaries of insurance coverage was substantial and growing. The percentage of Americans who felt that American health care needed to be fundamentally changed or completely rebuilt increased steadily in the late 1980s, exceeding 90 percent in November 1991.[21] What Starr and Wofford recognized, however, was a subtle but important shift in the character of public opinion. This shift involved not only an increase in overall public support for reform, but also a growing convergence of opinion among Americans of diverse viewpoints, circumstances, and characteristics.

Like public opinion about other major policy issues, general public sentiments about health care have remained relatively constant over the last half-century.[22] Support for medical spending and for the government to "do more" on health care, for example, has been consistently high, with large majorities (60 to 80 percent) favoring increased government spending and assistance. Along with public support for other government initiatives, support for government spending on medical care reached a low point between the mid-1970s and the early 1980s as the economy soured and antigovernment sentiments prevailed. Unlike other domestic programs, however, health care programs rapidly regained public support during the 1980s. By 1987 they were even slightly more popular than they had been in the mid-1970s. Interestingly, neither programs targeted to the poor nor general domestic programs regained the levels of public support they had enjoyed in the 1970s. Indeed, after examining national polling data collected between 1975 and 1989, Mark Schlesinger and Taeku Lee conclude that "only for health care have Americans become distinctly more supportive of government in the late-1980s than in the mid-1970s."[23]

Why did government involvement in health care become more popular relative to other government initiatives? The most likely answer is that health care, in comparison with other domestic policy priorities, became less socially divisive between the mid-1970s and the late 1980s. Although support for government involvement in medical care varies by income, age, education, gender, race, and degree of political involvement, these differences are substantially smaller for health care than for other areas of government policy and may in fact have narrowed slightly over the past fifteen years. More important, federal health initiatives do not evoke the same negative public association as do other redistributive policies, such as antipoverty programs. They are not strongly identified with racial

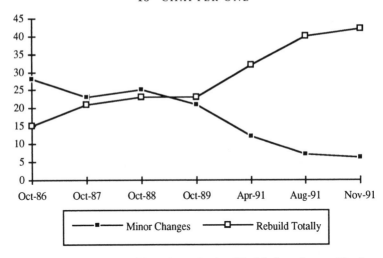

Figure 1.1   Percentage of Americans Saying Health Care System Needs to Be Totally Rebuilt versus Percentage Saying Minor Changes Needed (*source*: Rosita M. Thomas, *Health Care in America: An Analysis of Public Opinion*, CRS Report for Congress 92–769 GOV [Washington, D.C.: Congressional Research Service, October 1992], 10).

minorities or with the economically disadvantaged, and federal involvement in health care does not appear to be linked in the public's mind to a wider role for government in other areas of American society.[24]

In a number of important ways, then, health care appears to be different from other domestic policy priorities. It is not only more popular than antipoverty programs and general domestic initiatives, but also characterized by greater consensus between rich and poor, old and young. Yet support for greater government involvement in health care does not necessarily translate into support for comprehensive health care reform. Was there a parallel shift in public attitudes toward reform?

As figure 1.1 shows, the increase in public support for comprehensive reform in the years leading up to Wofford's victory was indeed considerable. In 1986 only 15 percent of Americans believed that the health care system needed to be "completely rebuilt," while more than a quarter felt it needed only "minor changes." By the time of the Pennsylvania election, the number of Americans who felt a complete rebuilding of the system was necessary had risen to 42 percent, while those who wanted only minor changes had fallen to 6 percent.[25]

The increase in public support for comprehensive reform in the years leading up to the Pennsylvania election was also quite rapid. Between October 1989 and November 1991, the number of Americans expressing support for a complete restructuring of the health care system jumped from 23 to 42 percent, while those supporting minor changes dropped from 21 to 6 percent. All told, by November 1991 more than 90 percent of Americans believed the health care system needed to be fundamentally changed or completely rebuilt—roughly 20 percent more than had felt that way two years earlier.

What explains this rapid increase in public discontent? Recent research on the dynamics of public opinion suggests that public sentiments mainly shift in response to observable changes in external conditions or to changing patterns of media coverage.[26] I have already outlined some of the changes in the structure and performance of the medical sector that might have prompted public concern—the increasingly visible burden of medical costs, the rising number of uninsured, the increasing stringency and pervasiveness of medical underwriting—but these trends had been under way for more than a decade before the sudden jump in public discontent occurred. No doubt they had some cumulative effect, but if that were the whole story, public support for reform would have built gradually over the course of the decade, rather than increase sharply between 1989 and 1991. Instead, the sudden increase in public discontent appears to have been linked to the national economic downturn that began in 1989 and worsened through 1991.[27] By promoting a sense of economic insecurity, the recession heightened public anxiety about the escalating cost of medical care and the fragility of employer-sponsored health insurance. Moreover, the recession was harder on white-collar and professional workers than were other recent economic downturns, forcing many middle-income Americans who had taken their personal health care arrangements for granted to face the prospect of losing their health insurance or having their coverage cut back. According to the public opinion data assembled by Schlesinger and Lee, all the factors associated with economic slumps—unemployment, disenchantment with the business community, and economic anxiety—increase public support for government involvement in health care, both in absolute terms and relative to other domestic initiatives.[28]

If the recession precipitated the rapid change in public opinion that polls picked up between 1989 and 1991, this would go a long way toward explaining why support for fundamental reform jumped so quickly and dramatically at the same time that Americans remained deeply ambivalent about its proper scope and direction. Americans expressed dissatisfaction with the medical system as a whole, but they remained overwhelmingly satisfied with the quality and accessibility—if not the cost—of the medical care they and their families received. In addition, the extent to which Americans were willing to sacrifice to enable reform remained unclear. Although most Americans supported an expansion of coverage to the uninsured, opinion surveys showed limited public support for restrictions on personal medical care decisions or increased taxation to fund reform. Moreover, the public remained ambivalent about the proper role of government in a reformed system. Polls indicated that Americans were convinced that government had to be part of the solution but at the same time fearful that it would botch the effort.[29]

Finally, public dissatisfaction with the status quo did not embody anything approaching a latent public consensus about the direction reform should take. In opinion surveys, Americans appeared quite ready to embrace any alternative to present insurance arrangements, including a national health insurance system funded through taxes. But when respondents were asked to choose among competing reform approaches, public support tended to split fairly evenly among the alternatives, with levels of support varying greatly with the wording of the survey questions.

These aspects of public ambivalence accord well with Daniel Yankelovich's three-stage model of opinion formation, in which members of the public become aware of a policy issue, weigh the consequences of alternative courses of action, and then arrive at a general conception of what should be done.[30] At the time of the Pennsylvania election, this last stage of opinion development—what Yankelovich terms "public judgment"—had not yet been reached. Although many Americans were anxious about the security of their health care arrangements, few understood the major options for reform being considered by policymakers or the trade-offs those options might entail. What emerged in the late 1980s and found expression in Wofford's stunning upset victory was a *negative* public judgment about a system of health care finance that Americans found too costly, unreliable, and inhumane. A corresponding positive judgment about the direction reform should take would prove more difficult for policymakers and the public to reach.

MEDIA COVERAGE OF HEALTH CARE REFORM

What role did the media play in drawing public and political attention to health care reform? Since Maxwell McCombs and Donald Shaw first examined the "agenda-setting function of mass media" in the 1968 presidential campaign, communications researchers have demonstrated conclusively that the media affect citizens' perceptions of issue importance.[31] There is also reason to believe that policymakers rely on media for their assessment of public concerns.[32] Whether media amplify the effects of other political actors or actively attempt to set the government agenda themselves, they can play an important role in raising public awareness about policy issues.

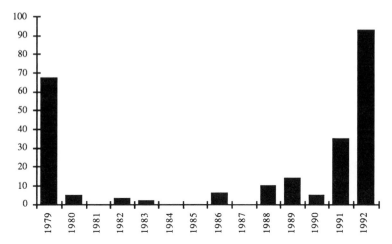

Figure 1.2 Frequency of Articles in *Christian Science Monitor, New York Times*, and *Wall Street Journal* Mentioning "Health/Medical Care Reform" or "National Health Insurance" (*source*: computerized search by author).

Media coverage of health care reform was almost nonexistent through the 1980s. Between 1980 and 1990, for example, three of the most widely read national newspapers—the *Christian Science Monitor, New York Times*, and *Wall Street Journal*—together ran a total of forty stories on health care reform or national health insurance. In not one of these years were more than fourteen stories printed, and in four—1981, 1984, 1985, and 1987—there was no coverage of the issue whatsoever. These figures stand in stark contrast to the last year of reform activity, 1979, when a total of almost seventy articles appeared in these three newspapers. As figure 1.2 shows, the total number of articles rose slightly in the latter half of the 1980s, but the real jump took place in 1991, as the total number of articles grew from five to thirty-five, only to be followed by another more dramatic rise in 1992 as the number of articles reached ninety-three.

These trends become clearer when we focus on the six years between 1987 and 1993 and expand the pool of newspapers. Figure 1.3 shows the number of articles mentioning health care reform that appeared in eight widely read newspapers between 1987 and 1993. As before, there is a slight drop in print-media attention in 1990 followed by surges of coverage in 1991 and 1992.

Juxtaposed against the public opinion data and Wofford's victory in 1991, these trends suggest that the press was reacting to, rather than driving, public opinion and political events. If this were the case, the media's role in raising public concern about health care would run

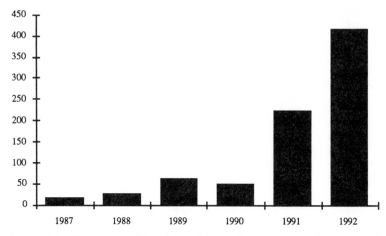

Figure 1.3   Frequency of Articles in *Atlanta Constitution/Atlanta Journal,*
Boston Globe, Chicago Tribune, Christian Science Monitor, Los Angeles
Times, New York Times, Wall Street Journal, and *Washington Post* Mentioning "Health/Medical Care Reform" (*source*: computerized search by
author).

counter to the traditional model of media agenda setting in which the
public "learns what issues are important from the priorities of the news
media."[33] In this instance, the reverse appears to have happened: media
coverage of health care reform responded to, rather than precipitated,
public and political concern.[34]

There are of course other plausible hypotheses. The rise in public concern and increase in news coverage occurred within a short enough period
that both the public and media may have been responding to a common
third factor—for example, a significant rise in medical costs or in the
number of uninsured. Identifying the exact causal process at work is difficult because public opinion, media coverage, and policymaking all mutually influence one another. The concept of media agenda setting implies a
one-way causal process whereby media coverage (the independent variable) changes public issue priorities (the dependent variable). Yet, as
Everett Rogers and James Dearing argue, "there is undoubtedly a two-
way, mutually dependent relationship between the public agenda and the
media agenda in the agenda-setting process."[35] Likewise, there is clearly
an interactive relationship between journalists and policymakers. The
great bulk of domestic news stories focus on people in government, and
media outlets are an important vehicle by which policymakers draw public attention to new policy issues.[36] At the same time, because people in
government demand timely political feedback, journalists often become

"stand-ins" for the national constituency, shaping policymakers' perceptions of the prevailing "national mood."[37]

The multiple paths of influence that connect the public, news media, and policymakers can make tracing an instance of agenda setting to its ultimate causal source difficult, if not impossible. In this case at least, the rise in public support for health care reform appears to have been a precursor to the increase in news media coverage, and perhaps a cause of it. But what seems most significant is that public opinion, media coverage, and political events all closely tracked one another. The sudden emergence of health care reform onto the national political agenda thus appears to be an example of an "amplifying feedback loop," in which the public, news media, and national policymakers all responded to the cues put forth by the others, creating a rapid cascade of attention to the issue.[38]

HEALTH CARE REFORM AND THE
CONGRESSIONAL AGENDA

In 1991 Congress faced a growing number of health care reform proposals. Yet there remained some trepidation among policymakers about addressing the issue. The federal government's last great foray into the wilderness of health care reform, the Medicare Catastrophic Coverage Act (MCCA), had been passed in 1988 and repealed the next year after outraged upper-income senior citizens revolted against the progressive taxes it levied on Medicare beneficiaries. Also ill-fated was the Bipartisan Commission on Comprehensive Health Care (the Pepper Commission). Authorized by the MCCA to come up with a series of recommendations for health care reform, the commission had quickly descended into partisan bickering. Its final recommendations, released in 1990, had been greeted with little fanfare.

Noticeably absent from the debate over health care reform was Republican President George Bush. In his 1990 State of the Union address, the president had called upon Health and Human Services Secretary Louis Sullivan to craft a response to the issue. But dissension within the administration and between Bush and congressional Republicans over the appropriate character of that response had left the White House on the sidelines and Republican members of Congress bereft of executive leadership.

While President Bush faltered, the Democratic leadership in the Senate pushed ahead with its comprehensive health care reform initiative, Health America. In early June, the sponsors of Health America—Senators George Mitchell, Ted Kennedy, Don Riegle, and Jay Rockefeller—made

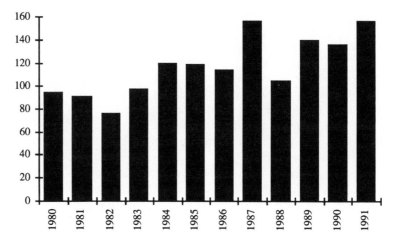

Figure 1.4 Frequency of Congressional Hearings on Health Care. Health care topics include the National Institutes of Health, health care costs, health insurance, Medicare, Medicaid, drugs, the Food and Drug Administration, medical facilities, nursing homes, medical education, mental illness, medical fraud and malpractice, long-term care, senior citizens' health, women's health, abortion, veterans' health, military health, AIDS, cancer, heart and lung disease, Alzheimer's disease, various other diseases, and medical research and development (*source*: data courtesy of Frank R. Baumgartner, Bryan D. Jones, and Jeffery C. Talbert, National Science Foundation project no. SBR-9320922, Frank R. Baumgartner and Bryan D. Jones, principal investigators).

an impassioned plea for support to an assembled hall of interest-group representatives and corporate lobbyists, warning them that the failure of the bill and its play-or-pay approach would open the door to more disruptive reforms.[39] But other Democratic members of the Senate and House wanted to go further. In the spring of 1991, Representative Marty Russo of Illinois, a member of the pivotal House Ways and Means Committee, introduced a single-payer proposal to replace all existing private and public insurance with a universal public program.[40]

One way to estimate changes in the level of congressional attention to health care is to count the number of hearings that were held on the topic by congressional committees and subcommittees.[41] Yet hearings have their shortcomings as a measure of agenda status. Many hearings on health care are concerned with routine or ongoing issues surrounding existing health programs, including the periodic reauthorization of programs. Many others concern topics only tangentially related to health care reform, such as medical research or the process by which new drugs are approved. As figure 1.4 reveals, the total number of congressional

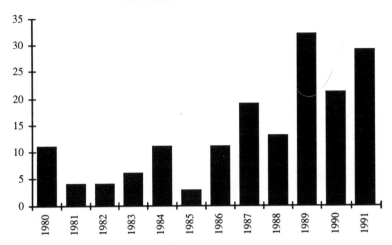

Figure 1.5   Frequency of Congressional Hearings on Health Care Costs or the Uninsured (*source*: data courtesy of Frank R. Baumgartner, Bryan D. Jones, and Jeffery C. Talbert, National Science Foundation project no. SBR-9320922, Frank R. Baumgartner and Bryan D. Jones, principal investigators).

hearings on health care remained consistently high from 1980 through 1991, exceeding 100 hearings per year after 1983 and topping 150 hearings annually in 1987 and 1991.[42] Although the number of hearings generally increased over this twelve-year period, the level of congressional attention remained remarkably high throughout. In every year from 1980 through 1991, Congress appears to have paid a considerable amount of attention to topics surrounding health policy.[43]

The picture looks somewhat different, however, if we consider only those congressional hearings that focused on medical costs or the uninsured.[44] Figure 1.5 shows the total number of congressional hearings that were held annually on these topics over the same twelve-year period. The volume of hearings is smaller in this case, and it increases more dramatically between 1980 and 1991. The number of hearings rises erratically through the mid-1980s, jumps sharply in 1989, falls back in 1990, and then rises again in 1991.

There is a similar but more dramatic increase in another indicator of legislative activity—the volume of legislation introduced in Congress.[45] Figure 1.6 shows the total number of bills on the subject of national health care introduced in each Congress from the 96th (1979 and 1980) through the 102nd (1991 and 1992).[46] The number of bills remains fairly meager until the 100th Congress (1987 and 1988), then rises precipitously, from 13 bills in the 96th Congress (1985 and 1986) to 63 in the 100th Congress to around 100 in both the 101st (1989 and 1990) and

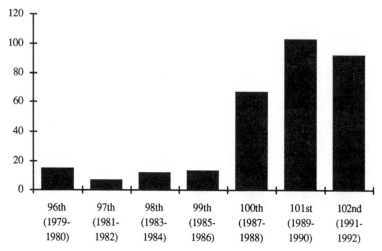

Figure 1.6 Number of Bills Introduced in Congress Related to "National Health Care" or "National Health Insurance." For the 96th and 97th Congresses, the subject code was "national health care"; for all others, it was "national health (insurance) care" (*source*: computerized search by author).

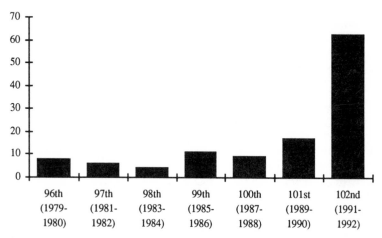

Figure 1.7 Number of Bills Introduced in Congress Related to "National Health Care" or "National Health Insurance," Narrow Definition. See note 47 for a description of the search parameters (*source*: computerized search by author).

102nd Congresses. Perhaps most surprising is the considerable legislative activity that surfaced in the 101st Congress, well before the Pennsylvania election. Indeed, the number of bills actually fell slightly in the 102nd Congress, from 103 to 92. However, this largely reflects the large amount of legislation pertaining to the MCCA that was introduced between 1987 and 1989. When tabulated using a more narrow definition of health care reform, the number of bills in the 100th Congress showed no increase, and the number in the 101st Congress rose only modestly.[47] By this narrower definition, as figure 1.7 shows, the real jump in legislative activity took place in the 102nd Congress, during which the number of bills rose from 17 to 63. About two-thirds of these bills—41 of the 63—were introduced after the Pennsylvania election.

Taken as a whole, the pattern of congressional hearings and legislative introductions suggests two basic trends in congressional attention to health care reform. First, there was clearly a significant degree of congressional attention to health care reform even before the Pennsylvania election, with the subject beginning to rise steeply on the congressional agenda in the late 1980s. Second, like both public support for reform and media coverage of reform, congressional attention to the subject appears to have jumped sharply in the 102nd Congress (1991 and 1992), in the run-up to and immediate aftermath of the Pennsylvania election.

MOMENTUM TOWARD REFORM IN CONGRESS

What explains the momentum toward health care reform in Congress in the years immediately preceding the Pennsylvania election? We have already surveyed some of the proximate causes—deteriorating conditions in American medicine, rising public anxiety, and a sharp economic downturn—but three others seem comparably important. The first was the increasing pressure public health programs were placing on state and federal budgets. By the late 1980s, the escalating cost of the two largest federal health programs, Medicare and Medicaid, was generating widespread unease in Congress. In 1982 Congress had passed legislation requiring the Health Care Financing Administration to develop new methods for paying hospitals under Medicare. By the time of the Pennsylvania election, Congress had also enacted legislation creating fee schedules for physicians serving Medicare beneficiaries. Despite these measures, however, the cost of public health programs continued to rise rapidly.[48]

A second proximate cause of health care reform's enhanced stature on the congressional agenda was the emergence in the late 1980s of a revitalized Democratic leadership in the House, centered around the chairs of the major fiscal committees and the Speaker of the House. A key reflection of the Democratic party's stronger leadership style was the aggressive legislative activism of the new Speaker, Jim Wright of Texas, who entered office in 1987 with an ambitious list of legislative goals that included catastrophic health insurance. Although it was President Reagan who first drew national attention to catastrophic health insurance with some offhand comments at a presidential news conference in January 1986, leading members of Congress quickly made the issue part of their own more far-reaching health policy agendas.[49] The return of the Senate to Democratic control in the 1986 election placed both houses of Congress in Democratic hands, and shortly thereafter Reagan's standing was further weakened by the Iran-Contra scandal. Wright and other members of the leadership were able to take advantage of Reagan's faltering stance, coupled with more than a decade of growth in the power of the Speaker and the Democratic Caucus, to pursue a partisan agenda more forcefully than the House leadership had since the beginning of Reagan's presidency. In the end, neither Wright, who resigned under a cloud of ethics violations in 1989, nor catastrophic health insurance, which was repealed the same year, proved to have much lasting impact. Yet the new assertiveness of the Democratic leadership on catastrophic health insurance and other policy issues marked the arrival of a congressional leadership more willing to define its policy commitments and use its expanded leadership prerogatives to achieve them, even in the face of presidential opposition.[50]

Finally, increased congressional attention to health care reform had a third important proximate cause: the growing demands for reform being voiced by the major stakeholders in the health policy domain. By the time of the Pennsylvania election, many of the organized interests in health care had expressed support for some kind of reform. Even the American Medical Association (AMA), the most vociferous opponent of reform in the past, had proposed an employment-based plan to improve access to medical care.[51] Other provider groups—such as the American College of Physicians and American Academy of Family Physicians—appeared willing to accept even more comprehensive reforms. Business was also beginning to countenance a greater federal role in the financing of medical care after more than a decade of futile attempts to handle costs on its own.

At first glance, this chorus of interest-group support for reform appears puzzling. As Lawrence Brown asks, "If a formidable phalanx of powerful groups throttled change in the 1980s, why did they seemingly cease to do so in the early 1990s?"[52] The answer, paradoxically, is that the seeds of interest-group discontent were sown by the very success of these powerful stakeholders in preventing substantial policy change—not just in the 1980s, but during most of this century. By the 1970s continued cost increases were driving both the government and private employers to take more active steps to rein in medical inflation. In the 1980s these efforts began to produce results but not exactly the results their architects had intended. Federal cost-containment initiatives were shifting costs onto the private sector, the growing microregulation of clinical decisions by insurers was irritating providers and patients alike, and corporate America's quest for lower insurance premiums was further segmenting the insurance market and lowering coverage rates among individuals and small firms. In the past, when the nation's capacity for absorbing rising medical spending appeared virtually limitless, stakeholders had seen little reason to challenge one another over the exact division of the spoils of medical progress. But now these same stakeholders saw the conflict as zero-sum—one group's gain came at the expense of another—and each believed that it was uniquely disadvantaged in relation to its antagonists. Accordingly, medical providers, insurers, and business all began to put forward proposals for reform that they believed would restore the proper balance.

If the new aggressiveness of the Democratic leadership and the changing stance of powerful stakeholders were important proximate causes of the increased congressional attention to health care reform, they also reflected a broader transformation of the structure of American health politics. This transformation can be viewed as the deep or underlying cause of the increased congressional attention to reform, for it significantly increased the probability of a renewed legislative push for national health care reform.

Mark Peterson describes this transformation as a shift from an "iron triangle," in which powerful private interests had privileged access to an oligarchically organized Congress, into a more open "policy network," in which power was widely dispersed among interest groups and individual legislators.[53] The point of departure for Peterson's analysis is the early postwar period, when the medical lobby and a cross-party conservative coalition in Congress effectively blocked consideration of President Truman's proposal for national health insurance. Led by the AMA, the organized interests opposing Truman's proposal were unified and powerful—more than a match for the scattered band of supporters of the bill. By the 1960s and the debate over Medicare, the interest-group community had grown more polarized and its opposing camps more evenly paired, leading one observer to describe the Medicare struggle as a classic illustration of "class-conflict politics."[54] But the crucial shift occurred in the two decades following Medicare's passage, as new "stake-challengers" entered the political arena and old stakeholders had increasing difficulty maintaining their traditional alliance. In 1945 the dominant groups in the health policy domain had been profit and nonprofit sector associations, with organized labor and citizen groups serving as the main political counterweight. From 1945 to 1985, and especially after 1970, the proportion of citizen groups and mixed profit-nonprofit organizations rose, while the proportion of profit-sector groups declined. More important, newer groups were more likely than their older counterparts to endorse increased government support for health care, even in sectors historically antagonistic to government involvement.[55]

Not only did the composition of interest groups in the health policy domain change in the decades after World War II, the aggregate number of groups increased as well. Since the 1960s, there has been a dramatic rise in the number of interest groups operating in all federal policy areas, but in none more so than health. The number of interest groups active in health and social policy rose from 674 in 1960 to almost 4,000 in 1990—an almost sixfold increase. In comparison, the number of groups in all other policy areas increased by about a factor of four over the same thirty-year period.[56]

Paralleling the transformation of interests in the health policy domain were dramatic changes in the organization of Congress. The oligarchic Congress of the Truman era, dominated by conservative committee chairs, soon ran afoul of the liberal tide of the 1960s. In 1964 liberal Democrats tamed the Rules Committee by reinstating the twenty-one day rule, which prevented the committee from stalling bills for more than three weeks. During the 1960s, congressional staffs grew significantly, providing members with new independent resources for policy advocacy. And beginning in 1971, the Democratic Caucus instituted a series of rule changes that expanded the number of subcommittees and increased their power vis-à-vis full committees.

These institutional reforms ushered in a new congressional order, more supportive of legislative entrepreneurship and less conducive to the formation of entrenched policy subsystems than the oligarchy before it. Even rank-and-file members now had the resources and discretion to play a leadership role on policy issues, and many more committees and subcommittees participated in the making of health policy. In the House, for example, health care issues were divided among no fewer than seven major committees. And for the first time, all but one of the House and Senate committees and subcommittees with a significant jurisdictional interest in health care reform were chaired by members who supported reform.[57]

This dispersion of leadership among congressional committees is evident in the distribution of congressional hearings on health care. From 1980 to 1991, hearings on health care were divided among more congressional committees than hearings on any other major policy issue before Congress. Furthermore, no single committee enjoyed clear jurisdictional dominance. The committees with the largest share of hearings—the House Select Committee on Aging and the Senate Labor and Human Resources Committee—each accounted for only around one-quarter of the total number of hearings held in their respective parent bodies. Four committees in the House and three in the Senate held more than one hundred hearings *each* between 1980 and 1991. No other policy area is characterized by this degree of jurisdictional fragmentation.[58]

The effects of congressional reforms on the prospects for achieving national health care reform were not uniformly favorable. Although the reforms broke the legislative stranglehold of baronial committee chairs, and with it the privileged influence of the medical lobby, they also made it difficult for congressional chairs and party leaders to construct coalitions and broker legislative compromise.[59] But the effects of these changes on the prospects for *addressing* national health care reform were not so ambiguous. Never before had so many members of Congress been poised to play a leadership role on the issue, or possessed the analytic resources needed to develop serious proposals for reform.[60] By the 1990s, the structure of power in Congress and the interest-group community was uniquely hospitable to a renewed legislative campaign for national health care reform.

THE IMPACT OF THE PENNSYLVANIA ELECTION

We have examined some of the major reasons why national health care reform was receiving serious consideration in Congress even before Harris Wofford won in Pennsylvania. These were the underlying and proximate causes of the increased congressional attention to health care reform, the factors that helped push the issue onto the congressional agenda. The Pennsylvania election was the catalyst—the "focusing event," to use John Kingdon's phrase—that transformed the building momentum toward reform into a whole-scale rush.[61] Without the deeper causes, Wofford's victory would not have had the effect it did. Without Wofford's victory, the deeper causes may not have produced a serious congressional response or may have produced one only after further years of accumulating pressure. Together, the momentum toward reform in Congress and the outcome in Pennsylvania pushed health care reform to the top of the national political agenda.

That the Pennsylvania election precipitated a stunning increase in public and political attention to health care reform is undeniable. The figures presented earlier concerning media coverage, congressional hearings, and legislative introductions all reveal a large jump in the agenda status of health care reform around the time of the election. As we shall see later in this chapter, the response of Washington politicians to Wofford's victory was prompt, unambiguous, and consequential. Why the Pennsylvania election was such an important catalyst, however, is less clear. Kingdon argues, for example, that elections are not a particularly prominent factor in agenda setting, counted as important in only 30 percent of his interviews and seven of his twenty-three case studies.[62] This conclusion seems to be in accord with the frequent observation that politicians need not worry much about reelection, or at least cannot do much about it. After all, nearly all incumbent members of Congress are reelected—more than 95 percent of House members in the 1980s—and their average margin of victory has increased since the 1960s.[63] It seems unlikely that this advantage could be wiped out by an incumbent's position on a single issue, even one as salient as health care reform. Indeed, much of the literature on congressional elections suggests that factors other than candidates' positions—such as national party tides, presidential popularity, and the state of the economy—are the main determinants of electoral outcomes.[64] Given this, why would members of Congress pay much heed to the outcome of a single Senate race?

To begin with, Pennsylvania's Senate race had several atypical features that made it especially visible and important. The most critical was its timing. The Pennsylvania election was the only off-year Senate race in 1991, and it occurred in the year before a presidential election. President Bush, who had seemed invincible in the wake of the 1991 military triumph in Iraq, was beginning to look more vulnerable on the domestic front, with polls showing a smaller percentage of voters believing he should be reelected than at any time in his presidency.[65] Furthermore, Bush and Thornburgh were closely identified with one another: Thornburgh had stepped down from the Bush cabinet to run, he had made his service in the administration a major campaign theme, and he had asked both Bush and Vice President Dan Quayle to campaign for him in Pennsylvania. From the outset, therefore, the Pennsylvania race had been viewed as an important harbinger of the 1992 presidential campaign.

Moreover, it is simply not true that the electoral constraints on members of Congress are so diffuse or weak that members can do whatever they please. Gary Jacobson has shown that despite the increase in incumbents' winning margins in congressional elections, House members are still as likely to lose their races as they were before the 1960s, because at the same time that electoral margins have risen, elections have grown more volatile.[66] Not only are incumbent members of Congress who won by large margins in previous elections more vulnerable to challengers than in the past, but incumbents are also less affected by national party swings than they once were.[67] Increasingly, they rise or fall on their own, rather than with their party or their party's presidential candidate. The net result is that members of Congress are probably no more certain of their reelection today than they were thirty years ago.

The uncertainty surrounding future elections explains why members of Congress appear more cautious than their healthy margins of victory in previous elections would seem to warrant. Critics of Congress routinely bemoan the lack of dispatch with which Congress responds to controversial or complex issues, citing it as evidence that Congress is insufficiently responsive to the wishes of the electorate. In many cases, however, delay or incrementalism may be the most prudent congressional response to an uncertain environment. As Keith Krehbiel argues: "Other things being equal, legislators would rather select policies whose consequences are known in advance than policies whose consequences are uncertain. Under conditions of relative certainty, legislators can plan and make the most of credit-claiming. . . . Under conditions of relative uncertainty, however, surprise and the prospect of embarrassment lurk beneath any policy choice."[68]

Krehbiel argues that members of Congress seek to reduce the degree of uncertainty inherent in the policy choices they make by agreeing to rules, procedures, and structures that encourage the development of policy-related knowledge. But the uncertainty of the policy process also leads legislators to search for issues with demonstrated public salience. After examining the agenda of the U.S. Senate, for example, Jack Walker concludes that for a new or previously neglected policy issue to emerge on the Senate agenda, "senators must believe that the proposed legislation will have broad political appeal."[69] This condition is particularly important when a policy issue benefits the unorganized over the likely opposition of the organized, for in these cases members of Congress need some assurance that the unorganized constituencies that stand to benefit from a policy change will reward them at the polls for taking action (or punish them for failing to take action). Once popular attention to a policy issue is confirmed, however, members of Congress are likely to rush to it to share in the rewards. As one House aide put it: "Politicians are terrific at figuring out when it is no longer fruitful to be a hold-out. When the public has come to some judgment about what they think needs to be done, and they think somebody is actually proposing that, then to be opposed to it carries some liabilities."[70]

In American politics, elections are a particularly important source of information about which issues and proposals have the greatest potential to elicit popular support. Although scholars question the concept of an electoral mandate, few people in and around government seem to share their skepticism.[71] The last ballot is barely cast in an American election before observers and participants begin to proclaim the grand meaning of the results. It may be that such biennial exercises in political diagnosis serve a special purpose in the American political system. Where parties are weak and government power is fragmented, election results provide a common basis for priority-setting and coordination. As David Mayhew notes, "Nothing is more important in Capitol Hill politics than the shared conviction that election returns have proven a point."[72]

But how do such shared convictions form? Marjorie Hershey argues that the ambiguity of election results creates powerful incentives for journalists, politicians, and other political activists to construct plausible explanations of the vote.[73] Journalists want to offer deeper explanations of election results than vote totals alone can offer, politicians use election results to plan their political strategies, and a wide range of activists want to promote interpretations of election results that advantage them politically. The formal campaign is therefore followed by a postelection struggle among "campaigners, consultants, party and group leaders [who wish] to get their explanations of the election results reported as if they were fact."[74] These dueling explanations are then winnowed down by the news media to a few chosen explanations that become the "conventional wisdom."

To see if such a process unfolded after Pennsylvania's 1991 Senate race, I performed an analysis of postelection media coverage similar to the one conducted by Hershey to examine coverage of the 1984 presidential election.[75] My results offer strong support for Hershey's central thesis that the number of explanations of an election presented in the news media declines over time. The number of different interpretations was highest on November 7, the second day after the election, when some thirty-five separate explanations of the vote appeared. It quickly dropped to fewer than ten distinct explanations per day, reaching zero several times after the second week. The drop reflected both a precipitous fall in the total number of articles mentioning the election and a decline in the total number of explanations offered per article. The day after the election, for example, the average number of explanations per article was more than six. By the end of November, it was around one.[76]

One of the most interesting results is the extent to which news media coverage of the Pennsylvania election focused on Wofford's victory rather than Thornburgh's defeat (see table 1.1). This finding is directly contrary to the pattern found by Hershey in newspaper coverage of the 1984 presidential election, which focused disproportionately on Walter Mondale's defeat. It seems likely that part of the reason for this discrepancy is that Wofford's victory in 1991 was much more startling than Ronald Reagan's in 1984. Even so, the sheer imbalance in newspaper coverage is striking. Almost three-quarters of the total number of explanations appearing in the print media after the Pennsylvania election attributed the outcome to Wofford's persona, his positions on key issues, his support coalition, and his campaign strategy. By contrast, only between 10 and 11 percent of the explanations focused on Thornburgh and

TABLE 1.1

Media Explanations of the Pennsylvania Election, November 6–30, 1991

Explanation	Number of citations	Percent of all explanations cited
Characteristics of Electorate	38	10.2
Anti-Washington/anti-incumbent mood	16	4.3
General anxiety/anger	12	3.2
Desire for change	6	1.6
Focus on domestic problems	3	0.8
All other	1	0.3
Characteristics of Wofford	277	74.7
Issues, Policies	215	58.0
National health care reform	95	25.6
State of economy	49	13.2
Anti-Washington	11	3.0
"America first"	10	2.7
General populism/progressivism	10	2.7
Taxes/tax cuts to middle class	8	2.2
Unemployment benefits	8	2.2
Anti-Bush administration	6	1.6
Foreign trade	6	1.6
General focus on domestic policy	4	1.1
Resentment toward "undeserving"	2	0.5
All other	6	1.6
Constituency	36	9.7
Middle class	23	6.2
Labor	11	3.0
All other	2	0.5
Personalistic	19	5.1
"Outsider"	8	2.2
Painted Thornburgh as "insider"	7	1.9
Good character/credentials	3	0.8
All other	1	0.3
Strategic	7	1.9
Set/controlled campaign agenda	5	1.3
Effective TV campaign	2	0.5
Characteristics of Thornburgh	39	10.5
Personalistic	19	5.1
Close ties to Bush	5	1.3
"Insider"	5	1.3
Arrogant	3	0.8
Lacked conviction	3	0.8
Too liberal	2	0.5
All other	1	0.3

TABLE 1.1 *(cont.)*

Explanation	Number of citations	Percent of all explanations cited
Characteristics of Thornburgh *(cont.)*		
Strategic	19	5.1
Bad campaign strategy in general	6	1.6
Emphasized résumé	4	1.1
Too negative	3	0.8
Ceded initiative in campaign	2	0.5
Gaffe by aide	2	0.5
Not negative enough	2	0.5
All other	1	0.3
Characteristics of Bush administration	13	3.5
Economic policies	9	2.4
Focused on foreign policy	3	0.8
All other	1	0.3
Characteristics of the Democrats **(no longer special-interest party)**	3	0.8
All other	1	0.3

his campaign. Another 4 percent or so of the explanations linked the vote to the Bush administration and its policies, while the remaining 10 percent focused on the mood of the electorate. Only a handful of explanations dealt with the electorate's perceptions of the Democratic party—a major topic in postelection coverage of the 1984 presidential race.

By every measure, the campaign theme most commonly cited in explanations of Wofford's victory was national health care reform. Fully 81 percent of the articles that appeared after the election made some reference to health care reform, if only to note that it was a key issue in the race. Wofford's endorsement of national health insurance was also by far the leading *explanation* of the Pennsylvania vote, accounting for more than a quarter of all explanations offered between November 5 and December 1. By comparison, the next most frequently cited explanation—Wofford's focus on the ailing economy—accounted for only about half as many explanations, or roughly 13 percent of the total. Furthermore, the argument that Wofford won because he championed national health insurance became increasingly prominent in the weeks after the Pennsylvania election, rising from roughly one-quarter of the total number of interpretations offered per day to between 50 and 60 percent by the last week of November (see figure 1.8). Clearly, therefore, this explanation sur-

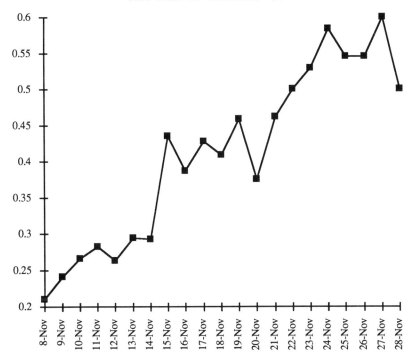

Figure 1.8   Wofford's Advocacy of National Health Care Reform (as a percentage of all explanations cited per day using five-day rolling averages) (*source*: content analysis of postelection media coverage by author).

vived the winnowing process to enter the conventional wisdom about the Pennsylvania race.

Indeed, very quickly after the election, a stock account of the results emerged that neatly tied together the three leading explanations of the vote: Wofford's support of national health care reform, his focus on the faltering economy, and his ability to connect with the politically crucial middle class. A *Washington Post* editorial on November 8, for example, described "the middle-class populism of Harris Wofford, who came out for health care and against unemployment."[77] On November 10, the *New York Times* pointed out that Wofford's successful campaign "had hammered away at related themes: that President Bush's policies had damaged the economy and particularly the middle class, and that the United States badly needs national health insurance."[78] And a *Washington Post* article on November 19 quoted a political scientist who argued that "health care was a subset of a much more complex set of motives. . . . [T]his was all about the fear of the middle class that their economic life is falling apart."[79] These three explanations—health care reform, the economy, and the middle class—together accounted for almost half of all explanations offered between November 5 and December 1.

Why were these explanations favored over others? And why, in particular, did Wofford's endorsement of national health insurance come to dominate media accounts of the election? In Hershey's model, the conventional wisdom emerges through a competitive process in which journalists and political activists construct explanations of "events [that] have no inherent meaning."[80] Yet it is worth questioning whether Hershey's constructivist account attributes too much latitude to those seeking to explain election results. After all, it would have been virtually impossible to discuss the Pennsylvania election in any detail without mentioning Wofford's support of national health insurance. Events may have no "inherent meaning" in the positivist sense that they embody some objective truth that need only be discovered, but this does not mean that competing interpretations of events are all equally valid or plausible. Rather, one would expect the range of acceptable interpretations to vary with the degree of ambiguity surrounding an event. Election results, because they are generally quite ambiguous, are particularly open to interpretation. Nonetheless, some explanations of election results may appear so self-evident in light of the available information that journalists and political activists find them difficult to ignore.

On this score, it is interesting to note the extent to which arguments linking Wofford's win to health care reform and the economy were promoted not by Democratic sources, but by key Republicans and the Bush administration. One might have expected Republican sources outside the Thornburgh camp to lay the blame for Thornburgh's defeat on Thornburgh and his campaign strategy. But one of the main reasons why these explanations appeared so infrequently in media accounts of the election was that very few Republicans offered them. Republican National Committee Chairman Clayton Yeutter called the Pennsylvania results an "aberration" without elaborating further.[81] Texas senator Phil Gramm, head of the National Republican Senatorial Campaign Committee, conceded that the election "turned into a referendum on Dick Thornburgh's resume versus [Wofford's] issues, and we lost that referendum."[82] Several other Republican senators were more explicit than Gramm about the appeal of Wofford's campaign themes. Senator Arlen Specter of Pennsylvania told reporters that the election carried "a very strong message" for the Bush administration about the "many, many domestic issues that have to be faced."[83] Arizona senator John McCain argued that the "election indicated clearly that the American people want the health-care issue addressed."[84]

Perhaps the most striking example of a Republican source casting the Pennsylvania vote as a vindication of Wofford's campaign platform was the postelection statements of President Bush. In a news conference the day after the election, Bush explained that the vote bore a "message" for his administration and for Congress: "When the economy is slow, people are concerned. They're hurting out there. They're concerned about their livelihood. . . . One of the messages in Pennsylvania: try to help people with health care."[85] As if to prove he had heard the message, Bush canceled a planned state visit to Asia and told reporters that the administration was now planning to develop its own health care reform proposal before the presidential election.[86]

If newspaper coverage is an accurate guide, then, there seems to have been a remarkable degree of consensus among political activists about the meaning of the Pennsylvania vote. It is of course possible that journalists screened out competing explanations of the election, perhaps out of sympathy for Wofford's policy positions. (Hershey found that Democratic sources were cited much more frequently after the 1984 election than Republican ones.) But the similarity between Republican and Democratic interpretations of the vote suggests that there really was widespread agreement among activists of both parties on the reasons for Wofford's win. Certainly, the prevalence of explanations citing Wofford's endorsement of national health insurance did not reflect careful analysis of survey data. Only five articles out of almost four hundred explicitly mentioned the exit poll that showed "national health insurance" at the top of Pennsylvanians' voting concerns.[87]

Not only did a wide range of activists put roughly the same "spin" on the Pennsylvania results, but they acted in accordance with this shared interpretation. The day after the election, a group of Senate Republicans led by John Chafee of Rhode Island and including Minority Leader Bob Dole took the opportunity to introduce their own proposal for reform, which offered refundable tax credits for the purchase of private insurance.[88] In the White House, Bush finally acceded to the inevitable and gave his health policy staff permission to develop a plan in earnest. Although it was clear that he would adopt an incremental approach similar to the tax-credit plan favored by Senate Republicans, the very fact that the administration was rushing to introduce a proposal indicated how far the outcome in Pennsylvania had pushed the debate.

For Democrats, a strategy for recapturing the White House in the 1992 presidential election had emerged. On the campaign trail, every major Democratic presidential candidate invoked Wofford's victory in declaring his support for national health care reform. In the Senate, the Democratic leadership launched a new effort to rally Democrats around their play-or-pay initiative and to coordinate their legislative activities with the leadership in the House. The Senate leadership also began to focus more directly on cultivating public support for reform, with Wofford joining Senator Rockefeller and Senate Majority Leader Mitchell in a five-state campaign to raise public awareness about the topic. In January alone, Democratic members of Congress held almost three hundred hearings on health care reform in their home districts or states. Even Senator Lloyd Bentsen, the cautious Democratic chair of the Finance Committee, became more outspoken in his support for reform, hinting that the public might be prepared for more fundamental change than he had previously envisioned.[89]

The response of members of Congress to the Pennsylvania election thus lent additional credence to the dominant interpretation of the vote. Convinced that Wofford's win was linked to his endorsement of national health insurance, politicians rushed to demonstrate their commitment to reform. This in turn reinforced the perception that the Pennsylvania vote reflected widespread public support for reform.[90]

The political bandwagons that form when new causes gain salience and popular support is one of the reasons for the presence of "positive feedback" in American politics.[91] Small changes may cascade into larger ones, single events may lead to whole series of events, and policy issues may expand quickly to involve all levels of the political system. Agenda change seems to occur swiftly as politicians lurch from issue to issue, only some of which are ultimately addressed. In many cases, agenda dynamics follow a pattern similar to the "issue-attention cycle" that Anthony Downs observed in American public attention to ecology: long-standing problems suddenly move to the center of political concern, then drift from the spotlight whether or not they are addressed.[92]

CONCLUSION

Harris Wofford's surprise victory in Pennsylvania brought to light the depth of middle-class discontent with the rising cost of health care and the insecurity of health insurance coverage. This discontent was a response to changes in the structure of American medicine that increasingly exposed insured, middle-class Americans to the financial insecurities of the working poor and the uninsured. These structural changes in turn resulted from the desperate attempt by American business to reduce the financial liability of employee medical benefits.

The outcome of Pennsylvania's Senate race alerted policymakers to the need to do something, but it provided little guidance as to what that something should be. Although public dissatisfaction with the status quo was almost palpable, opinion surveys revealed that most Americans remained ambivalent about the major proposals for reform.[93]

At the time of Wofford's stunning victory, three major approaches dominated the national debate: the single-payer approach, the play-or-pay approach, and the tax-credit approach. Not only was managed competition not among these leading reform models, but it had scarcely been mentioned on Capitol Hill or in the media. Yet less than a year after the Wofford election had secured the place of health care reform on the national political agenda, Bill Clinton would embrace managed competition en route to the presidency.

The following chapters turn to the question of why managed competition moved onto the national agenda in the wake of the Pennsylvania election. First, however, we must step back in time to explore the genesis of managed competition and its evolution over the last two decades.

CHAPTER 2

A Prescription for Reform

THE POLICY IDEAS embodied in managed competition are not new. The approach is rooted in a critique of American health policy that was first prominently advanced by economists and health policy analysts in the early 1970s. Building upon this critique, Alain Enthoven developed a market-oriented approach to universal health insurance that gained national attention in the late 1970s. Over the next decade, Enthoven refined his original reform design to address the concerns of critics. This model formed the basis for the managed-competition proposal developed by the Jackson Hole Group in 1991.

This chapter examines the genesis and evolution of managed competition and its sudden emergence onto the national political agenda. It explores how and under what influences managed competition developed over the last two decades and why it was embraced by medical industry leaders and key political actors in Washington. The chapter begins by analyzing the various strands of thought that fed into the managed-competition approach, then discusses the development of and response to Enthoven's 1977 Consumer Choice Health Plan, and then explains how the core ideas of the 1977 plan became the foundation of the Jackson Hole Group's proposal. The latter half of the chapter explains how the Jackson Hole model was brought to the attention of policymakers, and why critical elements of the proposal were adopted by political leaders in the aftermath of Pennsylvania's Senate race.

THE INFLUX OF ECONOMISTS INTO HEALTH POLICY ANALYSIS

Until the 1960s, neoclassical economists paid scarce attention to the health care "market." Although economic concepts and methods had been applied to the medical sector, relatively few neoclassical economists had concerned themselves with medical financing and delivery, and health economics as a distinct field had yet to emerge.[1] Most of the ideas about reforming the medical sector were being produced within the executive branch, by bureaucrats in the Social Security Administration who remained firmly committed to the goal of social insurance. To these "like-minded managers and policymakers," the notion of price competition in health services financing and delivery was anathema.[2]

It is difficult to know why interest in health economics increased as dramatically as it did in the 1960s and 1970s. Part of the reason, no doubt, was that economists were playing a more prominent advisory role in all areas of public policy. After languishing under Presidents Truman and Eisenhower, the White House's Council of Economic Advisors emerged as a powerful player in economic policy under Kennedy.[3] At roughly the same time, the percentage of presidential cabinet members with some graduate training in economics began to rise steadily—from 8 percent under Johnson to 21 percent under Carter. By 1975, 74 percent of the 257 social scientists who worked at the highest level of the federal civil service were economists.[4]

The late 1960s and early 1970s also gave rise to a new set of concerns about health policy that were particularly conducive to economic analysis. The passage of Medicare and Medicaid in 1965 shifted the focus of government involvement in medical care from access to cost. As medical inflation and the expense of newly enacted public programs rose, policymakers scrambled to bring order and efficiency to America's costly patchwork of programs.[5] These efforts not only demanded the *expertise* of economists, who entered government and consulting organizations in increasing numbers.[6] They also pushed the terms of discourse into the realm of economic analysis—away from the rhetoric of equity and justice and toward the language of cost, efficiency, and incentives.[7]

Finally, "rationalizing politics" was accompanied by a shift in the ideological climate surrounding American health policy.[8] Rising medical costs coupled with stagnating corporate profits first elicited widespread alarm within the business community in the early 1970s. Throughout the decade corporate leaders and business publications issued stinging de-nouncements of the cost and inefficiency of both American medicine and the regulatory framework that governed it. Although the complaints of corporate America rarely translated into political action, they signified a new willingness on the part of business leaders to attack the medical pro-fession—its erstwhile ally in the struggle against "socialized medicine"—as insufficiently responsive to competitive pressures. Far more important, however, were broader currents of intellectual change that were eroding not only the authority of the medical profession, but also the entire philo-sophical architecture that had guided social and regulatory policy in the 1960s and early 1970s.

These intellectual developments took place on at least three fronts. On the right, an emerging band of neoconservative intellectuals portrayed the social policies of the Great Society and War on Poverty as an elaborate power-grab by a "new class" of educated professionals. Neoconservatives challenged the philosophical and programmatic legacy of the sixties, warned that the state had grown burdened with conflicting and unattainable goals, and demanded an enlarged role for the market in the amelioration of social problems.[9] Their distinctive contribution to health policy—beyond a basic distrust of government intervention—was a skepticism toward the benefits of modern medicine and, by implication, toward the claims of those who wished to expand access to it.[10] Similar sentiments were echoed on the left by radical social critics like Ivan Illich, who charged that medicine was a repressive mechanism of social control that caused more disease than it cured.[11]

The most significant intellectual development of the 1970s, however, was associated with neither the far right nor the far left. It was the general rise to prominence of economistic approaches to public policy.[12] This intellectual vogue manifested itself in a number of ways—in the growing emphasis placed by government agencies on policy research and evaluation, in the burgeoning "policy analysis" movement in schools of public policy, in the ascendance of corporate-funded think tanks, and most visibly in the sudden receptivity of official Washington to academic critiques of regulatory policy. Coupled with the increasingly antigovernment political wind that began sweeping through Washington in the late 1970s, the economistic view of government policy crystallized into a simple but powerful conclusion: that government regulation was costly, inefficient, and frequently ineffective and that it should be eliminated or made to work in tandem with the market.

The increasingly strident critique of government regulation mirrored changes that were taking place in the field of economics. Most of the health economists who were entering government and America's universities in the 1970s did not adopt the theoretical outlook and normative canon that had guided the architects of Social Security and Medicare. By the late 1960s, monetarism and neoclassical economics were making a comeback in academia. As inflation rose and policymakers found it increasingly difficult to manage the economy, economists began to question the basic tenets of Keynesian fiscal policy.[13] Two of the most influential critics of Keynesianism, Milton Friedman of the University of Chicago and Martin Feldstein of Harvard, both wrote extensively on health care finance.[14] Friedman and Feldstein shared the view that in health care, as in other areas, government policy had interfered with the proper workings of the free market. Friedman went further and criticized the institutionalized market power of the medical profession, even calling for the abolition of licensing.[15]

THE NEOCLASSICAL CRITIQUE

It is not hard to see why neoclassical economists found the health care market wanting. The medical sector clearly does not fit the paradigm of "perfect competition"—the standard by which neoclassical economists judge an effectively functioning market. On the demand side of the equation, federal and state governments and large private payers such as the Blues have concentrated purchasing power that allows them to affect prices.[16] Patients, the "consumers" of health care, are poorly informed relative to suppliers, unable to accurately compare services, and insulated from the full costs of their medical decisions by third-party insurance.[17] On the supply side, there exist substantial barriers to entry, such as licensing and accreditation requirements for physicians and other practitioners. Health care providers make many of the most costly decisions concerning the delivery of care (opening the door to what economists call "supplier-induced demand"). And providers themselves are largely insulated from cost pressures, since insurance will pay for most of the care they give. For these reasons and others, the medical sector deviates greatly from an ideal-type perfectly competitive market.

The paradigm of perfect competition is both descriptive and normative—descriptive in that it is a heuristic yardstick for judging the structure and performance of a market, and normative in that neoclassical economists view the perfectly competitive market as the optimal means of husbanding and allocating scarce resources. So it was natural that once economists had recognized the shortcomings of the market for health care, they would begin to advocate measures to remedy its failures. A series of "procompetitive" prescriptions emerged in the 1970s, falling into three general categories: measures to induce consumer cost-consciousness, measures to decrease the market power of medical providers, and measures to encourage alternative delivery systems, such as HMOs.[18]

The consumer approach had two strands. The first, most clearly articulated by Feldstein, criticized the favorable tax treatment of health care benefits.[19] Feldstein argued that the policy of excluding employer contributions to health insurance from taxable income leads to "overinsurance." Workers demand and employers provide more generous insurance than they would if they were using after-tax dollars. Since insurance effectively shields patients from the cost of treatment, "excess" insurance leads them to demand care that they would otherwise forgo.[20] Following the path blazed by Feldstein, a steady stream of economists have argued for a reduction in—or the whole-scale elimination of—tax subsidies for the purchase of health coverage.

A second, similar strand of the consumer approach centered on the "old-time religion" of greater cost-sharing.[21] On this view, raising the out-of-pocket prices patients face for health services and health insurance reduces the amount of care patients demand and hence the total cost of health care to society at large.[22] Like those who attack tax subsidies, the advocates of greater cost-sharing believe that health insurance discourages patients from economizing. If there is to be health insurance, they argue, its distortional effects should be limited by taxing it like other forms of employee compensation, requiring that patients pay more of the cost of treatment out of pocket, or both.

A second set of procompetitive measures that emerged in the 1970s focused not on consumer behavior, but on the market power of medical providers. Friedman's scathing criticism of the medical "cartel" was a harbinger of this line of thought. In the 1970s, other academics, such as Duke University law professor Clark Havighurst, called for far-reaching deregulatory measures.[23] An outgrowth of the broader deregulatory agenda, the antitrust movement in health was given a boost by a series of court cases in the late 1970s and early 1980s that eroded the special treatment of the medical profession under law.[24] One by one, the profession's claims to immunity from antitrust challenge fell in the courts. Although some felt this litigation did not go far enough, few argued that the profession retained the degree of professional autonomy that it had once enjoyed.

Finally, a third set of procompetitive measures aimed to encourage cost-effective alternative delivery systems. Proponents of these measures, like the advocates of deregulation, wanted to break the medical profession away from the guild model of practice. Rather than advocate a more vigorous application of antitrust policy, however, they challenged the economic cornerstone of the guild model—traditional fee-for-service payment. In its stead, they proposed the development of "total health care delivery systems," in which patients pay in advance for the delivery of comprehensive care through an integrated network of providers.[25] In the early 1970s, Paul Ellwood led the charge on this front when he pressed the Nixon administration to pass legislation encouraging health maintenance organizations (a term that he had coined). In 1978 Harold Luft published an influential review of fifty-one studies comparing traditional insurance and HMOs.[26] He found that Kaiser-Permanente HMOs in California reduced total costs by 10 to 40 percent compared with conventional insurance. Similar results were obtained by the RAND Health Insurance Experiment conducted in Seattle in the 1970s.[27]

The embrace of prepaid group practice by the advocates of competition was somewhat ironic, given that "prepaid group practice was originally associated with the cooperative movement and dismissed as a utopian, slightly subversive idea."[28] But it was well in keeping with their indictments of the "perverse incentives" in the medical system. Alternative delivery systems had the virtue of addressing these structural incentives through market mechanisms rather than large-scale government involvement. Thus they were viewed by procompetitive reformers as a means for creating "a health maintenance industry that [would be] largely self-regulatory."[29]

THE CONSUMER CHOICE HEALTH PLAN
AND ITS CRITICS

Managed competition emerged as a potent combination of these earlier academic proposals and the experience of health industry executives. It was inspired by the Federal Employees Health Benefits Program (FEHBP), a comprehensive health insurance program for federal employees established in 1959. The FEHBP was the model upon which Scott Fleming, an official in the Department of Health, Education, and Welfare (HEW) who had been a senior executive at Kaiser, based a proposal for national health insurance that circulated within the Nixon administration in 1973.[30] What attracted Fleming to the FEHBP was that it allowed federal employees to choose among numerous health plans, including HMOs, yet the government contributed the same amount to help pay for the annual premium regardless of which plan an employee chose. Fleming felt that this gave federal employees an incentive to purchase less expensive plans and insurers a reason to compete among one another to attract enrollees.

Fleming's work was extended by Alain Enthoven, an economist with experience in health policy who had been assistant secretary of defense under Robert McNamara in the 1960s. After leaving the Pentagon, Enthoven spent several years on the board of directors of Georgetown University and headed the medical branch of Litton Industries, a major multinational conglomerate. When Carter was elected president in 1976, HEW Secretary Joseph Califano solicited Enthoven to develop a "first-class private sector plan" for the administration's consideration.[31] The result was the "Consumer Choice Health Plan: An Approach to National Health Insurance Based on Regulated Competition in the Private Sector."[32] Modeled in part after the FEHBP and Fleming's 1973 proposal, the Consumer Choice Health Plan was the first comprehensive procompetitive proposal for national health insurance. Although it did not receive the endorsement of the Carter administration, Enthoven's proposal became quite influential and served as the prototype for several initiatives that were introduced in the 96th and 97th Congresses.[33]

The Consumer Choice Health Plan would have allowed citizens to choose among government-qualified local health plans, which Enthoven envisioned as organized systems of care, such as HMOs and PPOs. Premium rates would be linked to actuarial categories based on such variables as age, sex, and geographic location. The government would subsidize the purchase of insurance with refundable tax credits equal to a fixed percentage of the average cost incurred by each actuarial category. Medicaid would be replaced by means-tested vouchers for the purchase of insurance, and Medicare beneficiaries would be encouraged to join organized systems of care. Private insurers that wished to participate would agree to accept all enrollees during annual "open-enrollment" periods, charge the same premium for the same benefits to all persons in each actuarial category, and offer at least one plan covering only a basic package of benefits. People who chose not to enroll in a qualified plan would be ineligible for tax subsidies or vouchers.

It is important to understand how the Consumer Choice Health Plan differed from some of the other procompetitive measures mentioned thus far. First, it sought to increase consumer cost-consciousness, but at the time of choice among insurance plans rather than at the time of treatment. Because tax subsidies and vouchers would not vary with the plan chosen, people would have an incentive to choose less costly plans. Once they were enrolled in a plan, however, out-of-pocket costs would be limited by law. This was very different from eliminating tax subsidies altogether or requiring that patients pay more of the cost of care when they became sick.

Second, Enthoven stressed that the real focus of his proposal was not patients but providers. "Physicians are the primary decision-makers in our health care system," he wrote to Califano. "But the present structure of the industry imposes very little responsibility on them for the economic consequences of their health care decisions."[34] The most important effect of bringing people into organized systems of care, Enthoven felt, would be to subject providers to fiscal constraints that would encourage them to adopt more cost-effective practice styles. In addition, Enthoven wanted the government to provide patients with more information about health care alternatives, so that they would not have to rely solely on the judgment of physicians.

Finally, Enthoven paid more attention than other procompetitive reformers to the problem of "risk selection" by insurers. Enthoven saw it as axiomatic that the health care market could not work as long as there were strong incentives for insurers to identify and avoid insuring individuals with high expected medical expense. This was why he included actuarial categories in the Consumer Choice Health Plan. Allowing insurers to vary premiums by actuarial category attenuated the incentive for insurers to seek out low-risk enrollees and systematically exclude high-risk ones. Furthermore, tax subsidies would be adjusted to reflect the higher premiums charged to high-risk groups, so people in more costly actuarial categories would not end up paying much more than average for health insurance.

Nonetheless, the Consumer Choice Health Plan did not escape criticism. Hard-core advocates of competition were attracted to its market flavor, but disliked the regulated half of "regulated competition." They found the subsidies, vouchers, and rules too burdensome, and the government role in the reconstituted system too great.[35] A more thoughtful set of critiques of the plan came from those who doubted the general premises of the free-marketeers.[36] They pointed out that the proposal would be open to abuse and manipulation. There were many creative ways in which insurers could select risk. Few of them would be prevented by the proposal. Insurers could include high deductibles or copayments in their plans, thereby discouraging those who expected to incur high medical costs from enrolling. They could tailor the benefit package so that healthier people would find the plan attractive. In fact, requiring insurers to charge everyone in a given actuarial category the same premium would create an added incentive to weed out high risks within each category. This was particularly true because the variables that Enthoven wanted to use to develop actuarial categories—variables such as age, sex, and geographic location—account for very little of the variance in individual medical expenditures.[37]

The plan's critics also pointed out that there were far too few HMOs in operation for Enthoven's proposal to be a viable model for national reform. While California, the upper Midwest, and several cities in the Northeast were home to large numbers of HMOs, there were fewer than two hundred HMOs nationwide, and national HMO enrollment had not yet reached 7 million people.[38] Moreover, many regions of the country had too few residents to support several competing integrated health plans.

Yet another problem identified by the plan's critics was that of "underservice." The specter of underservice emerges for the very reason that health economists find HMOs and other alternative delivery systems attractive. Because HMOs rely on prospective per capita payment ("capitation") rather than retrospective fee-for-service payment, they force their providers to operate within a fixed prospective budget. Ideally, this will encourage providers to use resources more carefully and efficiently. Unfortunately, providers might instead discriminate against those who need care most, either by underserving them or by persuading them to disenroll.

A final critique of the plan focused on its potential treatment of the poor. Yale policy expert Theodore Marmor, one of the most outspoken supporters of universal public insurance, worried that the voucher approach would lead to "income tiering."[39] Since the value of the premium vouchers could not exceed the cost of what Enthoven termed the "low option plan," the poor might be forced into plans that covered the fewest number of contingencies, while the middle class and wealthy would be able to enroll in more comprehensive plans.

Although these criticisms formed a powerful indictment of the Consumer Choice Health Plan, Enthoven refused to concede defeat. He began to think about ways to remedy some of the problems identified by his critics. In his mind, the most serious deficiency of the original proposal was its vulnerability to risk selection. "It became apparent to me," he would later write, "that my 1977–78 writings left the incorrect impression that what I was proposing was an unmanaged market system made up of competitive medical plans on the supply side, individual consumers on the demand side, fixed and fairly minimal rules, and only passive supervision of them by government." Enthoven concluded that "management" of the market required "intelligent active collective agents on the demand side . . . who contract with the competing health care plans and continuously structure and adjust the market to overcome its tendencies to failure." These collective agents, which Enthoven termed "sponsors," could be employers or public-sector agencies. Sponsors would contract with managed-care plans and protect patients from risk selection or underservice.[40]

The concept of sponsors evolved further through Enthoven's association with Paul Ellwood, the Minneapolis physician who had played an instrumental role in convincing the Nixon administration to introduce legislation supporting HMOs. Since the early 1970s, Ellwood had been holding health care forums in Jackson Hole, Wyoming. Most of the attendees at these forums were representatives of the medical industry, particularly the HMO industry. In 1973 Ellwood founded InterStudy, a nonprofit think tank for the study of issues concerning the HMO industry. A year later, he invited Enthoven to attend InterStudy's annual meetings in Jackson Hole.[41]

Ellwood, Enthoven, and many of the other participants in the Jackson Hole meetings were firmly committed to procompetitive reform. But they also recognized that the continued escalation of health care costs and the rising number of uninsured were weakening support for the medical sector and threatening its gains. The insurance market was deteriorating, the number of uninsured was rising, and the dramatic growth in managed-care plans was having little effect on national health spending, which continued to grow at an unprecedented rate.

A CONSUMER CHOICE HEALTH PLAN FOR THE 1990S

In the late 1980s, Enthoven teamed up with another health policy expert, Richard Kronick, to develop an updated market approach to national health insurance. What emerged from their collaboration was the "Consumer Choice Health Plan for the 1990s," a "universal health insurance plan based on managed competition."[42] Although similar to Enthoven's 1977 plan, the new and improved Consumer Choice Health Plan departed from its progenitor in several important respects and incorporated an entirely new element—a "public sponsor" of private insurance.

Like the original Consumer Choice Health Plan, Enthoven and Kronick's proposal had two central features: universal insurance coverage and a regulated market to control costs. To achieve universal coverage, Enthoven and Kronick proposed a play-or-pay system in which all employers would be required to either insure their full-time employees or pay a tax based on their total payroll. Nonworkers, part-time employees, and full-time workers whose employers chose to pay the tax would obtain coverage through a public sponsor established in each state. The main funding for the public sponsors would come from the payroll tax and from taxes levied on those who obtained insurance through a sponsor. Subsidies would be available on a sliding scale for the poor, reaching 100 percent of the average cost of a basic health plan for individuals and families beneath the poverty line.

To control costs, Enthoven and Kronick proposed a system of "managed competition." This system had two main components: a requirement that employers and the public sponsors make "fixed contributions" to the cost of health insurance and a limit on the amount of an employer's contribution that could be excluded from taxation. The term "fixed contribution" was somewhat misleading, since contributions could vary with the health-risk categories of the enrollees in each plan. As Enthoven and Kronick employed the term, a fixed contribution was one that did not vary with the health plan chosen by the individual subscriber. The employer's contribution would thus be limited to a fixed percentage (Enthoven and Kronick proposed 80 percent) of the average cost of a health plan that covered a basic set of services. Likewise, public sponsors would subsidize enrollee coverage up to the amount of 80 percent of the average cost of the health plans with which it contracted. Premiums could vary to reflect the actuarial risk of subscribers, but the contribution would be fixed at 80 percent of the average premium for a given risk category.

The second component of managed competition was a limit on the tax-favored status of health insurance. Enthoven and Kronick advocated capping the portion of an employer's contribution that could be excluded from an employee's taxable income at the amount of the fixed contribution. The subsidies for those purchasing insurance through a public sponsor would be similarly structured.

The fixed-contribution approach and the tax cap were the central elements of managed competition. Both measures aimed to encourage insurance subscribers to opt for less costly health plans. Since contributions and tax subsidies would be fixed, individuals who chose expensive plans would be required to pay the extra cost with their own after-tax dollars. In theory, this would lead people to choose managed-care plans rather than traditional insurance. Indeed, Enthoven and Kronick were clearly reluctant to retain a role for conventional fee-for-service insurance. Employers and sponsors would be required to offer "a choice of qualified plans, *possibly* including traditional insurance [emphasis added]." Traditional fee-for-service payment, they argued, gave doctors and hospitals "no incentive to find and use medical practices that produce the same health outcome at less cost."[43]

Competition among qualified health plans to attract enrollees would be "managed" by employers and public sponsors, both of which would be charged with the formidable task of counteracting the causes of market failure. Since the primary cause of such failure is the incentive for health plans to select risk, employers and sponsors would have to identify and group people according to their actuarial risk and reimburse plans accordingly. Sponsors could also require that the health plans with which they contracted offer standardized coverage, thereby preventing plans from manipulating the terms of coverage to attract healthier people.

Taken as a whole, the updated Consumer Choice Health Plan retained the core ideas and values of the proposal put forth by Enthoven in 1977. The main innovation of the plan was the public sponsors, which Enthoven had designed to address the fundamental problems with the original Consumer Choice Health Plan. Another significant departure was the replacement of tax-based financing with employment-based financing—an approach Enthoven had once bitterly criticized.[44] Nonetheless, the guiding assumption of the new Consumer Choice Health Plan was the same as that of the old: people would enroll in competing alternative delivery systems if they were required to pay the extra cost of more expensive health plans.

THE BIRTH OF THE JACKSON HOLE GROUP

By 1990 Enthoven and Paul Ellwood were worried. Both men were committed to a private-sector approach to health care reform, and both feared that the government was on the verge of assuming broad regulatory authority over the medical system. In February 1990 they convened a meeting in Jackson Hole of policymakers and reform-minded medical industry leaders to discuss "the crisis in the health care delivery system." Among those present at the meeting were Senator David Durenberger, ranking Republican of the Finance Subcommittee on Medicare and Long-Term Care; William Roper, director of the Centers for Disease Control; Bernard Tresnowski, president of the Blue Cross and Blue Shield Association; Thomas Pyle, InterStudy's chairman of the board and president of the Harvard Community Health Plan (an HMO in Brookline, Massachusetts); Kermit Knudsen, the chairman of the American Group Practice Association; and William Link, executive vice president of Prudential. (Link was also representing "the gang of five," an informal association of the five largest private insurers: Aetna, Cigna, The Travelers, Metropolitan Life, and Prudential.)

The participants in the meeting were frank and to the point. All of them agreed with Enthoven and Ellwood's grim assessment of the situation, and all recognized that their interests were on the line.[45] By the end of the four-day conference, the group had tentatively agreed to work with Enthoven and Ellwood to come up with a serious reform proposal. Before they left, Ellwood asked each of the members of the group to develop recommendations for the next meeting in Boston.

Not long after the meeting, Tresnowski enlisted the support of Lynn Etheredge, a health policy consultant based just outside of Washington, D.C. Etheredge was the consummate insider: pragmatic, knowledgeable, and committed to health care reform. He had worked in the Office of Management and Budget through four administrations, helped write three presidents' national health insurance plans, and developed an extensive network of contacts inside government. Tresnowski asked Etheredge if he would design the regulatory agencies that would oversee a reformed medical system, and he wanted Etheredge to present his ideas to the group in Boston.

On May 21, Etheredge outlined his proposal to Ellwood and the other members of the group. He thought that the group's reform ideas could be integrated into a comprehensive reform plan requiring minimal government regulation by creating federal standard-setting bodies that would certify private insurance plans. Etheredge's proposal envisioned the Securities and Exchange Commission as the prototype for a national health board, an independent agency that would both set the guidelines for a standard package of health benefits that all insurers would have to offer and cap the amount of insurance premiums that employers could exclude from federal taxation. To ensure compliance with the new rules, insurance plans would have to be registered by the board to qualify for federal tax exclusion. The standards for registration would be set by three smaller agencies.

These ideas were well received, and Ellwood asked Etheredge to incorporate them into a paper that would be discussed at the next meeting, which would be held in Jackson Hole in late summer. By that time, a procompetitive reform plan was beginning to take shape, and Etheredge's description of how federal regulation could foster private-sector reforms had evolved into a full-fledged set of recommendations for national health care reform. In addition, the group of industry leaders, policy experts, and public officials that had been meeting in Jackson Hole had begun to assume a distinct identity. Etheredge started referring to them as the "Jackson Hole Group."*

Sensing the growing momentum of the reform effort, Ellwood started reaching out to interested parties to bring them into the process. He was particularly interested in cultivating support among the large corporations that had been at the forefront of delivery system reform through the 1980s. Ellwood called Dr. Mary Jane England, the new president of the Washington Business Group on Health (WBGH), and asked her to come to Jackson Hole on behalf of the business community. England agreed and in early 1991 she flew out to Jackson Hole to represent the large employers of the WBGH.[46]

The Washington Business Group on Health was founded in the early 1970s by Willis Goldbeck, a corporate liberal committed to making big business a powerful player in national health policy. The first component of Goldbeck's strategy was to encourage large employers to manage their own medical costs. "Our biggest educational step has not been in dealing with business about government," he explained, "but to break business away from the providers. If there was to be a marker of what we have accomplished, it would be that we have broken down the myths that kept business as a passive purchaser and we have made them aggressive buyers."[47] In the 1980s, aggressive buying by big business took the form of internal company strategies to lower costs. Large corporations self-insured, raised deductibles and copayments, adopted utilization review, altered benefit design, and switched to managed-care plans.

The second part of Goldbeck's strategy was to make "big business a credible participant in national health policy."[48] The WBGH fought for the Medicare prospective payment system, which Congress passed in January 1983; it supported health planning regulation and the Professional Standards Review Organizations; and it endorsed various measures to gather national data on physicians and hospitals and to ensure that the

---

* A complete list of those who participated in the Jackson Hole meetings between 1990 and 1992 is contained in appendix B.

medical profession complied with antitrust law.[49] By 1990, however, the WBGH was adrift politically. Its membership had fallen to fewer than 160 corporations, down from more than two hundred in 1984.[50] Health care reform was moving onto the national agenda, but the Washington Business Group had not taken a position on the issue. According to Mary Jane England, who came from Prudential to head the WBGH in early 1990, the member corporations had not yet thought out the broader questions of national health care reform: "The Business Group had been [in Washington] and was credible, but had not been aggressive in moving forward what it felt the reform proposals should look like. . . . The business community had been out doing it, but had not translated what it was doing into a public policy agenda for Washington. . . . [The WBGH] had to convince the business community that some of the innovations that it had put in place could be celebrated and brought forward. It was that dynamic that brought the Business Group much more visibly into the public policy debate."[51]

The private-sector innovations that England wanted to extend to public policy were the new "organized systems of care" that big business was developing with large insurers. These new managed-care plans integrated the financing and delivery of care while using sophisticated computer systems to store medical records and manage claims. They represented corporate America's vision of an efficient and rational medical system. As one WBGH brochure raved: "Organized systems of care . . . establish a process and a structure for holding numerous fragmented providers accountable for the cost and outcomes of the care they deliver. Organized systems of care are the reward for the courage to change."[52]

By the time the WBGH began participating in the Jackson Hole meetings in late-February 1991, the preliminary policy paper written by Etheredge had evolved into a set of twelve recommendations for health care reform.[53] The first recommendation was the most important: "Seek national legislation for federal-government-directed implementation of the Jackson Hole Group recommendations." The other recommendations focused on the role of the private sector and government in the reformed health care system. Etheredge proposed a "pro-competitive regulatory structure" in which government authority would be limited to three responsibilities: designing the basic benefit package that all insurers would be required to offer, setting the standards by which private health plans would be certified, and revising federal tax policy to cap the tax exclusion for employer-provided health insurance at the cost of a basic benefit package. A dozen copies of the recommendations were circulated at the meeting in February and received almost universal support. As Etheredge recounted, "It was clear that we had a strong basic agreement on these key ideas."[54]

Also passed around at the February meeting was a discussion paper by Enthoven entitled, "A Route to Universal Health Insurance and Comprehensive Market Reform through Small Employment Group Market Reform."[55] The document laid out a strategy for reforming the small group market that relied much more heavily on the sponsors than the Enthoven-Kronick plan had. In the Enthoven-Kronick plan, the sponsors had been residual insurers for employees of small firms and individuals not covered through employment. In the discussion paper presented at the February meeting, however, Enthoven recast the concept of sponsors as "health insurance purchasing cooperatives" or HIPCs (pronounced HIP-icks). HIPCs would be nonprofit membership corporations, run by representatives of participating small employers, that would contract with health plans meeting federal guidelines for covered benefits and enrollment procedures. All workers in small firms would obtain insurance through the HIPCs, which would collect premiums from small businesses and their employees. The HIPCs would then reimburse contracting plans on a periodic basis, adjusting payments to reflect the actuarial risk of each plan's members.

Enthoven viewed the HIPCs as a mechanism for correcting the deficiencies of the small group market, which had been unraveling for more than a decade. Since small employment groups have fewer members over which to spread the risk of sickness or injury, premiums vary widely among small groups and some high-risk firms are refused coverage altogether. Furthermore, administrative costs are much higher for small groups than for larger ones, and most small firms do not have access to managed-care plans. Sponsor organizations could remedy these problems by aggregating the purchasing power of many small firms. The sponsor would offer several different types of health plans to the employees of participating firms, and it could require that the insurers whose plans it offered charge roughly the same premium to all individuals and employment groups.

FRAMING THE JACKSON HOLE PROPOSAL

Although the outlines of a proposal had been worked out, it was not until the summer of 1991 that Ellwood, Enthoven, and Etheredge sat down to formulate a comprehensive plan. At the February meeting, the members of the Jackson Hole Group had agreed that it was time for the various areas of consensus to be incorporated into a broad statement of the group's policy goals. The main problem faced by Ellwood, Enthoven, and Etheredge was deciding where to begin. Each of the men had brought their own ideas about reform to the Jackson Hole effort. Ellwood wanted the plan to incorporate a "health-outcomes strategy" in which measurements of the clinical outcomes of patients would be collected in a national database and used to develop guidelines for appropriate medical interventions.[56] Enthoven was committed to the tax cap and the fixed-contribution approach, both designed to encourage price competition in a decentralized private market. And Etheredge felt that the plan should focus on reforming the insurance market, in particular the small group market.

The three men finally decided that the core of the proposal should be a new relationship between providers and insurers. This relationship would take the form of "accountable health partnerships," organized networks of providers that integrated the finance and delivery of health care. These partnerships would be the groundwork for what Ellwood was calling "the 21st Century American Health System."

There were several reasons why Ellwood, Enthoven, and Etheredge decided to make accountable health partnerships the cornerstone of the Jackson Hole proposal. First, organized systems of care were at the heart of the procompetitive approach to universal health insurance. The necessary precondition of this approach, as Ellwood himself had argued over two decades before, was that private health plans be publicly accountable both for their cost and for the well-being of their subscribers. As far as Ellwood, Enthoven, and Etheredge were concerned, this kind of accountability could only be achieved if health plans were well-managed networks of providers operating within the constraints of fixed prospective budgets.

Yet advocating that physicians and hospitals form provider networks entailed political risks. After all, the medical profession fought tooth and nail for more than a century to preserve the guild model of medical practice. Indeed, until the late 1970s, the American Medical Association's "ethical prohibitions against all forms of contract medicine or underbidding by physicians" withstood all court challenges.[57] With impressive tenacity, physicians resisted public and private efforts to dismantle the "organizational structures that preserved a distinct sphere of professional dominance and authority."[58]

As recently as 1990, salaried compensation was "totally unacceptable" to 58 percent of physician leaders and "somewhat unacceptable" to 21 percent. Compensation on the basis of the number of patients treated annually fared almost as poorly: 66 percent of physician leaders viewed it as unacceptable while less than 5 percent found it "totally acceptable."[59] Likewise, most physicians bemoaned the growing encroachments upon their professional autonomy by managed-care plans, the federal government, and the utilization-review techniques of third-party payers. To many health care providers, particularly physicians, alternative delivery systems such as HMOs represented the worst of both worlds. Not only did they generally reimburse medical professionals on a salaried or per-patient basis, but they also encroached upon the clinical autonomy of the practitioners with whom they contracted.

Thus a second reason that Ellwood, Enthoven, and Etheredge organized their proposal around the idea of accountable health partnerships was to address physician concerns about alternative delivery systems. Of all the ideas that had come out of the Jackson Hole Group, Etheredge explained, accountable health partnerships "had to be the first one, because provider groups were not going to go along if this meant managed care as it had been done in the past. It had to be a completely new relationship among the players."[60] Portraying accountable health partnerships as a new relationship that preserved clinical autonomy was crucial because provider groups were an essential but weak link in the Jackson Hole Group's political chain. Although many physicians had attended the Jackson Hole meetings, only two provider groups had been officially represented.[61]

The belief of the Jackson Hole principals that accountable health partnerships would appeal to medical professionals was a measure of the changed political circumstances surrounding national health care reform. Even a decade earlier, attempts to enlist physicians in support of an enlarged role for organized systems of care would have seemed quixotic. But since the early 1980s much had changed: the federal government had clamped down on Medicare payments to providers, private insurers had placed stricter limits on doctors' clinical discretion, a growing number of physicians had entered group practice or joined organized delivery systems, and the medical community had continued to split into increasingly antagonistic specialty societies. The American Medical Association, once the undisputed "voice of American medicine," found itself torn among the diverse interests of the medical profession and forced to take increasingly ambiguous positions on matters of public and professional policy.[62] The leaders of the Jackson Hole Group hoped to take advantage of the increasingly diverse and ambiguous interests of the medical profession to attract the support of physician groups for a reform proposal predicated on the expansion of managed care.

There was a third and final reason to start with accountable health partnerships, one that had much less to do with Ellwood, Enthoven, and Etheredge than it did with the major private-sector interests that comprised the Jackson Hole Group. Accountable health partnerships were not simply a procompetitive aspiration but a new way of describing changes that were already taking place in managed care. They were modeled after the managed-care plans under development by large insurers to appeal to corporate purchasers of employee medical care services.

Since virtually all large firms self-insure and thus pay employee medical claims themselves, insurers that market to large corporations are not faced with the same incentives as those that market to small firms. The sine qua non of selling insurance in the small group market is risk selection—attracting employer groups with low expected medical expense and screening out or charging higher rates to employer groups with high expected medical expense. For insurers marketing their services to large corporations, on the other hand, the overriding imperative is to lower an employer's medical spending.

To be sure, keeping the cost of a health plan down depends a great deal on getting a favorable mix of risk. It is widely acknowledged that managed-care plans have benefited from "biased selection," the tendency for employees who are older or who require costly treatment to purchase traditional indemnity plans rather than health plans that limit their choice of providers.[63] As was mentioned in the last chapter, managed-care plans also achieve much of their savings by negotiating discounts with providers, who may offset these discounts by raising rates for other payers.

Nonetheless, since most large firms pay employee medical claims themselves, the insurance companies with which they contract are expected not to weed out high-cost employees, but to restrain total health care spending.[64] These insurance companies do not even sell insurance, if insurance is understood as a mechanism for spreading financial risk, but rather promise managerial expertise and access to discounted medical care services. Using large groups of employees as a battering ram, managed-care plans negotiate substantial discounts with hospitals and physicians or pay providers on a fixed per diem basis.[65] The modus operandi of these plans is to develop large networks of discounted providers whose clinical decisions can be closely monitored, and then penalize patients who seek care from nonparticipating physicians and hospitals. This is what Lawrence Brown terms the "managerial imperative," or the imposition of "administrative discretion between what patients demand and what physicians supply."[66]

If any group had a privileged voice in the Jackson Hole Group, it was the large insurers that were on the forefront of delivery system reform. In attendance at the critical meeting in early 1990, for example, were Bernard Tresnowski of Blue Cross/Blue Shield, William Link of Prudential (who was also representing the "gang of five"), Thomas Pyle of the Harvard Community Health Plan, and David Lawrence of the Kaiser Foundation Health Plan. Other meetings hosted Richard T. Burke, the president and CEO of United HealthCare Corporation (a national managed-care conglomerate); Michael Stocker of U.S. Healthcare (another national HMO chain); John Troy of The Travelers; Ted Kelley and Alan Maltz of Aetna; John Moynahan, Jr., of Metropolitan Life; and G. Robert O'Brien and Robert E. Patricelli of Cigna.

These men came to see in the threat of health care reform a golden opportunity to capitalize on their companies' heavy investments in managed care. They were scornful of the pervasive risk selection that went on in the small group market and eager to distance themselves from it. To them, the future was in managing the delivery of care, not just paying for it—in managing risk, not just avoiding it. [67] In their view, the small group market needed fundamental reform—that is, if reform meant aggregating the purchasing power of small firms and giving them access to managed-care plans.

This position put the large insurance companies and managed-care conglomerates at odds with the great bulk of commercial insurers, which not only profited from the status quo but lacked the capital and expertise to develop managed-care plans. Indeed, the Jackson Hole Group was one expression of a gathering intra-industry struggle between insurers that handled large corporate accounts and those that operated in the small group market.[68]

The concept of accountable health partnerships clearly had great appeal among the large insurance companies that were active in the Jackson Hole effort. A national health plan based on competition among sophisticated managed-care plans would make these insurers the rightful heirs of the private medical system. And Ellwood, Enthoven, and Etheredge were not about to dissuade them from thinking as much.

DRAFTING THE JACKSON HOLE PROPOSAL

In late August, Ellwood and Etheredge wrote the first of the four policy papers that would come to be known as the Jackson Hole proposal. The first paper contained a broad overview of the proposal and the reform philosophy upon which it was based, but it focused in particular on accountable health partnerships.

Ellwood and Etheredge began their exposition of the proposal by painting a dire future for the private medical system in the United States:

> Hyperinflation in U.S. health services without commensurate increases in value is leading critics to demand increasing public intervention, global spending limits, area-by-area and service-by-service budgets, and elimination of a multiple-payer, private insurance industry. The private insurance industry and the private practice of medicine face a formidable challenge. In addition to providing financial protection, both private carriers and provid-

ers must justify their independence from extensive government controls or from being supplanted by a government program by proving they can produce better health, [create] satisfied patients and payers, and slow the rapid rise of health care costs.

At stake is whether the 21st century American health system will be built around competitive markets. . . . Without effective markets, the government will be forced to regulate and take over health care financing and to ration medical care spending and services.[69]

As Etheredge put it, "We essentially told these guys, 'Either you get behind our reform agenda or you don't have a future.'"[70]

Topping that agenda were accountable health partnerships, health plans that would be "publicly accountable for their cost (in dollars) and effectiveness (in terms of their impact on clinical status, function, and well-being) . . . as well as for patient satisfaction." These health partnerships, Ellwood and Etheredge explained, would be structured to effectively deliver a standard package of benefits defined by law. They would also agree to hold an annual open-enrollment period and offer community rating. Creating such accountable health partnerships would be difficult, Ellwood and Etheredge conceded, but there was no other choice. "For the American health insurance industry," they wrote, "minor reform, let alone business as usual, are not sufficient to assure a future role in the new health care system."

And yet Ellwood and Etheredge saw a light at the end of the tunnel. Segments of the private health sector, they argued, had the capacity to lead America into the twenty-first century: "Some health insurance firms have the immediate potential—the leadership, customer base, capital, and management skills—to improve the way medicine is practiced by taking an active interest in the effects of medicine on their policy holders' health." Whether they would seize on this potential was unclear. "Health insurers are not uncontested heirs to these responsibilities," Ellwood and Etheredge warned. "The opportunity to shift their resources and emphasis from risk-spreading and bill-paying to clinical and quality of life-enhancing functions is now at hand. At issue is whether this transition can be achieved quickly enough, and whether it will be sufficient to forestall massive public intervention into the U.S. health care system."[71]

Here were all the elements of the strategy that had led Ellwood, Enthoven, and Etheredge to structure their proposal around accountable health partnerships. First, there was a call for a market approach to health care reform—an approach that explicitly rejected "government controls." Second, there was an emphasis on a new relationship between insurers and providers. Finally, there were references to those health insurance firms with "the leadership, customer base, capital, and management skills" to build the foundation of the twenty-first century American health system.

The remainder of the policy document was devoted to a discussion of the major points of the Jackson Hole proposal, and these points were discussed in three separate documents.[72] In the second policy document, Enthoven explained the managed-competition approach to market reform and the role of health insurance purchasing cooperatives within it; in the third, Ellwood focused on the standard package of health benefits; and in the fourth, Etheredge described the proposed national health board and the three standard-setting organizations that would advise it.

Taken together, the four policy documents represented a fairly detailed proposal for health care reform, one whose structure closely followed the Enthoven-Kronick plan. The Jackson Hole proposal would have achieved universal coverage by mandating that all firms insure their full-time employees (a payroll tax would be levied on employers to cover the cost of insuring part-time workers). It was not a play-or-pay plan, however, since firms would not have the option of paying a tax in lieu of covering their employees.

The essential elements of managed competition—the tax cap and fixed-contribution approach—were of course included in the plan, but with a new twist. While developing the HIPCs, Enthoven had come up with an ingenious method for determining the amount of the fixed contribution. Since each HIPC would have jurisdiction over a specific region of the country (the number and geographic distribution of the HIPCs was left unclear in the proposal), the fixed contribution could be adjusted to reflect geographical variance in insurance premiums. Enthoven advocated that the amount of the contribution be limited to the price of the least expensive health plan offered by the HIPC in each region. This limitation would hold for all employers; even if a firm was larger than one hundred employees and thus did not purchase insurance through a HIPC, its premium payments on behalf of employees could not exceed the cost of the lowest-priced plan contracting with the local HIPC. In addition, only contributions up to this amount would be exempt from taxation. Thus workers who wanted to buy more expensive coverage would have to use their own after-tax wages to pay the difference between the price of the least expensive plan and the plan in which they wished to enroll.

Firms with fewer than one hundred employees would be induced to purchase insurance through a regional purchasing cooperative. The HIPC would also insure all people not covered through employment (such as part-time workers) or by Medicare or Medicaid. Enthoven suggested that the total number of individuals covered by each HIPC be around 1 million. The HIPCs would contract only with certified plans covering the basic package of health benefits. (By this time, Enthoven was convinced that the managed-competition approach would work best if coverage were standardized.) People who obtained coverage through a HIPC—and, in the case of workers in small firms, their employers— would send premium payments to their purchasing cooperative. The HIPC would in turn reimburse health plans on the basis of their total enrollment, adjusting the payments to compensate health plans that enrolled higher-risk individuals.

The whole system would be governed by an independent national health board advised by three private-sector organizations. Although state governments would select and designate HIPCs, the national health board would be responsible for formally approving and registering each purchasing cooperative.

The four policy documents outlining the Jackson Hole proposal were completed by early September and began to circulate among the members of the Jackson Hole Group and nationally through an informal network of industry leaders and policy analysts. While some health policy experts and a few congressional aides were aware of the plan, Ellwood, Enthoven, and Etheredge did not publish the proposal or call a press conference.[73] As Etheredge explained: "The general assumption was that . . . much of what we were discussing was pretty academic. It was kind of a blueprint. The political process wasn't ready to act."[74]

THE ADVOCACY OF THE *NEW YORK TIMES*

Even without active lobbying by the Jackson Hole Group, the amount of attention being paid to its managed-competition ideas was growing. The main cause of this heightened interest was a series of editorials in the *New York Times* advocating comprehensive health care reform through managed competition. In late-May 1991, the editorial board of the *Times* ran a two-part series spelling out the reasons for health care reform and endorsing managed competition. This series was followed by a steady stream of editorials praising managed competition and its proponents. By the end of 1992, the *New York Times* had run some twenty-six separate editorials endorsing managed competition or criticizing alternative reform proposals.[75]

The author of these editorials was Michael Weinstein, a journalist and member of the newspaper's editorial board with a doctorate in economics from MIT. When the editorial board, under the leadership of editorial page editor Jack Rosenthal, had chosen to focus on health care reform, Rosenthal had asked Weinstein to stake out the newspaper's position on the issue. After looking at the various reform approaches, Weinstein found himself drawn to the theory of managed competition. "To my mind," he explained, "the notion of health reform that Enthoven had drawn up far surpassed anything else I saw or read."[76] Although managed competition had received no coverage in the popular press, Weinstein was immediately convinced that the *New York Times* should enter the nascent reform debate by endorsing it.

Under normal circumstances, Weinstein might have been told to find a new policy to advocate. Not only was it risky to endorse an obscure proposal, but it was also time- and resource-consuming. Most editorials focused on policy issues that were already in the limelight and widely understood by the newspaper's readership. Health care reform met neither of these criteria. It was just making its entrance onto the national political stage, and few readers understood the intricate reform proposals being discussed in Washington. Moreover, the editorial board could not easily address issues that required a long-term commitment of resources. Space on the editorial page was limited, and writers were busy. It was not always possible to explore the details of a specific policy issue, especially if those details tended toward the arcane.

But Rosenthal found the idea of blazing a trail on health care reform attractive. He wanted reform to be one of the few issues that the editorial page would take the time to fully address. As Weinstein explained: "It isn't normal that you carry on a sophisticated and at times quite technical debate about policy on an editorial page. But [Rosenthal] recognized that it was going to be the most important domestic debate of the next several years. . . . What Jack Rosenthal has said about this precise issue is that we were engaged in what journalists used to call a crusade. We thought this was an extremely important domestic issue, we thought we had something extremely important and right to say, and we were on a crusade to get this policy to the forefront of public debate and to see that it eventually came to be."[77]

The editorial board's decision to launch a "crusade" on health care reform reflected Rosenthal's belief that it was the mission of the editorial page to provide its readership with in-depth commentary on important policy topics. In the late 1980s, he and his predecessor, Max Frankel, had pushed the editorial board to designate a few policy issues as "causes"— issues on which the board would take a clear, consistent stance over time. The board chose the causes as a group, based on their sense of which were most pressing and politically timely. Once an issue was chosen, it was usually assigned to a single editorial writer, who researched the issue, developed an initial position for the editorial board to debate, and wrote all the editorials. It was a process that encouraged editorialists to focus on overlooked or emerging topics and gave them considerable freedom to stake out complex positions and present them at length.[78]

Although it was Rosenthal who committed the *Times* to the cause of health care reform, it was Weinstein who singled out managed competition as the newspaper's chosen approach. Weinstein was receptive to the idea-system that had evolved out of the neoclassical critique. He accepted without reservation Enthoven's arguments about market failure in the medical sector, as well as the prescriptions that flowed from those arguments. In May, for example, in the first *New York Times* editorial, Weinstein echoed Enthoven's claim that the principal problem with the present system was fee-for-service payment. In the second editorial, he proposed that health care reform be organized around managed-care plans and that enrollment in such plans be encouraged by changes in the tax code. And in June, Weinstein waxed that "a little-known system called managed competition . . . can control costs, improve care, and guarantee coverage to every American."[79]

About this time, Weinstein also began to communicate with the leadership of the Jackson Hole Group, which was well aware of the strategic importance of his editorials. The group encouraged Weinstein to continue pushing for managed competition and invited him to Jackson Hole for their next conference. Enthoven in particular kept Weinstein up to date on the evolution of the approach and the progress being made by the Jackson Hole Group.[80] At the group's behest, Weinstein traveled to Jackson Hole to attend a meeting in February 1992.

Weinstein's editorials were an amazing windfall to the Jackson Hole Group—and not just because of their highly favorable treatment of the group's proposal. It was equally important that the *New York Times* publicized the managed-competition approach long before other major national newspapers paid it notice. In 1991, the first year that the term *managed competition* appeared in any large national newspaper, the *New York Times* printed four articles specifically mentioning the approach (three were editorials written by Weinstein), while no other major national newspaper ran an article containing the term. In 1992, with managed competition gaining adherents in Congress and on the campaign trail, the *New York Times* still ran more than half the total number of articles mentioning managed competition. And while other national newspapers caught up in 1993, managed competition was by this time already a subject of intense political concern (see figure 2.1).

Because of their tenor as well as their timing, the *New York Times* editorials were an unqualified boon for the advocates of managed competition. By bringing the principles of managed competition to the pages of the popular print media, the *New York Times* increased their respectability and spelled out their political appeal. Moreover, by pushing a relatively obscure approach into the spotlight, the *New York Times* raised the level of attention being paid it, particularly in Washington. As Weinstein put it: "The editorials made a policy that would have otherwise been

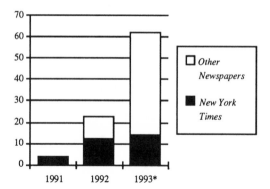

Figure 2.1 Frequency of Articles in the *New York Times* and Other Major National Newspapers Mentioning "Managed Competition," 1991–93. (*Source*: computerized search by author of the *New York Times, Wall Street Journal, Washington Post, Christian Science Monitor, Los Angeles Times, Chicago Tribune, Boston Globe, USA Today*, and *Atlanta Constitution/Atlanta Journal*). *Articles for 1993 include January through May only.

buried in an academic journal from the seventies a matter of public discourse. We brought a policy to the public with a name, a label, and a rationale. . . . We made it coherent; we made it an object of explicit public discussion. I think we legitimized it for many in Congress."[81]

This notion of legitimacy is important to understanding the media's effect on policymaking. Policymakers—elected and appointed public officials, interest-group leaders, and other people closely associated with them—rely on the media for cues not only about the agenda status of political problems, but also about the potential political viability of alternative proposals to address them. They are therefore more likely to take notice of and become familiar with a proposal if it has been discussed in the *New York Times* or another prominent media outlet. Of course, policymakers will rarely be swayed by a few articles or newscasts, but they may be more likely to take a proposal seriously and examine it carefully if it has already appeared in the popular press. After all, an important part of their work consists in remaining abreast of current events and ideas, especially those that relate to their areas of expertise. As one Senate staff member explained: "I can remember [the senator] first taking a really good look at managed competition when the *New York Times* came out with a series of editorials praising the concept. He said to me, 'I need to know more about this, not so much because it is an intriguing idea, but because if the *New York Times* endorses it, then people are going to start talking about it. So I have to be able to talk about it.' "[82]

The impact of the *New York Times* editorials is best understood in the context of the Wofford election. While the editorials brought the concept of managed competition to a broad audience, including many members of Congress and congressional staff, their effect was greatly magnified by the sense of urgency that beset Washington in the wake of Wofford's victory. What the editorials did was put the idea of managed competition into popular circulation at the same time that many policymakers were desperately searching for ideas about health care reform. As Etheredge pointed out: "What really made [people aware of managed competition] was the Wofford election. That's when things really started to take off. . . . Suddenly politicians knew they needed a plan, and those that did not want a [single-payer] system needed something they could support that was intellectually responsible."[83]

The *New York Times* capitalized on the moment. The day after the election, an editorial by Weinstein used the election to illustrate the need for a national health system based on managed competition. Several days later, Weinstein wrote an editorial laying out a set of criteria for judging the merit of national health care reform proposals. Not surprisingly, the only proposal that met his test was managed competition.[84]

Nonetheless, the success of the editorial board's "crusade" was largely a product of the propitious moment at which it had been launched. In the wake of the Pennsylvania election, many policymakers—especially those who were uncomfortable with the current menu of reform approaches—began to search for plans they could support. By skillfully juxtaposing managed competition with the three major approaches to health care reform currently under consideration—the tax-credit approach, the play-or-pay approach, and the single-payer approach—Weinstein made managed competition appear fresh and original. And by portraying it as a middle-of-the-road approach, one that did more to address the underlying problems in American medicine than tax credits but that was more market-oriented than either the play-or-pay or single-payer approaches, he rang a receptive chord among many policymakers, particularly conservative Democrats in Congress.

THE SUPPORT OF CONSERVATIVE DEMOCRATS

For much of the twentieth century, conservative southern Democrats have been a powerful retarding force in American social policy. Even after the Democratic party in Congress became more northern and western during the New Deal, it continued to be controlled by its southern wing, whose members dominated the seniority-based committee system. From the waning of the New Deal to the mid-1950s, southern Democrats held together a regnant conservative coalition that was generally hostile to new social initiatives, including major social programs in health.[85]

This all changed in the 1960s. Large liberal majorities and catalyzing presidential leadership opened the door to civil rights legislation, the War on Poverty, the Great Society, and—in health policy—Medicare and Medicaid. This tidal wave of legislation was followed by far-reaching institutional reforms, mainly in the House, that weakened full committees and their chairs relative to subcommittees, multiplied the resources available to individual legislators, increased the importance of floor activity, and augmented the power of the Democratic Caucus and Speaker. In the process, southern Democrats were stripped of their institutional power as well as their racial agenda, and the southern wing of the Democratic party lost its distinct identity along with much of its clout.[86]

To some extent, the pendulum has swung back. Southern and western Democrats have become an important conservatizing force in the party, but on economic issues rather than racial ones. With the consecutive election defeats of Carter and Mondale and the continued migration of southern voters into the Republican fold, a growing number of Democrats, particularly those from the South and West, advocated that the party move toward the ideological "center" to attract voters back to the party ticket. Many of these so-called New Democrats alleged that reforms in the presidential selection process had opened the party to activist groups and thereby weakened its stance.[87] In the mid-1980s, a contingent of southern Democrats defected from the Democratic National Committee and formed the more conservative Democratic Leadership Council (DLC). One of the leading figures in the DLC was Arkansas Governor Bill Clinton, who headed the organization from 1990 to 1992.

In 1991 the largest contingent of southern conservative Democrats in Congress was the Conservative Democratic Forum (CDF) in the House of Representatives. Formed after the 1980 election, when the House was closely split along partisan lines, the CDF had provided President Reagan with the votes he needed to pass his budget in 1981.[88] In the Senate, two archetypal southern Democrats were David Boren of Oklahoma and John Breaux of Louisiana, both avowed centrists. These members of Congress were much more likely to vote in alliance with Republicans than were other Democrats.[89] They religiously opposed taxes and government regulation and generally favored granting broad discretion to the market on matters of social and economic policy.

On health care reform, however, conservative Democrats had not yet staked out their position at the time of the Pennsylvania election. Most had been waiting for an acceptable health care reform proposal to emerge—one that relied heavily on the private sector, was supported by the business community, required little in the way of new taxes, but that also represented a serious and credible attempt at reform. None of the prominent approaches then under discussion in Washington met these standards. The single-payer approach was out of the question, and the Republican tax-credit schemes were far too incremental. Conservative Democrats might have been expected to embrace one of the various employment-based plans grouped under the rubric of play-or-pay, since the approach was being touted by many in Washington as the "pragmatic road toward national health insurance."[90] But play-or-pay involved a payroll tax and perhaps regulation of provider payment rates, both of which were distasteful to conservative Democrats. Thus, when it became clear that they could no longer ignore health care reform, southern Democrats were faced with a Hobson's choice. Should they support the play-or-pay approach, which had been endorsed by the Senate Democratic leadership and the Pepper Commission, or the relatively limited tax-credit proposals under development by Republicans?

One CDF member who found this dilemma more troubling than most was Representative Jim Cooper of Tennessee. Cooper and his young aide, Atul Gawande, started to focus on health policy in the late 1980s. After sponsoring a few modest pieces of health legislation, Cooper turned his attention to health care reform and, according to Gawande, set about "finding a health reform approach that would be attractive to moderate and conservative Democrats."[91] Although Gawande left Cooper's office in 1990, his successor, Anand Raman, took up where he left off. By the time of the Pennsylvania election, Cooper and the CDF were fully committed to joining the legislative push for health care reform.

Yet none of the plans under consideration appealed to Cooper or his staff. As Raman lamented: "There was the single-payer approach, a couple of play-or-pay variations, and the Republican approach, which was a very sad incremental thing. There was always a desire to find something to support. It became more and more frustrating. We were quite content to let someone else introduce a bill we could support, but nothing came along." The one idea that did spark the imagination of Cooper and his staff was managed competition, but no member of Congress had introduced legislation embodying the approach. Cooper had seen the *New York Times* editorials and had also read the position papers of the Jackson Hole proposal, but as Raman explained, "It was not apparent on its face that the Jackson Hole Group recommendations were a good basis for legislation, partly because those papers are particularly dense and when you read them it's not apparent what the grand scheme of things is."[92] Thus it was not until the beginning of 1992 that Cooper and Raman—in concert with Representative Mike Andrews of Texas, another CDF member, and his health policy aide, Dave Kendall—finally decided to transform the Jackson Hole proposal into a bill.

On January 22, Raman and Kendall met with Ellwood and Etheredge over breakfast at a hotel across from the White House.[93] During the meeting, Ellwood invited Raman and Kendall to the Jackson Hole Group's annual conference, and in early February the two congressional aides flew out to Jackson Hole to meet the group's members and learn more about the proposal. At the meeting, they plotted their subsequent legislative course with Ellwood, Enthoven, and Mary Jane England, who offered to put the resources of the Washington Business Group on Health at their disposal.

Although Raman and Kendall consulted frequently with the principals of the Jackson Hole Group and worked closely with the WBGH, it quickly became clear that the CDF bill would part with the Jackson Hole proposal in one important respect—it was not going to mandate that firms pay for health insurance. This was a critical omission. Eighty-five percent of the uninsured live in families headed by workers.[94] Therefore, the only way to achieve universal coverage and at the same time preserve the employment-based system of health insurance is to require that employers insure their employees or, as in the play-or-pay approach, tax firms that do not insure their employees and use the revenues to fund a residual public program. Yet the CDF saw another side of the problem of the working uninsured: nearly two-thirds of all uninsured workers are employed in firms with one hundred or fewer employees.[95] An employer mandate would therefore disproportionately affect small business, an extremely important constituency in the South. The CDF members, loathe to antagonize the small business sector and generally wary of mandates and payroll taxes, believed that the goal of universal coverage was one that could wait.

The CDF bill differed from the Jackson Hole proposal in another respect—it set the cutoff firm size for the purchasing cooperatives at one thousand employees rather than one hundred employees (and would have allowed states to raise that cutoff to ten thousand). This represented a far less significant departure than the omission of the employer mandate. Raising the cutoff for mandatory participation in the HIPCs from one hundred employees to one thousand employees increased the affected population from about 40 percent of the employed population to roughly 60 percent.[96] But without the requirement that employers provide health insurance to their employees, the concept of mandatory participation rang hollow. Under the CDF bill, firms smaller than the cutoff size would be required to join a HIPC if they wanted to purchase tax-advantaged health insurance. But they were still allowed to decide whether to insure their employees in the first place.[97]

Although the CDF bill was largely complete by April, Cooper did not formally introduce it until September in order to allow the other members of the CDF to provide input.[98] Not long thereafter, an identical bill was introduced in the Senate by David Boren and John Breaux, whose staff had become interested in the CDF's work during the drafting process.[99] With the exception of the employer mandate and the higher cutoff firm size, the CDF bill followed the Jackson Hole model to the letter.[100] Indeed, none of the ideas contained within it was new. Many stretched back to the original Consumer Choice Health Plan, some had grown out of the more recent evolution of Enthoven's work, and others had come out of Enthoven's association with Ellwood, Etheredge, and the members of the Jackson Hole Group. The CDF took these ideas, embodied in the Jackson Hole proposal, and transformed them into a fully drafted piece of legislation with the support of an influential group of conservative Democrats. In doing so, the CDF helped complete the process of making managed competition a credible policy approach.

THE PRESIDENT'S "COMPREHENSIVE HEALTH CARE REFORM PROGRAM"

Conservative Democrats were not the only politicians pressed to act by the Wofford election. The outcome in Pennsylvania had even more foreboding overtones for the Bush administration, which had studiously avoided taking a stand on health care reform. The unexpected defeat of Thornburgh, a politician who was in many ways a true Bush Republican, left Bush feeling that he had little choice but to develop a health care reform plan for the 1992 presidential campaign.

Within the Bush administration, health care reform had been a subject of debate for some time. Although some high-ranking aides supported the development of a presidential proposal, others, including White House Chief of Staff John Sununu, counseled against it. After the Pennsylvania election and Sununu's resignation, the field was cleared for administration officials who supported the development of a plan—such as Gail Wilensky, the chief health policy adviser to the president; Richard Darman, the director of the Office of Management and Budget; and Deborah Steelman, one of the president's top campaign advisers. Wilensky, a health economist, strongly believed that government responsibility should be limited to creating an effective market in the medical sector. This sentiment was shared by Darman, who had publicly praised Enthoven's model of managed competition, as well as the tax-credit scheme proposed by the conservative Heritage Foundation, early in 1991.[101] Steelman, for her part, was well versed in the details of the Jackson Hole model. While chairing the Bush administration's Advisory Council on Social Security, she had attended the crucial Jackson Hole conference of

February 1991 and had lobbied extensively on behalf of Aetna, a key member of the Jackson Hole Group.

The plan that President Bush finally presented on February 6, 1992, was an uneasy compromise between the tax-credit proposals championed by the Heritage Foundation and Senate Republicans on the one hand, and the Jackson Hole proposal on the other.[102] The cornerstone of the president's plan was a set of tax credits and deductions to help low-income and middle-class individuals purchase insurance. For all but the very poor, however, the value of the credit or deduction was extremely low, and the credit phased out rapidly with rising income, thereby creating significant work disincentives. Even then, the plan neglected to specify how the credit and deduction would be funded.[103]

The plan also included some elements, in equally watered-down form, of the Jackson Hole proposal. For one, it would have encouraged the formation of "Health Insurance Networks" to aggregate the purchasing power of small employers and thereby lower administrative costs. Yet these voluntary small-employer purchasing groups were a far cry from the HIPCs envisioned by the Jackson Hole proposal.[104] The president's proposal also endorsed the concept of "coordinated care" (presumably a new way of saying managed care), but its support for managed care boiled down to a relatively limited set of initiatives designed to eliminate state laws regulating managed-care plans and to increase the participation of Medicare beneficiaries in organized delivery systems. The plan would also have required states to develop a bare-bones "basic benefit package" for purchase by tax-credit recipients. Its boldest provisions required that insurers marketing to employer groups and tax-credit recipients phase out experience rating and certain underwriting practices.

Even though the president's plan fell short of expectations, the fact that it paid lip service to the principles of managed competition indicated just how influential the paradigm for reform embodied in the Jackson Hole proposal had become. As a Senate staff member who had worked on the president's plan pointed out: "The Bush plan wasn't that far from a lot of things that were in the CDF plan. . . . These same elements were coming up in all these different plans."[105]

CONCLUSION

Since the 1992 presidential election, journalists and policy advocates have advanced two conflicting views of the Jackson Hole Group. The first portrays the group as a collection of seasoned policy experts, closely attuned to the changes taking place in American medicine, who constructed a reform proposal so intellectually compelling that the Clinton administration found it impossible to ignore. Shortly after the election, for example, the *New York Times* described the Jackson Hole Group as "Hillary Clinton's Potent Brain Trust on Health Reform"—"a loose-knit group of experts" that was alternately "one of the most important influences in the shaping of the Clinton plan," the source of "much of the basic blueprint" of the administration's reform strategy, and "one of the most important intellectual forces as Hillary Rodham Clinton moves toward a health-care plan." Alongside the story, the *Times* printed a quarter-page photograph of Paul Ellwood and other group members gravely talking strategy in the living room of Ellwood's Jackson Hole condominium.[106]

A second and less charitable view of the Jackson Hole Group has been forwarded by advocates of a Canadian-style single-payer system. In this view, the Jackson Hole Group was not a coterie of brilliant policy experts who developed a compelling blueprint for reform but a group of threatened medical industry leaders who sought to forestall further-reaching reforms by sponsoring a proposal that safeguarded their interests. "Stripped of rhetoric," charged the outspoken single-payer supporters David Himmelstein, Sidney Wolfe, and Steffie Woolhandler in early 1993, "managed competition is a plan to save the biggest private insurance companies and sacrifice patients' rights to choose their doctor." The "central theme" of managed competition, they warned, is to "find a way to keep insurance giants such as Aetna and Prudential at the heart of health care."[107]

Yet neither of these views accurately describes the Jackson Hole Group or the role it played in the rise of managed competition. As will become clear in subsequent chapters, the group was neither the sole nor the most immediate influence on the development of the president's proposal. Nor was it simply a collection of disinterested policy experts whose ideas were so logical, well-tested, or congruent with current political realities that they seeped into national policy deliberations on their own accord. The ideas were important, but their influence and credibility hinged upon their strong base of support among powerful private interests.

On the other hand, the conspiracy view of the Jackson Hole Group— that it was merely a pawn of insurance executives bent on twisting the group's proposal to their own sinister ends—ignores not only the intellectual precursors of the Jackson Hole proposal but also the well-developed reform philosophies of Ellwood and Enthoven. The intellectual principals of the Jackson Hole Group may have structured their proposal and crafted their entreaties so as to appeal to the major private interests that comprised the group. Yet the ideas embodied in the Jackson Hole proposal had a lineage that far predated the medical industry's interest in managed competition.

It is tempting to see this intellectual lineage as the true source of the

Jackson Hole Group's influence. After all, procompetitive ideas have assumed a prominence in U.S. health policy debates unmatched in any other country. Even before neoclassical economists began to develop specific reform proposals, providers and insurers invoked free-market ideology to challenge the legitimacy of government intervention. In the 1970s, President Nixon "embraced the powerful market symbolism" of HMOs with the HMO Act of 1973.[108] In the 1980s, President Reagan did the same by encouraging Medicare beneficiaries to join HMOs. Even Medicare's sophisticated regulatory scheme for paying hospitals was cloaked in market rhetoric when it was adopted in 1983. Surely if it had not been the Jackson Hole proposal, it would have been a similar set of procompetitive ideas that captured the imagination of politicians and interest groups when health care reform burst onto the national political agenda in 1991.

But would it have been? The Jackson Hole proposal shared aspirations and assumptions with earlier procompetitive initiatives, but it was far more comprehensive than anything federal policymakers had debated or enacted in the past. Past competitive reforms had been more rhetoric than reality—relatively incremental measures accompanied by grandiose claims and either opposed or grudgingly accepted by medical interest groups. The Jackson Hole proposal, by contrast, was explicitly framed as a blueprint for universal health insurance, and it was supported not just by policy experts but also by a significant segment of the medical industry. Moreover, before the proposal's release in 1991, other procompetitive prescriptions had not figured prominently in the emerging national debate. The Republican tax-credit schemes, with their incremental gestures toward the market ideal, were widely considered inadequate, while the Heritage Foundation's far more comprehensive proposal was dismissed as unworkable. Although the Jackson Hole Group clearly benefited from its procompetitive credentials, therefore, the appeal of market symbolism and the legacy of procompetitive efforts cannot be the whole story behind its success.

One critical reason for the success of the Jackson Hole proposal was its close connection to medical industry leaders. To a degree unmatched by other advocates of procompetitive reform, the policy experts who developed the Jackson Hole proposal sought to build a support coalition for their ideas among key industry players. They succeeded in doing this, first, by dramatizing the threat of government intervention in medical care and, second, by drawing connections between their ideas and the changing interests of industry actors. Of course, both these strategies depended to a considerable extent on trends that Enthoven and his colleagues could exploit but not influence, namely, the momentum toward health care reform in Washington and the migration of large insurance companies into managed care. Nonetheless, it took skillful policy advocacy to convince the industry leaders in the Jackson Hole Group that a reform proposal based on managed competition was congruent with their interests.

However, constructing an alliance in support of managed competition was only part of the challenge that the principals of the Jackson Hole Group faced. The other part was bringing their reform model to the attention of policymakers in Washington. In this effort, they were greatly assisted by Pennsylvania's Senate race and the favorable editorials run by the *New York Times*. When Wofford won in Pennsylvania, politicians who were uncomfortable with the single-payer and play-or-pay approaches and interested in a reform design more comprehensive than the tax-credit model began to search for alternative policy ideas. The steady stream of editorials supporting managed competition helped pave the way for conservative Democrats and the Bush administration to embrace aspects of the Jackson Hole model in the wake of the Pennsylvania election.

Although the Jackson Hole Group obviously could not have foreseen the Pennsylvania result or the editorial support of the *Times*, the intersection of the group's advocacy efforts with these promotional factors is entirely consistent with the notion of positive feedback presented in the first chapter. After all, the timing of those fateful meetings in Jackson Hole was far from accidental: the Jackson Hole Group hoped to preempt competing policy proposals before the debate over national health care reform began in earnest. As Enthoven explained: "[The members of the Jackson Hole Group] were thinking about coming up with a health care plan for a new administration. . . . Costs were getting so big. Problems of access were multiplying. Perhaps a newly elected administration . . . would need a reform plan."[109] The Jackson Hole Group was reacting to the same set of circumstances that caused the *Times* to launch an editorial crusade, the same set of circumstances that prompted Harris Wofford to make national health insurance the centerpiece of his campaign. As we shall see in the next chapter, Enthoven and his colleagues were not the only policy advocates hoping to leave their mark on the dawning national debate.

CHAPTER 3

The Liberal Synthesis

Despite sharp ideological differences between
their advocates, the single-payer model of
national health insurance and managed
competition are not wholly opposed.
—Paul Starr

They have taken all our words and changed them
completely so they mean something else. The
HIPC has turned into the Canadian
government-run system.
—Lynn Etheredge

THE PRECEDING CHAPTER, as much an intellectual history as an analysis
of political events, focused on the genesis of managed competition and its
emergence as a leading framework for national health care reform. With
the benefit of hindsight, this focus seems natural. The reform approach
endorsed by President Clinton during the 1992 presidential campaign
does owe a large intellectual debt to the founders of managed competition, and it would be impossible to understand why President Clinton
embraced it without the analysis of the previous chapter.

But the focus of the last chapter must have surprised anyone familiar
with the long struggle for comprehensive health care reform and its recurrent tribulations. In most people's minds, health care reform is identified
not with political conservatives (and certainly not health economists) but
with liberals and organized labor—with Truman, Ted Kennedy, and the
AFL-CIO rather than Alain Enthoven and the Conservative Democratic
Forum. Indeed, until the 1970s, conservatives argued against any form of
government intervention in health care while liberals fought the good
fight for national health insurance, suffering several numbing defeats in
the process. Did liberal advocates of national health insurance suddenly
disappear from the scene in the eighties, convinced that competition was
the cure?

For a time, they did retreat. Bloodied from the unsuccessful battles of
the 1970s, and aware of the futility of championing national health insur-

ance in the face of a hostile administration and an apathetic public, liberal advocates of health care reform contented themselves with pushing for gap-filling measures while preventing Presidents Reagan and Bush from reversing the social policies of the past. Beginning in the late 1980s, however, the liberal struggle for national health insurance picked up momentum and took a new direction. This new strategy was embodied in the term *single payer*, which first came into general use at the end of the decade. Employed most commonly to describe Canada's national health insurance system, the term manifested a new awareness by liberals that government-funded health insurance was not only a way to provide universal insurance coverage, but also a powerful mechanism for containing health spending.

This new policy understanding opened the door to a fundamental transformation of managed competition. At the same time that the Jackson Hole Group was pushing managed competition onto the public agenda, a second set of political actors was moving the proposal toward the philosophical framework of the single-payer approach, with the hope of creating a reform model that would bring to fruition the long liberal struggle for comprehensive health care reform.

LIBERALS AND THE LONG STRUGGLE FOR REFORM

The first campaign for compulsory health insurance took place in the waning years of the Progressive Era.[1] In 1912 former President Theodore Roosevelt campaigned on a platform that endorsed mandatory workingman's insurance against the cost of sickness (a cost that then consisted primarily of lost wages rather than medical expenses). But Roosevelt's defeat by Woodrow Wilson left the task of promoting social insurance to less prominent social progressives. Beginning in 1915, the American Association for Labor Legislation (AALL)—a small coterie of academics, physicians, and professional philanthropists—took up the charge at the state level, modeling their reform proposal on the German system of compulsory health insurance for wage earners. The legislative portion of the AALL's efforts began in 1916 with high hopes and the tepid support of the American Medical Association. It ended not long thereafter amidst an ideologically charged climate of "polemics and name-calling."[2] Strident opposition to the bill came from the business community, commercial insurance companies, and the medical profession (which withdrew its initial approval). America's entrance into the First World War put the final nail in the coffin of compulsory health insurance.

The issue of health insurance remained dormant until the New Deal, when officials of the Roosevelt administration advocated its inclusion in the Social Security Act. Yet nothing came of their recommendations during Roosevelt's lifetime. The virulent opposition of the AMA led Roosevelt and his key advisers to fear that including a contributory health insurance program in the bill would jeopardize its passage. In the 1938 midterm elections, conservatives gained the upper hand in Congress and forged a Dixiecrat-Republican alliance against additional social programs. Although Roosevelt vowed to fight for the program, he never returned to it with sustained enthusiasm. Bereft of presidential sponsorship, public health insurance was destined to become "an orphan of the New Deal."[3]

After Roosevelt's death, Harry Truman vowed to complete the New Deal's unfinished legacy by incorporating health insurance into the Social Security system. But the response to Truman's proposal in Congress was far from encouraging. Despite his unexpected 1948 electoral victory, Truman was unable to extricate his national health insurance bill from the congressional committees with jurisdiction over federal social programs. In 1950 the Korean War broke out, the conservative coalition on Capitol Hill was reinvigorated, and national health insurance disappeared from the political agenda as it had twice before.

Nonetheless, the rate of private insurance was on the rise. During World War II, fringe benefits up to 5 percent of wages had been exempted from wartime wage and price controls, encouraging employers to provide health insurance to their workers. As a consequence, the number of Americans enrolled in group hospital plans had risen almost fourfold between 1942 and the end of the war—from fewer than 7 million to more than 26 million.[4] After the war, employer-sponsored health insurance continued to expand as unions won the right to bargain collectively for health benefits and the government exempted health plans from federal taxation.

Ironically, while the postwar expansion of private insurance offered a protective umbrella to many Americans, it also helped to insulate the very segment of society—wage laborers—that had historically been the target of proposals for public health insurance in the United States and abroad. But as health insurance spread into the workplace, a new collection of vulnerable groups emerged—the aged, the indigent, the unemployed—groups that now appeared even more underprivileged than they had when private insurance was rare. The elderly in particular did not share in the benefits of America's expanding private welfare regime. They were sicker and poorer than the rest of the population but rarely enjoyed health insurance after retirement. The starkness of their plight inspired the frustrated reformers in the Truman administration to formulate a new strategy for enacting national health insurance. Rather than try to win universal health insurance in one fell swoop, they would first champion federal hospital insurance for the aged.

The "Medicare" strategy, as it came to be called, was adopted by John F. Kennedy during his 1960 presidential campaign. Upon taking office, however, Kennedy found that the most difficult legislative task would be to force the congressional committees with jurisdiction to report the bill. The most recalcitrant among them was the House Ways and Means Committee, whose members were openly hostile to the initiative. Of the twenty-five members of the committee, ten were Republican and six were southern Democrats opposed to the bill. The powerful committee chairman, Wilbur Mills, had just engineered the passage of the 1960 Kerr-Mills bill—a means-tested, state-administered insurance program for the elderly poor—and was not about to let the Medicare bill out of committee. Even if he had, the bill was short some twenty-three votes in the House.[5]

This all changed with the election of 1964. The Democrats gained more than a 2-to-1 majority in Congress, and Lyndon B. Johnson returned to the White House in an electoral landslide. The question now was not whether a health insurance bill for the aged would pass but what form it would take. The administration was committed to compulsory hospital insurance through Social Security. The Republicans had been pressing for a more generous voluntary insurance plan that covered physician fees. In a savvy political move, Mills proposed combining the two bills and expanding the Kerr-Mills program to cover the medical costs of the nonelderly poor. Mills's "three-layer cake" sailed through Congress, and Johnson signed the program into law on July 30, 1965.[6]

The effects of the Medicare program were profound and immediate. In keeping with the long struggle by reformers to appease the AMA, the architects of Medicare ceded nearly all control over the new program to the medical profession. The opening section of the bill read, "Nothing in this title shall be construed to authorize any federal official or employee to exercise any supervision or control over the practice of medicine."[7] The remainder of the legislation carried out this mandate to the letter, even leaving the determination of fees to the medical providers who treated Medicare beneficiaries. Not surprisingly, the initial cost of the program outstripped even the most expansive expectations voiced before passage. In the decade following Medicare's enactment, federal health care outlays rose from less than $10 billion to more than $40 billion and from 2.6 percent of total federal spending to nearly 9 percent.[8] The escalating cost of the program, as well as the rampant medical inflation it exacerbated, led to the "self-sustaining participation" of the federal government in American medical care.[9] The program gave rise to a new federal health bureaucracy charged with managing the billions of dollars in public health care expenditures. Moreover, by providing access to a significant portion of the previously uninsured, as well as nationalizing a large portion of national medical expenditures, Medicare made the problem of the uninsured less salient to policymakers than that of medical costs.

The 1970s began with the widespread recognition of a "crisis" in American health care. Stinging indictments of the medical complex and its exorbitant price tag came from liberals and conservatives alike. On Capitol Hill, the number of bills for national health insurance grew rapidly, and one—the Health Security plan introduced by Senator Ted Kennedy—was receiving serious congressional consideration. Universal health insurance had returned to the national agenda for the first time since Truman's Fair Deal—this time as a result of growing concern over medical costs.

But contradictions inhered in the sudden attention paid to reform. The political imperative in the 1970s was to "rationalize" medical care, and that meant, first and last, reducing its cost to both government and business. Business in particular demanded that American medicine be made more efficient and less expensive—a goal that illustrated well the ideology of "corporate rationalization."[10] The Nixon administration was also more interested in rationalizing health care than in promoting national health insurance, and officials within the Department of Health, Education, and Welfare began to plot a strategy to counter the political challenge from congressional liberals. In early 1970, several HEW officials including Assistant Secretary Lewis Butler met with Paul Ellwood, who argued that HMOs were the answer to America's health care woes. Immediately taken by the idea, the HEW officials proceeded to sell it to an initially skeptical administration. Here was a way to address what the president had admitted to be "a massive crisis" in health care without adding to the federal health care bureaucracy or measurably increasing government spending.

In February 1971, Nixon unveiled a "national health strategy" in a special message to Congress.[11] In addition to financial incentives for the development of HMOs, the president proposed a "National Health Insurance Partnership" to guarantee working Americans coverage through their employers while providing a less generous package of benefits to low-income families. Although the administration policy was not well received in Congress, the prospects for national health insurance seemed to be markedly improving. Nixon introduced another, more comprehensive national health plan early in 1974 and even went so far as to proclaim that "comprehensive health insurance is an idea whose time has come in America."[12]

Nixon's idea of comprehensive health insurance, however, had arrived too early. In what would prove to be a great blunder, labor unions and liberal advocates of national health insurance decided to hold out until after the 1974 midterm elections in the hope of passing Kennedy's Health Security plan. With the Watergate scandal coming to light, the prevalent wisdom among congressional liberals was that Nixon's days were numbered. Although this assessment proved correct, with Nixon went national health insurance. As Paul Starr laments, "If the name on the administration's plan had not been Nixon and had the time not been the year of Watergate, the United States might have had national health insurance in 1974."[13]

During the 1976 campaign, Jimmy Carter pledged his support for national health insurance largely to attract the support of organized labor. He was far from eager to push for a comprehensive program once in office, fearing that national health insurance would strain the budget and imperil his anti-inflation efforts. At first, Carter held off on introducing a national health insurance plan and instead proposed new federal regulations to control hospital costs. Finally, under pressure from Senator Kennedy and Finance Committee Chairman Russell Long, the Carter administration introduced its own program in 1979. The plan, not to be fully implemented until 1983, would have required that employers provide their workers with a minimum package of benefits, expanded public coverage for the poor, and created a government health care cooperative from which the remaining uninsured could buy health insurance. The proposal's limited scope reflected Carter's own reluctance to press for the program, as well as the divisions within his administration over the proposal. The president was convinced that a national health plan needed to be preceded by cost controls and phased in over time to avoid burdening the federal budget or fueling inflation.[14]

Neither the president's national health plan nor Senator Kennedy's proposal ever made it to the floor of the House or Senate. The president's hospital cost containment legislation was twice reported to the House floor and soundly defeated each time by the hospital industry and the growing antiregulatory forces in Congress. During the floor debate, Representative David Stockman of Michigan vilified the bill, claiming that it exemplified the misguided regulatory efforts of the decade. The antigovernment rhetoric of the opposition encapsulated what was becoming an increasingly strident neoconservative critique of American social and economic policy.

The election of Ronald Reagan in 1980 crushed any remaining hope for comprehensive health care reform. National health insurance vanished into the "social policy black hole of the 1980s," where it would languish for a decade.[15]

FROM NATIONAL HEALTH INSURANCE
TO SINGLE PAYER

Since the New Deal, the ideas of liberal health reformers have undergone two important changes. Until the late 1960s, liberals were guided by the principle of social insurance. The most ardent proponents of national health insurance were officials in the Social Security Administration, who naturally supported a compulsory and contributory health insurance system administered by the federal government.[16] The guiding principle of these officials and their allies was equity. Compulsory health insurance was a way to ensure that all citizens, whether rich or poor, had access to the benefits of mainstream American medicine.

But the sharp economic downturn in the early 1970s raised doubts in the liberal mind about the economic and political feasibility of comprehensive reform. Advocates of universal health insurance continued to focus on equity, but they were beset by a nagging fear that the cost of national health insurance would be too great. In 1945 President Truman had freely admitted that an extension of health insurance coverage to the uninsured would require substantial new spending.[17] No politician dared say that in the 1970s. The Medicare program was consistently over budget, medical inflation had reached double-digit rates, and economic growth had slowed. Reformers were placed on the defensive, forced to justify the programs already in place. Accordingly, the emphasis in liberal thought shifted away from equity to cost containment, and the two priorities increasingly appeared to be at odds.

By the late 1980s, liberals were beginning to reevaluate the trade-off between cost and access that many of them had accepted as valid. Contrary to the promises of the defenders of competition, medical costs were not slowing as managed-care plans proliferated and cost-sharing increased. Indeed, they were rising more rapidly than they had in the 1970s.[18] More important, the number of uninsured was also climbing, and no one doubted that health care inflation was largely to blame. Furthermore, the performance of American medical arrangements appeared increasingly substandard in international comparison. Over the 1980s, health care spending per capita had grown faster in the United States than abroad. By the end of the decade, the United States was spending substantially more per capita on health care than any other advanced industrial democracy.[19] At the same time, however, some thirty-five million Americans were without health insurance on any given day. To explain this cruel paradox, liberals pointed to the inefficiencies in American medicine—the high administrative costs, the fragmentation of financing, the overuse of expensive medical technologies—and with renewed confidence claimed that national health insurance was the key not only to ensuring universal access, but also to controlling costs.

Thus the debate over health care reform experienced a strange reversal. In the 1970s, the foes of regulation on Capitol Hill and in the private sector attacked the programs championed by liberals as inefficient and expensive. In the late 1980s, the private sector was the object of derision as liberals went on the attack. Publicly financed universal health insurance was increasingly portrayed by liberal reformers not only as a vehicle for achieving greater equity in the distribution of medical care, but also as the key to achieving a more efficient and less expensive medical system. Liberals co-opted the ideology of rationalization and turned it against their opponents.

This new political strategy, the second adaptation of liberal thought, was embodied in the term *single payer*, which first came into general use in the late 1980s.[20] Technically, the term refers to a single public insurer for a defined set of medical services (or a set of public insurers each covering an exclusive subnational region, such as a state or province). This is to be contrasted with an "all-payer" system, in which multiple payers, both public and private, reimburse physicians and hospitals at fixed, negotiated rates.

The single-payer and all-payer approaches draw their inspiration from the medical financing arrangements found in other advanced industrial democracies, including Canada and the nations of western Europe. In these countries, insurance coverage is universal or virtually so, and public or quasi-public agencies bargain with providers to determine a total budget constraint for health care. In some cases, such as in the all-payer systems of Germany and the Netherlands, people obtain insurance from regionally or occupationally based "sickness funds," which in turn negotiate reimbursement rates with providers in a formalized bargaining process overseen by the government. In other cases, such as in the provincially based single-payer system of Canada, government is the primary insurer and budgets are determined through direct negotiations between public agencies and providers. Other models exist as well. Britain operates a National Health Service in which most hospitals are publicly owned and general practitioners receive a small public salary along with other payments. Yet all these systems—whether all-payer or single-payer, predominately private or predominantly public—share the common features of universality and binding budget constraints.[21]

The rationale behind budgeting in these countries is straightforward enough. People should be protected from the costs of medical care. Society should be protected from the costs that might accrue if people went without treatment because they did not have insurance and could not afford to pay for care themselves.[22] But ensuring that everyone has medical insurance creates one problem to solve another. Now rather than being unable to afford medical care, people face little or no price constraint at the time of treatment. And neither do providers, for there is now no functioning system of market signals to keep them from doing or charging too much. Thus government or its agent steps in to make sure that health expenditures are kept in line with what society can afford. In practice, this might entail determining a schedule of fees that physicians can charge and updating it regularly to reflect changes in input costs, service volume, and clinical technology; setting prospective budgets for hospitals based on prior operating costs and expected changes in case mix; and controlling expenditures on such expensive capital goods as facilities and new equipment. These measures, or some combination thereof, are often referred to as "global budgeting," with "global" denoting total health expenditures of a nation or subnational region. Global budgets are a hallmark of both single-payer and all-payer systems, although in single-payer systems global budgeting is generally more explicit and the government more directly involved.

When the term *single payer* first slipped into the lexicon of reformers in the late 1980s, it was almost invariably employed to contrast the U.S. and Canadian medical systems. Canada consolidated its national insurance program in 1971. At that time, the medical care systems of the United States and Canada closely resembled one another. Since then, however, U.S. and Canadian health spending have diverged significantly. By 1990 the United States was spending 12.1 percent of its gross domestic product on health, compared with 9.3 percent in Canada, and unlike Canada, the United States still left millions of its citizens uncovered.[23] Liberals argued that the key to Canada's success was universal coverage and financing through a monopsonistic payer.[24] As Theodore Marmor, a leading proponent of a Canadian-style system, expressed this new liberal consensus, "Arrangements that produce universality also produce cost control."[25]

To be sure, the Canadian system had received attention from reformers in the past. Between 1977 and 1979, Senator Kennedy and HEW Secretary Califano independently made several trips to Canada to explore its provincial health insurance model.[26] But Canadian national health insurance quickly slipped from the consciousness of American health policymakers when Ronald Reagan embarked down a sharply different path in 1980. In the latter half of the 1980s, however, the level of interest in Canada rose once again, reaching unprecedented heights. Congressional committees, national media outlets, and the general public all began to look northward for instrumental lessons about how to deal with America's medical problems. The virtues of the Canadian single-payer system were touted by citizen groups, such as Citizen Action, Consumers Union, and Public Citizen, and by two renegade provider groups—the Physicians for a National Health Program and the National Association of Social Workers. The biggest volley on behalf of the supporters of single payer came in early 1991, when Representative Marty Russo of Illinois introduced a single-payer plan modeled after the Canadian system.[27]

But the return of government health insurance to the national agenda (in its new guise of single payer) was tinged with irony. Organized labor, which had led the charge for comprehensive reform in the past, was weaker than it had been at any other point in the postwar era, with national union membership hovering at around 16 percent of the workforce.[28] Although some labor unions had restated their long-standing commitment to government-provided health insurance, the AFL-CIO was deadlocked on whether to press for a single-payer plan or an employment-based approach. The ambiguous statements of the AFL-CIO leadership made it clear that the union was not yet ready to invest its waning resources in a long, drawn-out battle for a single-payer system.

Likewise, the liberal reformers of yesteryear were wary of repeating past defeats. Senator Kennedy, the long-time champion of health care reform, was convinced that the only politically viable road to universal coverage was an employment-based plan. Many supporters of the single-payer approach were dismayed to see Kennedy embracing the same type of reform design that he had stalwartly rejected during the Nixon years.[29] The time was finally ripe for true reform, they argued, and the play-or-pay approach that Kennedy and other members of the Senate Democratic leadership supported was deeply flawed.

Not only had national health insurance lost the committed support of its original proponents, but health care reform had also emerged on the national political agenda at a time when several factors augured poorly for the single-payer approach. For one, there was the perceived antitax sentiment among the voting public and, in particular, the upper-income citizens who stood to gain the least from a single-payer plan. Few members of Congress could forget the backlash from the upper-income elderly that had prompted the repeal of the progressively financed Medicare catastrophic program. Many legislators were simply not prepared to vote for a health care reform plan that entailed substantial tax increases, even if taxes replaced private premiums.

Related to this general concern about new taxes was the fiscal pressure created by the federal budget deficit. The supporters of single payer liked to point out that the deficit was driven in large part by runaway public health care spending. If costs could be controlled systemwide, they argued, national health insurance could actually reduce the deficit. But many policymakers remained unconvinced by this logic, and most were highly reluctant to put several hundred billion dollars of private spending onto the public ledger.

Another indication that the single-payer plan faced an uphill battle was the high level of public distrust of government. Under Eisenhower, 75 percent of Americans said they trusted the government "to do what was right." By the early 1990s—in the wake of the upheavals of the 1960s, Watergate, Iran-Contra, and several of the worst economic recessions since the Great Depression—the proportion of Americans who trusted government had fallen to 23 percent.[30]

Although rooted in contemporary events, this generic public distrust of government is just one expression of the antistatist ethos that has so captured observers of American political culture from de Tocqueville on.[31] For much of this century, organized medicine effectively challenged national health insurance by calling into question the legitimacy of state action. The medical lobby skillfully portrayed reformers as agents of a sinister foreign presence intent on stripping Americans of their cherished freedom. "Would socialized medicine lead to socialization of other phases of American life?" asked one AMA pamphlet decrying Truman's national health insurance program. It answered: "Lenin thought so. He declared: 'socialized medicine is the keystone to the arch of the Socialist State.'"[32] While the specter of socialism had lost its visceral effect by the early 1990s, opponents of a single-payer plan still had at their disposal a vast array of potent cultural symbols and idioms—rationing, Kafkaesque bureaucracy, and the like—that fed the citizenry's darkest fears of public power. Could the advocates of a single-payer system successfully overcome this deep-seated public contempt for government?

Finally, and perhaps most important, other nations had instituted statutory national health insurance programs at a time when the organization of health care financing and delivery was vastly different than the current configuration in the United States. Many European nations have had systems of national health insurance for close to a century. Germany established the foundation of its national system of compulsory health insurance in 1883. Other European nations followed Germany's lead in the early twentieth century. With the exception of local mutual benefit funds, none of these nations had to contend with well-established organizations managing the finance and delivery of medical care. In Germany, opposition to state control of medicine came from the Social Democratic and Progressive parties, which opposed the compulsion of labor by the state.[33] In other European nations, the medical profession represented the biggest barrier to reform.[34] Even in Canada, a laggard on the road to national health insurance by European standards, the main political opponent of the provincial medical plans and of their consolidation was the Canadian Medical Association.[35]

Reformers in the United States, on other hand, faced a different set of circumstances in the beginning of the 1990s. A decade of expansion in the medical industry had spawned a vast array of health care organizations, ranging from staff-model HMOs to "managed" fee-for-service health plans and encompassing myriad hybrids in between. Spanning the fifty states were network upon network of health care providers connected by webs of sophisticated information technology and equipped with the latest marvels of American medicine. Although none of these innovations seems to have measurably improved U.S. health outcomes or slowed the growth in health spending, these diverse medical plans were not going to forfeit their central position within the medical sector without a fight.

Herein lies the paradox. Health care reform emerged onto the public agenda mainly because of middle class discontent with the trends of the last decade. These trends, I argued in the first chapter, were largely brought on by the effort of American employers to reduce their spending on medical care benefits. And yet these trends also gave rise to new health care organizations run by people who wished to preserve—and, if possible, enlarge—the role of their organizations within the medical system. Thus the same forces that created effective public pressure for comprehensive reform also created new roadblocks to its achievement. Old stakeholders were weakened, but new ones had sprung up in their place. And liberal reformers were left to wonder whether they should challenge or propitiate these new political actors.

HEALTH USA AND THE LIBERAL ADAPTATION

In July 1991 Senator Bob Kerrey of Nebraska, who sat on no major health committees, introduced a national health insurance plan that became influential among liberal reformers.[36] Designed by UCLA professor Richard Brown and drafted by Kerrey aide Gretchen Brown, the Health USA Act of 1991 adapted the pure single-payer approach to incorporate competing private and public health plans. Its financing structure followed the social insurance model, but rather than make the government the primary insurer, funds were funneled back to approved private and public health plans. Health USA thus represented a new variation on the concept of a single payer. Financing was unitary, but health care delivery was pluralistic.

Health USA addressed several of the perceived drawbacks of Congressman Russo's more centralized single-payer model. State governments, rather than a federal agency, would administer the program. The state program would serve as the payer of last resort, insuring all individuals who failed to enroll in a private plan. The states would also be in charge of paying private health plans, although about 90 percent of the funding would come from the federal government.

The plan would have allowed people to choose from a variety of private health plans, including HMOs. For each enrollee, the state would pay private plans a fixed payment adjusted to reflect the actuarial risk of the enrollee. All approved private health plans would be required to abide by federal rules banning discriminatory practices, limiting the extent of cost sharing, and prohibiting additional premium charges. Plans would only be allowed to compete by offering enrollees additional benefits or higher quality services.

Yet competition among private and public health plans was not intended to be a cost-containment mechanism, as it was in managed competition. To control costs, the Kerrey plan relied on global budgeting and all-payer rate regulation. Revenues from a national payroll tax and several other new federal taxes would be collected in a national trust fund from which state programs would be funded. The state-run plans and other fee-for-service plans would reimburse physicians on the basis of a negotiated fee schedule, while hospitals would be required to operate within the constraints of prospectively negotiated annual budgets. Thus cost control would come through central financing and limits on the amount providers could charge for covered health care services.

The idea that emerged with Health USA—and that had not been seriously considered by liberals in the past—was that fixed, per capita payments to health plans could preserve elements of the private insurance market while serving as a powerful instrument to control costs. The proponents of HMOs had long pointed out that capitation forced plans to operate within the constraints of fixed prospective budgets, but liberals had generally assumed that the most effective way to contain costs was to regulate reimbursement rates under a fee-for-service payment system. This may have been the case a decade ago, but the 1980s witnessed the proliferation of integrated health plans and multispecialty group practice. To preserve these diverse private health plans, a national health program would have to reimburse them on a per-capita, rather than a fee-for-service, basis.

Perhaps more important, fixed capitated payments set by the government can be a much more effective cost-containment mechanism than negotiated fee schedules. To some extent, fee schedules can be subverted by hospitals and physicians. Providers and practitioners may react to a reduction in payment levels by increasing the volume of services, or they may treat patients in practice settings where reimbursement levels are higher. In contrast, fixed capitated payments to integrated health plans create strong incentives for the efficient use of available resources, and the reimbursement system is not as vulnerable to the common techniques that are used by providers to get around fee schedules (although it is more vulnerable to other abuses, such as risk selection and underservice).

The Kerrey plan treated capitation as a way to both cap spending and grant plans flexibility in allocating their limited resources among services. This was not managed competition by any stretch of the imagination. The theory of managed competition, in keeping with its neoclassical origins, posited that price-conscious consumer choice would lower costs. The managed half of managed competition—the HIPCs, the standardized benefit package, and the national guidelines for accountable health partnerships—was designed to prevent nonprice competition among plans, such as competition on the basis of risk selection. In contrast, the Kerrey plan rejected the idea that price competition would effectively lower costs. It represented an attempt to meld the advantages of a single-payer system, such as administrative savings and equitableness, with some of the flexibility and diversity inherent in a multi-payer system.

For members of Congress who disliked play-or-pay but were uncomfortable with Russo's plan, Health USA was an important breakthrough. The plan had its greatest impact in the Senate, where several senators adopted aspects of Kerrey's approach. During his campaign for the Senate, Wofford and his campaign aides took a deep interest in the plan, partly because it had the backing of Paul Starr, and used it as the basis for a set of principles they released to the press late in the campaign. After the election, Wofford joined forces with Senator Tom Daschle, a freshman from South Dakota, to develop the American Health Security Plan.[37] Daschle's single-payer plan borrowed heavily from Health USA, especially in its delegation of broad responsibility to the states.

Despite the support it received from Wofford, Daschle, and a few other left-leaning senators, Health USA was still found wanting by many Washington insiders. In the first place, the plan required a substantial increase in federal taxes. Many questioned whether citizens would recognize that new taxes replaced premiums they had once paid out of pocket and through lower cash wages. Public opinion surveys indicated that the level of support for the adoption of a national health insurance plan was inversely related to the tax burden it entailed.[38] Collecting taxes at the federal level, moreover, might lead citizens to fear that their premiums would be lost or mismanaged.

Another area of concern was the plan's reliance on rate regulation. Not only was such regulation fiercely opposed by providers and distrusted by conservative Democrats and Republicans, but its efficacy was also a subject of debate. Although a considerable body of research has amassed over the last two decades documenting the ability of rate-setting efforts to slow medical inflation, many advocates of increased competition in medical care argued that the global application of such regulation in the United States would either fail to control costs or create perverse incentives. Regulated rates were "administered prices," they argued, and as such did not reflect the true economic costs of medical services. If rates were set too low relative to underlying costs, rationing or discrimination against high-cost patients might result. If rates were set too high, regulation might become a form of cost-based reimbursement, sparing providers of the fiscal pressures needed to close down facilities and improve efficiency. The inability of the opponents of rate regulation to agree whether budgeting would lead to draconian rationing on the one hand or generous cost-based reimbursement on the other hinted at the true source of their concern. It was not the choice of administrated prices over market prices. In health care, market pricing is not really an option. Markets respond only to consumer preferences backed up by dollars. True market pricing of medical services would require not only the abolition of health insurance (which reduces financial barriers to care), but also the outright denial of medical treatment to those unable to afford it. Administrated medical prices are therefore unavoidable. Even managed competition does not obviate them since the revenue that health plans receive from purchasing cooperatives may not match the cost of treating patients.[39] The crucial question is *who* should administer prices—private health plans or public regulators. To the critics of rate regulation, this was a responsibility best left to the private sector. Public regulators, they argued, did not have the requisite expertise to develop appropriate pricing mechanisms and would put political considerations ahead of rational economic analysis. It was this fundamental belief, not some dispassionate analysis of economic incentives, that motivated their opposition to regulatory efforts.

The two perceived drawbacks of the Kerrey plan—federal taxes and rate regulation—were, not coincidentally, the two most commonly criticized aspects of the single-payer approach in general—not coincidentally, because Kerrey's plan was single payer in a new guise. It rejected a government monopoly of health insurance, but it retained the philosophical and programmatic beliefs that lay at the core of the single-payer approach. A far more significant reinterpretation of the single-payer concept was soon to emerge.

THE GARAMENDI PLAN AND THE LIBERAL SYNTHESIS

California is a state where concern about taxes and the feasibility of rate regulation takes on a special significance. The passage of the state's Proposition 13 in the late 1970s was a harbinger of the income tax cuts of the early Reagan years.[40] Proposition 13 and income tax indexing ushered in a severe fiscal crisis that in the early 1980s prompted legislators to attempt an overhaul of MediCal, the state's Medicaid program. MediCal reform had been attempted and thwarted in the past. In 1978 State Senator John Garamendi had proposed substantial reform of the MediCal system, including the implementation of statewide rate-setting, but the bill had been defeated by hostile legislators and the California Medical Association (CMA). In 1982, however, state legislators in alliance with California's business leaders were able to pass a market-based MediCal reform plan over the strident objections of the CMA.[41]

The victory of procompetitive reform in California was due in part to the prevalence of Kaiser-type HMOs in the state. In 1978 California was home to almost half of the nation's HMO enrollees.[42] By 1992 the Pacific region had a higher percentage of its workers enrolled in managed-care plans than any region in the country, with 47 percent of the region's workers in HMOs and 36 percent in PPOs and POS plans.[43] In California, therefore, the question of how to include organized systems of care in the framework of health care reform was far from academic.

When John Garamendi became California Insurance Commissioner in 1990 and pledged to reform the state's ailing health care system, concern about taxes and the effect of reform on managed care returned to the forefront of California politics. Garamendi was clearly in favor of far-reaching reform, and his political statements suggested that he supported an approach that had many of the characteristics of a single-payer plan. In 1991 he announced that he was creating an advisory panel of health policy experts from throughout California and charging them with the task of developing a proposal for reform.*

The advisory committee was placed under the leadership of Deputy Insurance Commissioner Walter Zelman, who had run against Garamendi in the Democratic primary. With the help of Linda Bergthold, a health policy specialist who knew Garamendi from the Peace Corps, Zelman began to assemble the advisory panel in the latter half of 1991. From the outset, Zelman encouraged the committee members to be open-minded rather than doctrinaire. For that reason, he specifically excluded from membership on the committee two prominent health policy experts who lived in California: Alain Enthoven and Richard Brown. As Zelman explained: "I avoided putting on [the advisory panel] people who were already affiliated with one concept or another. The two people that stood out in my mind were Enthoven and Rick Brown. Those two I decided to leave off."[44]

As the advisory panel began to debate the merits and demerits of different approaches to reform, it became apparent that there was strong support for a single-payer plan within the group. Many of the health policy experts on the committee wanted a tax-financed system that broke the

---

* The complete membership of the committee is listed in appendix C.

linkage between employment and health insurance coverage. There was less support, however, for the regulatory structure that was associated with the single-payer approach. Most of the panelists felt that rate regulation was neither politically viable nor desirable in a state with such a large managed-care presence.[45]

Some of the experts were familiar with Enthoven's recent work on sponsors. Richard Kronick, the coauthor of the Consumer Choice Health Plan for the 1990s, was a member of the committee, and he pushed the sponsor idea from the start. Many of the committee members thought the plan should incorporate an entity similar to the HIPCs in the Jackson Hole proposal to manage competition among private health plans. But the Jackson Hole model was employment-based, and it explicitly rejected some of the key tenets of the single-payer approach. How could a single-payer system incorporate competition without sacrificing its philosophical foundation?

Part of the answer was to be found in Kerrey's plan. It rejected the pure single-payer model and allowed for limited competition between private and public health plans. However, the Kerrey plan relied forthrightly on all-payer rate regulation, which the committee had already rejected as a cost-containment mechanism. The panelists began to think about ways in which the single-payer approach could be carried out without regulating payment rates or relying solely on competition to control costs.

The compromise that emerged late in 1991 was a striking synthesis of the managed-competition and single-payer approaches. At its core was the idea of a "single sponsor"—a HIPC covering every citizen in California. Whereas the purchasing cooperatives that had originally been designed by Enthoven were meant to address the problems in the small group market, Garamendi's advisory panel envisioned the HIPC as a single payer of all health plans in California. The HIPC would cover everyone in the state, not just nonworkers and those employed in small firms. Coverage would be financed through a payroll tax on employers and employees. Since the revenue from the tax could not rise faster than wages, the state purchasing cooperative would finance plans from a fixed budget that could increase no faster than the state's population and wage base. Like the Kerrey plan, then, the system would operate within a global budget for health care spending.

Unlike Kerrey, however, the committee did not endorse the use of rate regulation to control costs. Instead, it borrowed from Enthoven's notion of encouraging cost-conscious consumer choice by limiting contributions to a fixed amount. As in the Jackson Hole proposal, payments by the HIPC to health plans would be tied to the price of the lowest-cost plan in the region (and adjusted to take into account the actuarial risk of the plan's enrollees). Californians would thus have to pay extra for plans that were more expensive than the lowest-priced plan in their region. The panel believed that this would encourage them to enroll in low-cost organized systems of care.

As in both the Kerrey and Jackson Hole proposals, insurers would be required to offer a standard package of benefits (although they could also offer plans with more generous coverage). The amount of cost-sharing within plans would be limited by law, and plans would be prohibited from denying coverage to individuals for any reason. Furthermore, limits would be placed on the amount by which a plan's premium could exceed the price of the lowest-cost plan. Plans that were not able to compete on these terms would be ineligible to participate in the program. To ensure that all plans enrolled a mix of socioeconomic groups, participating health plans would be required to accept a fixed percentage of low-income Californians at no additional charge to the enrollee. This provision was meant to militate against the problem of income-tiering, which seemed likely to plague the Jackson Hole model.

The plan was released by Garamendi in February 1991, shortly after President Bush introduced his Comprehensive Health Care Reform Program.[46] The policy documents accompanying the Garamendi plan touted the plan's originality, its rejection of the dominant approaches to reform, and its pragmatic synthesis of competition and regulation:

> Ultimately, this proposal does not fit easily into any of the three major categories of health care reform approaches: the incremental approach, employer-based reform such as pay or play, or the single payor approach. It suggests a different, hopefully more productive blending of competitive and regulatory forces than might be achieved through any of these other approaches. It is hoped that this proposal will move California's health care debate forward, and that all concerned individuals and entities will remain willing to review new approaches, and to resist tendencies to classify new ideas according to older jargon and frameworks.[47]

What was being promoted was a new health care reform paradigm—not just for California but for the entire nation. The Garamendi plan synthesized the single-payer and managed-competition approaches, and its effect would be profound.

After the plan was released, Zelman sent it to a number of members of Congress, and he and Garamendi started to lobby for it in Washington. (Zelman called it "proselytizing.") Garamendi even hired a Washington lobbyist to arrange meetings with members of Congress who might be interested in the approach.[48] In late March, Zelman toured Capitol Hill to drum up support for the approach among members of Congress and their staffs.[49] In the Senate, Zelman and Garamendi found a receptive audience in Daschle, Kerrey, and Wofford. Senator Jeff Bingaman of New

Mexico was also highly supportive, and he and his staff began to develop a bill incorporating aspects of the Garamendi approach.[50] These Senators believed that a national program could be built from the ground up, with most states creating a program similar in structure to the Garamendi plan but some adapting the single-sponsor approach to suit local circumstances.

The *New York Times* also offered its support for the Garamendi plan. In drafting the proposal, Zelman had tried to present it in a way that would appeal to Michael Weinstein at the *Times*. "I knew [Weinstein] was playing a significant role," Zelman explained. "Since I knew he was writing a series of editorials, I was very conscious . . . of what the *New York Times* was going to think." Shortly before releasing the proposal, in fact, Zelman and Garamendi made a pilgrimage to New York to obtain Weinstein's editorial benediction. "We went to Weinstein's office," recounted Zelman, "and . . . we discussed [the proposal with him] for an hour. He was obviously very intrigued by it. . . . We released the proposal, and a few days later he wrote this glowing editorial . . . and we were nationally famous."[51]

Weinstein's editorial was indeed glowing. Calling the Garamendi plan a "model for every state," Weinstein described the proposal as an "artful" combination of competition and regulation. "The beauty of the plan can perhaps be best appreciated by understanding what it would not do," gushed Weinstein. "It would not rely on employers to insure employees; so workers would no longer be bound to particular jobs to maintain their coverage. The plan would not resort to rigid price controls, which would inevitably lead to rationing. And it would not put medical decisions in the hands of bureaucrats."[52] In a second editorial on the proposal in April, Weinstein wrote that the Garamendi plan was "a Jackson Hole-compatible plan that would include every Californian and could be instituted with only minimal help from Washington." He concluded his commentary by linking the Garamendi and CDF proposals with the work of the Jackson Hole Group: "The longer Congress keeps looking vainly to national insurance, universal tax credits or employer-paid plans, the better managed competition looks. All at once, two managed competition plans have become part of the debate. Jackson Hole-compatible deserves to be the standard by which to judge all the rest."[53]

The editorial was a stunning endorsement of managed competition, but it raised the question of what the ubiquitous label *managed competition* really meant. Weinstein had failed to point out the deep differences between the Garamendi plan and the Jackson Hole proposal. In the Garamendi plan, the HIPC would cover the entire population of California. In the Jackson Hole model, the HIPCs would only cover workers in firms with fewer than one hundred employees. The Garamendi plan broke the linkage between employment and health insurance, while the Jackson Hole proposal was employment-based. And the Garamendi plan placed a limit on total health care spending—a measure that the members of the Jackson Hole Group bitterly opposed. These differences defined two views of managed competition—one born of the neoclassical critique, the other of the liberal synthesis.

PAUL STARR AND THE LIBERAL COMPROMISE

One health policy expert who took a greater interest in the Garamendi plan than most was Paul Starr. Although Starr had contended in "The Middle Class and National Health Reform" that the prospects for comprehensive reform were better than in the past, he still feared that none of the major reform approaches would be able to break the political impasse that had blocked reform efforts in the past. Philosophically, Starr was closest to the single-payer camp, but his sociological work had emphasized the power of vested interests, particularly the medical lobby, to block reform.[54] Starr doubted whether a Canadian-style plan was politically viable in the United States, or even desirable given the changes American medicine had undergone over the last decade.

What worried Starr most about the ideology of single-payer supporters was their eagerness to supplant organized delivery systems with government fee-for-service insurance. Starr had admired prepaid health plans since his decade-long study of the history of the medical profession in the United States. In the 1970s, he had authored several essays extolling HMOs as a critical counterweight to the market power of the medical profession. Unlike HMO proponents on the right, Starr was less concerned with the competitive forces that could be unleashed by the spread of HMOs than he was with the broader institutional changes that might result. In Starr's view, prepaid health plans represented a potential source of "countervailing power" in medical care—an institutional means by which the diffuse interests of patients could be brought to bear against the concentrated interests of the medical profession.[55]

Although Starr had hinted at the reform design he supported in his earlier writings, it was the Garamendi plan that helped him translate these abstract musings into a fully developed proposal for reform. Starr had received a copy of the Garamendi plan from Harris Wofford, who had been Garamendi's supervisor in the Peace Corps. He was immediately taken by the plan, finding many of its central features similar to his own ideas about reform. In Starr's view, the Garamendi plan contained the seeds of a legislative compromise—a plan that would cover all Americans through insurance purchasing cooperatives, while using managed competition *and* global budgeting to control costs. Liberals would get universal coverage and a budget on overall national health care spending. Conservatives would get cost-conscious consumer choice and competing private health plans.

Starr saw the HIPCs as the crucial component of this compromise strategy. He wanted the HIPCs to be inclusive, preferably covering the entire population in a region, and to act as a powerful countervailing force on behalf of consumers. These monopsonistic buyers would use their market clout to restrain costs and guard against abuses. Covering most of the population through the HIPCs would also sever the tie between employment and health insurance coverage. Employers would still contribute to the cost of coverage, but all workers in a region would be allowed to choose from the same set of plans, even if they changed jobs.

Starr's vision of reform also included a national budget for health care spending. The mechanism of global budgeting he prescribed amalgamated the approaches taken under the Kerrey and Garamendi plans. In the Kerrey plan, the budget would be set at the national level and enforced state-by-state through capitated payments to health plans and through the use of negotiated rates by fee-for-service plans. In the Garamendi plan, total spending depended on the amount of taxes collected annually (which, in turn, depended on wage levels) and the choices made by individuals about health plan enrollment.

Starr wanted to include the budgetary discipline of the Kerrey plan, but he felt that rate regulation should only be used in states where other measures proved insufficient. A budget would be arrived at for each HIPC based on the price of the lowest-cost plan. Once it was set, a national health board would limit the annual growth in capitated payments to health plans. The HIPCs, in turn, would bargain with health plans to make sure that they met federal expenditure targets. Each HIPC would offer one fee-for-service plan, which would be forced to operate within the constraints of a fixed budget (equal to the number of enrollees times the risk-adjusted capitated payment). Thus, rather than allow numerous fee-for-service plans to reimburse physicians and hospitals on the basis of regulated rates, as the Kerrey plan proposed, Starr wanted each HIPC to contract with a single fee-for-service insurer. This also distanced Starr from the Jackson Hole Group, which clearly wanted to phase out fee-for-service insurance.

Finally, Starr was equivocal about financing. The plan could be funded through a payroll tax designed to cover the cost of the least expensive plan, with workers picking up the tab for more expensive plans using their own after-tax dollars (as in the Garamendi plan). Alternatively, employers could be required to pay a set percentage of the low-cost premium, leaving workers to pay the difference between the employer contribution and the cost of the plan in which they enrolled (as in the Jackson

Hole proposal). The latter approach had the advantage of requiring little new federal spending. It had the disadvantage of being less progressive than a tax-based plan and of being extremely unpopular among employers, especially small employers. One solution to these problems that was considered by Starr was to cap employer and employee liability at some fixed percentage of payroll and personal income.

None of the features of Starr's compromise proposal was original. Taken together, they constituted a national plan blending the managed-competition and single-payer approaches and justified by much the same political rationale as the play-or-pay approach.[56] But even if the approach was not new, Starr was able to surround it with a compelling set of arguments buttressed by his own deep understanding of the history and politics of health care reform in the United States. He assembled his arguments into a short book—a manifesto, more precisely—that he would publish in October 1992.[57] Starr also began to share his ideas with members of Congress and fellow health policy experts. In early May, he presented a rough outline of his approach in testimony before the Senate Finance Committee.[58] A week later, he met in Washington with Garamendi, Zelman, and Senators Bingaman, Daschle, Kerrey, and Wofford.[59] An outgrowth of the meeting was a decision by Starr to seek funding for a conference on managed competition that would be held shortly after the presidential election. The message Starr had taken away from the Pennsylvania election was that health care reform might help the Democrats recapture the White House. If a Democrat could upset President Bush, Starr wanted his plan to be at the forefront of this new president's domestic agenda.

CONCLUSION

By early 1992, American health care reformers were advancing two divergent versions of managed competition. On one side, the supporters of the Jackson Hole model were arguing that managed competition was a mechanism for injecting market forces into American medicine. They emphasized the fixed-contribution approach and the cap on tax-free employer contributions. On the other side, a small band of maverick policy experts was portraying managed competition as a way to realize many of the ends of the single-payer approach without government insurance or extensive regulation of provider rates. They focused on the purchasing cooperatives and stressed that managed competition should be backed up with a national budget on health care spending.

This second version of managed competition—what I have called the "liberal synthesis"—built on ideas that had been circulating in the health policy community for many years. None of the individual ideas that comprised it was original, and many of them had appeared in much the same combination in other reform proposals. As early as 1979, for example, Senator Kennedy introduced a reform bill based on regulated competition among private health plans that shared many similarities with Kerrey's proposal.[60] Nonetheless, the liberal synthesis represented a much more distinct break from earlier liberal thinking about national health insurance than the Jackson Hole proposal did from the neoclassical critique. All the concepts had been forwarded before—universal private insurance, managed competition, purchasing cooperatives, budgeting through capitation—but not in the same combination or with the same emphasis. The inclusive purchasing agents contained in the Garamendi and Starr proposals, for example, may have drawn inspiration from the managed-competition and single-payer approaches. They may have resembled the Federal Employees Health Benefit Program, or even European sickness funds. Yet they were given new functions and framed in new terms and embedded in a matrix of institutions not envisioned by other reform proposals. The underlying concept may not have been original, but its context and presentation were. So too with other key elements of the approach.

If the liberal synthesis was not a familiar collection of established ideas, however, it was also not a complete departure from the proposals it assimilated and recast. As this chapter has shown, the liberal synthesis owed a large intellectual debt to the ideas embodied in the Jackson Hole proposal. This is a debt that the architects of the liberal synthesis have been acutely reluctant to acknowledge. Paul Starr, for example, has emphasized that he had no involvement with the Jackson Hole efforts and only read the Jackson Hole papers after he had finished the first draft of his book.[61] Linda Bergthold made it clear that the proposal developed by the Jackson Hole Group "wasn't known as important by most people" on Garamendi's advisory committee.[62] In a certain sense, Starr and Bergthold are correct. There was indeed very little overlap between the participants in the Jackson Hole deliberations and the loose network of reformers who developed the liberal synthesis. Although members of Garamendi's advisory committee were familiar with the Jackson Hole proposal, the proposal itself clearly did not have much effect on the committee's work. It would be futile, therefore, to try to trace a direct line from the Jackson Hole proposal to the liberal synthesis. No such line exists. The path of influence I am describing is more subtle. It involves the diffusion of ideas, assumptions, and symbols. The argument is not that Starr or the California advisory committee simply reinvented managed competition in liberal guise but rather that they accepted many of the beliefs animating Enthoven's vision of reform—beliefs about the logic of competition, the architecture of institutions, and the capacity of government. Perhaps most important, they adopted much of the rhetoric associated with managed competition, most conspicuously the term *managed competition* itself. These strategic choices were not made uncritically, nor would they prove immune to future revision. Yet they are absolutely critical to understanding the genesis of the liberal synthesis—and the political dynamic that would soon propel it to the center of national debate.

CHAPTER 4

The Campaign

The debate over health care reform is over.
Managed competition has won.
—*New York Times*, October 1992

It was one of those rare moments that captured the mood of an entire presidential campaign. On October 15, 1992, Carole Simpson was moderating the second televised debate between the three remaining candidates in the 1992 presidential race: President George Bush, Governor Bill Clinton, and Texas businessman Ross Perot.[1] The format of the debate was that of a television talk show, with questions being asked by an audience of 209 carefully selected, uncommitted voters. One of the audience members had asked Clinton to describe his proposal for containing health care costs, and the Arkansas governor was outlining his reform plan.

The way to "control the costs and maintain the quality," Clinton explained to the audience, was to implement "a system of managed competition" in which most Americans would be "covered in big groups." Under such a system, he claimed, people would be able to choose their doctors and hospitals from a wide range of health plans, but there would be "an incentive to control costs." In addition, Clinton pledged to create "a national commission of health care providers and health care consumers that set ceilings to keep health costs in line with inflation plus population growth." He concluded by promising to send a health care reform package to Congress within the first hundred days of his presidency.

Up next was President Bush. After blaming high medical costs on malpractice lawsuits, the president launched into an attack on Governor Clinton's proposal. "I want to keep the quality of health care," the president argued. "That means keep government out of it. I don't like the idea of these boards. It all sounds to me like you're going to have some government setting prices. I want competition."

Finally, the ebullient Texas billionaire launched into a tirade of populist imagery, twice evoking laughter from the audience with his well-timed witticisms and, all the while, skillfully side-stepping the question at hand. The solution was simple, he told the audience: "You've got to reassert your ownership in this country, and you've got to completely reform our government. And at that point, [programs] will just be like apples falling from a tree."

The debate drove home the vast gap between the candidates on health care reform. Clinton had evinced a deep commitment to reform and appeared well versed in the details of his plan. President Bush, on the other hand, had seemed defensive and poorly informed. Did he really believe that rising malpractice claims were to blame for the inexorable escalation in health care costs? Every reputable study of the problem had concluded that the cost of "defensive medicine" (that is, tests and procedures performed by physicians solely to avoid malpractice claims) was negligible compared with total health care spending.[2] As for Ross Perot, he had asked Americans not only to reform the health care system, but to overhaul the entire political system en route. Home-spun charm notwithstanding, his was a stock answer—suitable for any issue and used for almost every one.

Public opinion polls bore out this gap. Regardless of which candidate they supported, surveyed voters believed that Clinton would do a better job than either Bush or Perot in responding to the problem of providing affordable health care to all Americans.[3] The gap between the candidates on health care reform was also reflected in the results of the presidential election itself. Although health care played a less prominent role in the 1992 presidential election than it had in Pennsylvania's 1991 Senate race, "it was an important secondary factor in influencing voter judgements."[4] Among those who voted for Governor Clinton, health care was second in salience only to the economy, and of the significant number of voters ranking health care reform as one of the most important problems facing the country, 67 percent supported Clinton compared with 19 percent for Bush.[5]

The previous two chapters traced the paths of two policy streams that carried managed competition onto the national political agenda. These chapters shed light on the process by which managed competition emerged from relative obscurity to become a leading framework for health care reform. Yet managed competition was not *the* leading framework for reform until the election of President Clinton. This chapter turns to the question of why Clinton embraced managed competition during the 1992 presidential campaign.

THE EARLY CAMPAIGN

Although Clinton began the presidential campaign supporting a play-or-pay proposal similar in structure to Health America, his endorsement of play-or-pay in the early primaries did not reflect any real commitment to the approach. If anything, it indicated the strength of the consensus in Washington that play-or-pay was the only viable middle road to health care reform. By late 1991, this approach not only had the support of the Senate Democratic leadership, but was also the basis for a proposal that had been introduced by the National Leadership Coalition for Health Care Reform—a coalition of large employers and labor unions.[6] Written by health policy specialist Kenneth Thorpe, the National Leadership Coalition proposal contained more stringent cost-containment measures than the Senate Democratic leadership bill, including national expenditure targets and mandatory rate setting.

Initially, Clinton and his campaign strategists had hoped to coast through the early primaries without endorsing a detailed reform proposal. Two of the top campaign directors, James Carville and Paul Begala, had worked on the Wofford campaign and were convinced that Clinton should steer clear of specifics early in the campaign. But Clinton, unlike Wofford, was running against candidates who were strongly in support of national health care reform. Senator Kerrey, for one, had made national health insurance the centerpiece of his campaign, and former Senator Paul Tsongas was advocating a managed-competition plan much like the Enthoven-Kronick proposal. Kerrey in particular was chiding Clinton for not forwarding a reform plan of his own.

Under these circumstances, the Clinton campaign needed to define its position on health care reform. Early in the campaign, campaign advisers asked Ron Pollack, the director of the health care advocacy group "Families USA," to prepare a statement that might form the basis of the governor's position. In September 1991, during a policy meeting arranged by Democratic pollster Stan Greenberg, Pollack had tried to convince the governor to endorse the play-or-pay approach.[7] Clinton had apparently been impressed by Pollack's arguments about the political advantages of play-or-pay, and Pollack had remained in contact with the campaign since. The campaign's request for a policy statement reached Pollack around midnight on the eve of a planned vacation, and by dawn, he had drafted a document outlining a set of goals for health care reform and a general approach to achieving them. He faxed it off to Clinton's advisers before leaving town.[8]

The task of writing up the governor's proposal fell on Bruce Reed, the issue director for the Clinton campaign and the policy director of the Democratic Leadership Council. Reed wanted to distance Clinton from Senator Kerrey, who was advocating his single-payer hybrid, as well as from the congressional Democrats who were supporting play-or-pay. Pressed for time, and not well versed in health policy, Reed took the play-or-pay structure of the Democratic leadership plan, melded it with the strong national health board envisioned by the National Leadership Coalition, and wrapped up the whole approach in Pollack's ambitious-sounding rhetoric. He showed the plan to Clinton, who was campaigning in New Hampshire with his wife, and the three worked it over for several hours in a cramped hotel room. The proposal was released in early January along with a promise by Clinton that his "uniquely American" approach would require no new taxes.[9]

Not long thereafter, the Clinton campaign started to receive advice from the Washington Advisory Group on Health, an ad hoc assembly of Washington-based health policy experts. The Advisory Group had been put together by Bruce Fried, a health policy specialist with the Wexler Group, a large Democratic consulting firm in Washington. In early January, Fried had given Bruce Reed some office space in the Wexler Group's building and had offered to assemble a coterie of health policy consultants to help the campaign. When Reed assented, Fried had pulled together a core group of health policy experts, most of whom were associated with play-or-pay, to help the campaign on health care reform.[10] Among them were Kenneth Thorpe; Marilyn Moon of the Urban Institute; Bob Berenson, a former aide to Jimmy Carter; and Judy Feder, a Georgetown professor who was widely credited with inventing the idea of play-or-pay while staffing the Pepper Commission.

Meanwhile, the Bush administration was vilifying the play-or-pay approach. In early January, Health and Human Services Secretary Louis Sullivan and Labor Secretary Lynn Martin used a one-sided interpretation of an Urban Institute study to castigate the Senate Democratic leadership for supporting play-or-pay.[11] The theme of this and later attacks was that play-or-pay would wipe out struggling small firms and create an enormous, underfunded public plan that would be forced to "ration" health care.

Partly because of the Bush administration's hostility to play-or-pay, the Clinton campaign became increasingly uncomfortable with the approach as the primary season unfolded. The Bush administration was savaging play-or-pay whenever the opportunity arose, and it had singled out the payroll tax as the target of its rhetorical pyrotechnics. Most of these attacks were directed not at Clinton, but at the Senate Democratic leadership, which was struggling to bring its play-or-pay bill to the floor. As Senator Kennedy's top health policy aide explained: "We were working terribly hard with this group of interested Senators to try to put something together that could get up to a floor vote. . . . We felt . . . that had we got it up in the Congress, we might have been able to force Bush into a posture of compromise where we could have ended up with a signed bill."[12]

In late January, the Senate Labor Committee approved the Senate Democratic leadership initiative on a straight party-line vote. In response to pressure from organized labor and single-payer advocates, the leadership had included enforceable national spending targets and mandatory all-payer rate setting in the bill, thereby bringing it much closer to the National Leadership Coalition proposal. Ironically, however, the Senate

Democratic leadership's efforts were provoking increasingly harsh and targeted criticisms of play-or-pay from the Bush administration and congressional opponents of the proposal. The charge that provoked the most alarm among Clinton's advisers was the Republican claim that play-or-pay was a backdoor attempt by congressional Democrats to create a universal public insurance program. Nothing could be more damaging to Clinton's New Democratic credentials, campaign aides believed, than for the governor to be closely identified with the single-payer approach or the Democratic leadership in Congress.[13]

Thus, while the Washington Advisory Group (which by late spring had swelled to over thirty-five members) continued to argue that Clinton should remain true to play-or-pay, some of the campaign staff began to toy with the idea of managed competition. Clinton and some of his aides were familiar with the Garamendi plan: Garamendi was the California director for the campaign, and he and Clinton had spoken about the plan with one another shortly before it was released.[14] Clinton had reportedly been quite enthusiastic about the approach, telling Garamendi and Zelman that it was an intriguing hybrid.[15] Bruce Reed knew about the Conservative Democratic Forum bill through Jeremy Rosner, the vice president for domestic policy at the DLC's Progressive Policy Institute, who was helping Anand Raman and Dave Kendall draft the CDF bill. Reed had also had been in touch with Atul Gawande, Representative Cooper's former health policy staffer.[16]

But these early rumblings within the Clinton campaign did not provoke a substantive shift in the governor's position on health care reform. No policy change could take place without Clinton's approval, and he was too busy struggling through a bruising set of primaries to think about health care reform. Moreover, James Carville and campaign pollster Greenberg felt strongly that Clinton should express his support for reform in general, but not for a specific plan. Instead of changing its focus on health care reform, therefore, the campaign retreated into ambiguity. Atul Gawande, who joined the campaign in June, recalled that the campaign position "was deliberately general. There were elements in it that allowed it to be potentially managed competition or potentially a play-or-pay scheme with rate regulation. Rather than dive into that whole debate, it was thought better to keep it general."[17]

THE POLITICS OF AMBIGUITY

By the close of the primary season, the Clinton camp had turned obfuscation into an art form. In June the campaign put together Clinton's policy manifesto, *Putting People First*. The chapter on health care promised to "cap national spending," "take on the health insurance industry," "stop drug price gouging," "establish a core benefit package," "develop health networks," and "guarantee universal coverage."[18] A critical question left unanswered, however, was how all these laudable goals would be met. To be sure, some specifics were offered. Universal coverage would be achieved by guaranteeing "every American a *core benefit package* . . . either through his or her employer or . . . [through] a high-quality public program."[19] But how would the public program be funded? Would the program contract with private health plans or reimburse providers itself, and if the latter, how would payment rates be determined?

To muddy the waters even further, the campaign excised from the book all references to the costs and savings of the plan. Clinton's adviser and long-time friend Ira Magaziner had estimated that health insurance coverage for the uninsured could be funded entirely through Medicare and Medicaid cutbacks and the savings realized by making the system more efficient. The Washington Advisory Group on Health was incredulous of Magaziner's numbers, and one of its members, Joshua Wiener of the Brookings Institution, estimated that the plan would require at least $40 billion in new spending. Magaziner and Wiener debated the numbers in an eleventh-hour conference call that ended when Bruce Reed suggested that the figures be omitted entirely. A relieved Clinton agreed, and Reed removed the figures before the book went to press.[20]

In July the *New England Journal of Medicine* featured an article on health care reform ostensibly written by Clinton that laid out "the key elements" of Clinton's health plan.[21] But the article was deliberately vague in several crucial areas. There was no mention of financing or the way in which universal coverage would be achieved. Although the plan purportedly combined regulatory and competitive cost-containment measures, the relationship between the two was unclear. Commenting on the article, Alain Enthoven pointed out that it contained words "to please supporters of both options."[22] Princeton health policy specialist Uwe Reinhardt was more critical: "There is no mention in Clinton's paper of the politically charged word 'mandate,' and he is . . . reluctant . . . to identify the source of financing for his plan. Indeed, the Governor's paper could accommodate quite a range of specific policy options. . . . [The proposal] is woefully incomplete with respect to many crucial aspects of a health care system."[23]

At the convention in New York, Clinton buried his health care reform package in a flurry of populist imagery, vowing to "take on the health care profiteers and make health care reform affordable for every family."[24] Now that he was the official Democratic candidate, Clinton and his advisers were especially wary of opening the campaign up to attacks from the Bush administration and congressional Republicans.

Despite the deliberate ambiguity of the governor's public statements, however, the Republicans continued to hammer away at the payroll tax in play-or-pay, claiming that it would devastate America's small-business sector. Atul Gawande, now the health and social policy director, began to worry that Clinton's vague position was doing him more harm than good. "By the middle of the summer," he recalled, "the Republicans were successful in portraying our plan as play-or-pay. Not only did they constantly talk about it as play-or-pay, but the media started to believe it. Then it became a debate about a 7 to 9 percent payroll tax, a debate about taxes in general that was putting us on weak ground."[25]

To make matters worse, the coherence of the campaign's position on health care reform was collapsing under the weight of its multiplying health policy advisers. In the wake of the convention, the ranks of the Washington Advisory Group on Health had swelled to more than sixty health policy experts—each of them with specific advice about the direction Clinton should take. As the members of this teeming gaggle of health policy specialists jockeyed among one another to win the governor's ear (and perhaps a coveted position within a Democratic administration), the campaign began to lose what little direction it had on health care reform.

Furthermore, a rift was opening up between the Washington Advisory Group and the campaign's two health policy principals, Gawande and Magaziner. The relationship between the leading figures in the Washington Advisory Group and the governor's two closest health policy advisers had always been strained. (A top member of the Washington Advisory Group wryly noted that the two advisers "thought the Washington Advisory Group was a communist front."[26]) As Gawande and Magaziner moved toward the managed-competition approach, the gap between them and the Washington Advisory Group grew larger. Several of the most influential members of the Washington Advisory Group, notably Judy Feder, Marilyn Moon, Kenneth Thorpe, and Joshua Wiener, were highly skeptical of managed competition. Feder had written to the *New York Times* in January criticizing managed competition and advocating global budgeting and negotiated fee schedules instead.[27] And many of her colleagues within the Washington Advisory Group shared this sentiment.[28]

Gawande and Magaziner, on the other hand, found managed competition increasingly appealing. Gawande had been in contact with Representative Cooper and the principals of the Jackson Hole Group, which in July had separated itself from InterStudy to become a nonprofit lobbying organization. He was also speaking frequently with the DLC leadership, and in particular with Jeremy Rosner, who was painting the CDF bill as paradigmatically New Democratic.[29] The DLC was convinced that the CDF framework would allow Clinton to distance himself from the Democrats on Capitol Hill who were advocating play-or-pay and those with a more liberal bent who wanted a single-payer system.

Magaziner did not enjoy Gawande's ties to the conservative Democrats, but he did have a much closer relationship with Clinton and knew that the governor was uncomfortable with the reform design the campaign had been advocating. Although Magaziner's background was in business consulting, he had recently completed a study of medical care in Rhode Island that had impressed Clinton enough to make Magaziner an informal health policy adviser to the campaign. Compared with Gawande, who had been deliberately brought on board by Reed to push the campaign toward managed competition, Magaziner was something of an enigma. His role in the campaign was hazily defined, his views on health care reform were not well known, and his area of expertise was industrial—not health—policy. But Magaziner also had the formidable advantage of being the only health policy adviser besides Bruce Reed who could take his ideas and concerns directly to the governor. This gave him a degree of influence over Clinton's position on health care reform that neither his ambiguous role in the campaign nor his relative unfamiliarity with health policy could attenuate.

Despite his limited expertise, Magaziner brought to the campaign some core convictions about health care reform. Perhaps most important was his belief that there was a tremendous amount of waste that could be squeezed out of American medicine if the proper framework for administrative and clinical decision making were established.[30] This conviction grew out of Magaziner's experience as a business consultant and his study of medicine in Rhode Island. It reflected a general faith, revealed in Magaziner's earlier ventures into public policy, that delicately calibrated regulation of private industries could restructure market incentives to promote socially desirable ends.[31] And it was a belief that distanced Magaziner from the members of the Washington Advisory Group, who were less sanguine about the prospects for short-term savings from simplification and standard-setting alone.

Magaziner parted with the Washington Advisory Group on other issues as well. He had deep reservations about the play-or-pay approach, especially the residual public plan, and he worried that the campaign had become excessively wedded to the views of its Washington-based health policy advisers. The disagreement over the figures in *Putting People First* represented a first attempt by Magaziner to move the campaign away from the Washington Advisory Group and assert himself as a major player in the development of Clinton's reform proposal. Magaziner's second attempt would lead the campaign to the liberal synthesis.

Magaziner had expressed his concerns about play-or-pay to Harvard professor Robert Reich, an old friend of Magaziner's who was advising the campaign on economic policy. In July Reich mentioned to Magaziner that he had recently read a manuscript on health care reform written by a colleague on the editorial board of *The American Prospect*, Paul Starr. A phone call between Magaziner and Starr followed in which Starr explained the key features of his approach and the rationale behind them. Magaziner asked Starr to send him a copy of the manuscript.[32]

Magaziner was immediately taken by Starr's erudite exposition of the Garamendi-style approach. Ever since fighting to reorganize the college curriculum as a student at Brown in the sixties, Magaziner had been known for his distinctive style of problem solving. He would immerse himself in the history and dimensions of a problem, analyzing every aspect, every potential solution, and then he would develop a tightly integrated approach to addressing it.[33] From the outset of the campaign, Magaziner had been searching for just such a conceptual approach to health care reform.

This put Magaziner at odds with the Washington Advisory Group, whose members thought Magaziner was an original thinker but woefully ignorant of the realities of Washington politics. Yet Magaziner's penchant for grand solutions made him the perfect contact for Starr and, through Starr, for Walter Zelman.[34] After all, Starr and Zelman were portraying the Garamendi plan as a new paradigm for health care reform that rejected the polarizing rhetoric of the past. Although the seasoned policy experts of the Washington Advisory Group were quick to dismiss such lofty claims, Magaziner was instinctively drawn to them.

With Magaziner and Gawande going in one policy direction and the Washington Advisory Group in several others, the campaign was losing ground on health care reform. Clinton himself seemed to have lost confidence, and when he spoke on the issue, he seemed uncertain about what approach he was advocating. As Bruce Fried explained, "During the primaries, Clinton was passionate on health care reform, but he lost his grounding on health care after the convention."[35] In contrast, the Bush campaign was finding its stride on the issue and honing its strategic assault on play-or-pay. Polls conducted by the Henry J. Kaiser Family Foundation showed that Bush was gradually eating into Clinton's wide lead on health care reform.[36] Between July and August, a growing percentage of voters contended that Bush would do a better job than Clinton in responding to the problems in American medicine. The politics of ambiguity was weakening Clinton on one of his strongest issues.

THE POLITICS OF DISCOVERY

By August, Gawande and Magaziner were convinced that the campaign needed to articulate a new policy direction on health care reform. The problem was how to get away from the payroll tax and the large public plan without being accused of abandoning earlier commitments. The two advisers wanted the plan to include elements of managed competition— such as purchasing cooperatives and incentives for consumers to choose low-cost plans—but also retain the enforceable national health budgets that the campaign had been supporting since January. This would be an approach much like the Garamendi and Starr proposals, with global budgets enforced through capitated payments to competing private health plans.

In early August, Gawande met in Washington with Bob Berenson, Paul Ellwood, Lynn Etheredge, Judy Feder, Bruce Fried, Jeremy Rosner, and Walter Zelman to get their input. The meeting was mostly a discussion of reform concepts, and although the participants differed among themselves, there was a general agreement that Clinton needed to distance himself from play-or-pay. Gawande was already convinced that Clinton should endorse an approach combining managed competition and global budgets. The main purpose of the meeting was to, in his words, "take the temperature of the policy community out there about the approach."[37]

On August 10, Gawande and Magaziner convened a meeting of some twenty-five people active in health policy to discuss a new health care framework for the campaign. Magaziner had invited people from outside the campaign who supported the managed-competition approach, including Starr and Zelman. In addition, the meeting included Feder, Thorpe, and several other members of the Washington Advisory Group. Also present were a number of health policy experts who were unaffiliated with the campaign, including Henry Aaron of the Brookings Institution and Larry Lewin of Lewin-VHI (a large health policy consulting firm in Virginia). Finally, Gawande brought in New York pediatrician Irwin Redlener and several "more political people," such as Karen Ignani of the AFL-CIO, Christopher Jennings of the Senate Aging Committee, and Jack Lewin, the director of Hawaii's employment-based comprehensive health program.[38]

Unlike the meeting of a few days earlier, this one was more confrontational and filled with what one participant described as "a lot of posturing."[39] Gawande began by laying out the proposal that he and Magaziner wanted the campaign to adopt—a plan that would allow for competition among managed-care networks within a budget set by the states. Everyone began to offer advice, but few challenged the proposal outright. In fact, the bulk of the meeting was devoted to criticisms of play-or-pay. Most of the meeting participants had come to recognize that the campaign leadership was going to abandon play-or-pay. No one wanted to seem wedded to an outmoded idea or to risk disfavor with the top figures in the campaign. Thus the meeting turned into a something of a bidding war, with each person at the table arguing more vociferously that the campaign should drop play-or-pay and embrace a new approach.

As the meeting's end neared, Magaziner argued that play-or-pay was a "quagmire." He felt that the Clinton proposal should grant the states broad latitude to adapt a managed-competition framework to local circumstances. Although Magaziner's pronouncement provoked a short debate about the extent to which states should be allowed to fashion their own approach, there was broad agreement that state flexibility should be a centerpiece of the plan. The most contentious issue turned out to be not the design of the plan, but how detailed it should be. Starr argued that the proposal should be as specific as possible, but most of the meeting participants, especially the more politically minded people, wanted to remain fairly vague. Sensing the unpopularity of his position, Starr retreated.

Finally, Gawande went back over the plan that he had presented at the beginning of the meeting, listing off its essential components. Despite the intensity of the meeting, the plan had not changed. Indeed, Gawande and Magaziner had set up the meeting not to amend the plan, but to build support for it within the health policy community. By bringing a large number of people into the decision-making process and making them feel as if they had contributed to the proposal, they sought to quell the dissension over health care reform within the campaign organization. As Gawande explained: "There is no such thing as getting a consensus on [health care reform]. If what I had done was gone into that meeting and said, 'Tell me what kind of plan you guys have,' we would have gotten nowhere. It was really an effort to see whether moving the details to this level would be something that could gain a wide range of policy support and political support."[40]

Nonetheless, the August meeting was not simply democratic ritual; the participation it permitted was not purely symbolic.[41] It served to bring new views into the campaign and to build support for those views within the campaign and the broader policy community. More important, the meeting provided a forum for airing and adjudicating disputes among the campaign's advisers. The meeting participants who were sympathetic to managed competition had a chance to explain the approach and its political logic. The participants who were hostile to managed competition had an opportunity to voice their reservations and suggest possible avenues of compromise.

The question remains, however, why the members of the Washington Advisory Group went along with the turn toward managed competition. The motives no doubt differed from adviser to adviser, but there seem to have been at least three main reasons. First, nearly all the meeting participants, including the Washington-based advisers, viewed play-or-pay as a political liability. Not only were Republicans gearing up for a new round of attacks on the approach, but Clinton himself was uncomfortable with the payroll tax and the large public plan. Gawande and Magaziner presented the participants in the meeting with two options: cling to play-or-pay or move toward managed competition. Thus framed, the choice was easy.

Second, the members of the Washington Advisory Group were placated by assurances from Gawande and Magaziner that any proposal embraced by the campaign would incorporate tough cost-containment provisions, including a national budget on health care spending and a regulatory backup in the event competition failed to control costs. In contrast to Gawande and Magaziner, who were attracted to managed competition as a policy prescription, Feder and others in the Washington Advisory Group viewed the turn toward managed competition as more of a symbolic gesture—a bow to the rhetoric of competition without much change in the core structure of the campaign's proposal. As long as the proposal retained the tough cost-containment measures they supported, therefore, the members of the Washington Advisory Group were willing to discard the rhetorical baggage associated with play-or-pay in favor of a fresher sounding approach

Third, and most important, the Washington Advisory Group went along with the turn toward competition because they did not have much of a choice: the balance of power within the campaign decisively favored Gawande and Magaziner. Gawande was part of the formal campaign organization, and his connection to Bruce Reed gave him access to the campaign leadership. Magaziner was a close and trusted friend of Clinton, the only health policy adviser with direct ties to the governor. By contrast, the Washington Advisory Group was far removed from the day-to-day operation of the campaign. None of its members belonged to the campaign organization in Arkansas, and none enjoyed an independent channel of communication to Clinton. None, therefore, could claim to speak for the campaign leadership or for Clinton with the same credibility as Gawande and Magaziner.

Gawande and Magaziner were at an advantage not just because of their positions within the campaign, but also because they were able to make a much stronger case than the Washington-based advisers that their views about reform were consonant with Clinton's. It was well known within the campaign, for instance, that Clinton did not like the payroll tax and public plan that play-or-pay entailed. Moreover, there was no denying how intrigued Clinton had been by the Garamendi plan when he had spoken about it with the California Insurance Commissioner during the early primaries. And even if Clinton had shown no previous interest in the approach, it would have been impossible for the campaign's advisers to ignore the striking congruence between Clinton's political philosophy and the ideas and assumptions embodied in the liberal synthesis. Indeed, when asked why the campaign moved toward managed competition, most members of the Washington Advisory Group were quick to point out the approach's appeal to Clinton's ideology and political instinct.[42]

It would therefore be a mistake to treat Clinton's proposal for reform as if it were simply the end result of bargaining and infighting among his campaign advisers. The struggle for power within the campaign did play a role in shaping Clinton's proposal, but only within the limits set by advisers' perceptions of what Clinton would support. Viewed in this way, the August policy shift was an effort to bring the campaign's position more closely in line with Clinton's conception of government and with his wider campaign agenda. Clinton could now speak confidently of being a new kind of Democrat who would harness market forces to achieve the liberal ideal of universal insurance coverage. He was freed of the burden of defending himself against Republican charges that he was proposing a huge tax increase to fund a government-run health care system. And because he had thrown his weight behind an approach that had not featured prominently in the national debate, he could portray himself as rising above the stale thinking and false dichotomies that had defeated efforts at compromise in the past.

Embracing a relatively obscure approach carried other immediate advantages as well. It meant that the campaign would meet fewer challenges to its claims about the budgetary impact of the plan or the amount of new taxes it would require. It also meant that Clinton would appear to be throwing his support behind both wings of the Democratic party. The proponents of single payer or play-or-pay might be chagrined that Clinton had moved closer to the Conservative Democratic Forum and the Democratic Leadership Council. But until the details of the proposal were hammered out, they would be reassured by his commitment to universal coverage and his endorsement of budgeting. The more conservative Democrats might chafe at the notion that budgets and competition could be combined. For a time, however, they would accept Clinton's assurances that budget caps would only take effect if managed competition failed to contain spending. In effect, the campaign had managed to make Clinton's proposal more specific and more ambiguous at once.

The remainder of August was spent working on the plan to prepare it for Clinton's approval. It was not until September, while Clinton was campaigning in East Lansing, Michigan, that Gawande and Magaziner were able to brief the governor on the new proposal. They brought with them Feder, Thorpe, and Ron Pollack. Gawande opened the meeting with a brief summary of the governor's position on reform and how it had evolved over the last few weeks.[43] Feder and Thorpe then presented the proposal in greater depth, with Thorpe laying out the estimated cost of the proposal and the savings that might be achieved. Finally, Pollack closed the meeting with an explanation of the rhetoric that Clinton could use to present his proposal and to distinguish it from President Bush's.[44]

Clinton was ecstatic about the new proposal, pumping his fist in the air in approval at various points in the meeting. Once Clinton had approved the plan, the campaign hurriedly prepared a speech on the proposal, as well as an eight-page press statement to be released simultaneously.

On September 24, flanked by New Jersey Governor Jim Florio and Senators Jay Rockefeller and Harris Wofford, Clinton presented his new plan in a special speech at Merck pharmaceuticals in Rahway, New Jersey. The proposal that he described was remarkably similar to the Garamendi and Starr proposals. Employers would be required to cover their employees. Smaller firms would receive tax credits to help them purchase coverage, and their employees would purchase coverage from large cooperatives. Individuals would be given, in Clinton's words, "real incentives to be in managed care networks, so that the costs can be held down by the forces of the marketplace." The networks would be given a fixed payment for each enrollee, thereby "limiting a network's total spending without interfering at all with its practices." As he neared the end of his speech, Clinton laid out the programmatic philosophy of the plan in no uncertain terms: "We've got to quit having the federal government micro-manage health care and instead set up incentives for the private sector to manage the cost. . . . This is a private system. It is not play-or-pay. It does not require new taxes. It will preserve what is best about the present health care system."[45]

The eight-page outline of the plan released the same day embellished these themes, claiming that the plan would "improve quality, expand choice, and control costs through a strategy of competition within a budget." Competition would be encouraged through the creation of "publicly-sponsored purchasing groups" that would "band together small businesses and individuals to buy private coverage." The purchasing groups would contract with managed-care networks, which would "receive a fixed amount of money . . . for meeting a consumer's full health needs." The budget would be set first at the national level, then at the state level, and then translated into capitated payments to health plans. To meet the global budget targets, each state would also establish fee schedules to be used by fee-for-service insurers.[46]

To distance itself from the payroll tax, the campaign had abandoned the central element of play-or-pay—the tax-funded public plan. Instead, all employers would be required to contribute to the cost of their workers' health insurance. But this created new problems. The main reason for the tax-financed plan in play-or-pay was to protect low-wage employees and small firms. Standard economic theory suggests that workers' money wages or other fringe benefits will fall to offset the cost of an employer mandate. For workers at or near the minimum wage, this adjustment cannot take place and job losses may result.[47] By ensuring that no firm paid more than a modest percentage of payroll to cover its workers, the play-or-pay approach aimed to limit the negative employment impact of a mandate.

The Clinton campaign recognized the difficulties with the pure mandate, of course, and the proposal included several measures to lessen its effect. Small firms would be eligible for subsidies and would be phased into the new system. They would also have access to community rates negotiated by a large, monopsonistic purchasing cooperative. (In this sense, the purchasing cooperatives took the place of the public plan in play-or-pay.) Whether these measures would be sufficient was an open question, but the single overriding imperative of the campaign was to distance itself from the word *tax*. As Senator Kennedy's top aide pointed out: "Play-or-pay got tagged as being a payroll tax. . . . Clinton was scared to death of being portrayed as a guy who wanted to impose new taxes, so he needed something else."[48]

The Clinton camp was extremely vague about several key aspects of the plan. They were careful not to draw attention to the twin pillars of managed competition—the fixed contribution and the tax cap. Advocating that people pay the difference between the lowest-priced health plan contracting with a purchasing cooperative and the one in which they enrolled was dangerous during a presidential race, and instead the campaign spoke vaguely of creating "real incentives" for individuals to enroll in managed-care plans. The plan also did not specify a cutoff firm size for the purchasing cooperatives or explain how payments to plans would be adjusted to reflect the actuarial risk of their enrollees.

Despite all its ambiguity, the plan represented a clear policy shift. On the surface, the most significant aspect of this shift was the replacement of the play-or-pay mechanism with the straight employer mandate. Far more critical, however, was the campaign's endorsement of a managed-competition structure based on purchasing cooperatives and competing private health plans. Another significant aspect of the new proposal was the idea that a national budget could be enforced through capitated payments to health plans rather than through all-payer rate regulation. This idea was part of a more general philosophy expressed in the plan—that the government's role in the health care system should be limited to developing broad guidelines within which the private sector would operate. Not only was Clinton abandoning the idea of a residual public plan and all-payer fee schedules; he was also proposing to fold Medicaid into a private system managed by the purchasing cooperatives.[49] This was a path to universal coverage taken by no other nation.

The Merck speech of September 24 left the campaign staff feeling heady and confident. Clinton had redefined his position, and the Bush camp was in disarray trying to formulate a response. But the celebration was short-lived. On September 27, the lead editorial in the *New York Times* announced that Clinton's health care plan "was just a skimpy statement of principles . . . [that] sounded as if they were written by a warring committee, with incompatible ideas jousting for supremacy and crucial details left out." The editorial (which had been written by Michael Weinstein, of course) continued: "Some words raise the nightmarish prospect that Mr. Clinton will try to run health care by dictating prices in ways doomed to fail. Other words suggest he would rely on competition to keep prices down. . . . Mr. Clinton owes voters a cleaner accounting."[50]

The Clinton campaign was thrown into a panic. Gawande and Thorpe called Weinstein and tried to convince him of the error of his assessment. Paul Starr dropped in on Weinstein in New York to repeat the message in person.[51] John Garamendi was asked by the campaign to write to the *New York Times* to set the record straight. In the letter, which was printed in early October, Garamendi expressed "surprise" that the *Times* disapproved of Clinton's plan. "A careful reading of that proposal," he wrote, "suggests that the Governor is clearly moving in a direction so effectively advocated by you in recent months. The Clinton proposal calls for a managed competition model in which insurers and health maintenance organizations compete for consumer support over price and service."[52]

To ensure that Weinstein had heard the message, the health policy staff prepared a press release expressing Clinton's commitment to managed competition. The release denied that Clinton had ever supported rate regulation. The budget targets would be met through managed competition and, if necessary, restrictions on the rate of growth of the capitated payments to private health plans. All-payer rate regulation would only be used during the "transition" and only where the penetration of managed-care plans was too low to support managed competition. To drive the point home, the release quoted Clinton as saying, "Managed competition, *not price controls*, will make the budget work and maintain quality."[53]

Weinstein was swayed. On October 10, in the first sentence of the lead editorial, he triumphantly announced, "The debate over health care reform is over. Managed competition has won." In glowing prose, the editorial sung the praise of managed competition and its newest champion, who had "wavered between managed competition and price controls" but had finally seized upon "the only reform that has a realistic chance to control costs as coverage is extended to millions of uninsured Americans." "Congress now faces a delicious prospect," Weinstein concluded. "Come January it can start with a managed competition blueprint, dot the i's and send the President, whether his name is Clinton or Bush, a bill he'd be proud to sign."[54] Managed competition, it seemed, was a fait accompli.

CONCLUSION

On November 3, 1992, just one year after Harris Wofford's surprise victory in Pennsylvania, Bill Clinton was elected president of the United States with 43 percent of the popular vote (and more than 53 percent of the two-party vote). Americans went to the polls in higher numbers than in recent elections, handing Clinton a healthy 5.6 percent victory margin over President Bush and voting almost two-to-one in favor of a new administration. In the House, turnover was unusually high—in part because of the revelation that hundreds of House members had regularly overdrawn their checking accounts with the House bank.[55] But despite the higher congressional turnover and Clinton's plurality victory, the partisan distribution in Congress barely budged. The Senate remained narrowly divided along partisan lines, with Democrats holding three fewer than the sixty seats necessary to break a filibuster. In the House, the Democrats lost ten seats in a relatively placid general election. Nonetheless, the survival of Democratic majorities meant that, for the first time since the Carter administration, the House, the Senate, and the White House were all in Democratic hands.[56]

If the election results painted a picture of continuity alongside change, the same could not be said of the gathering debate over national health care reform. In the one short year that separated Wofford's triumph in Pennsylvania from Clinton's election as president, health care reform had traveled from the periphery to the center of national debate. Just as rapidly, managed competition had emerged from relative obscurity to become a leading framework for national health care reform. The approach had been transformed from a conceptual paradigm into a specific reform proposal, from a proposal into a credible alternative on Capitol Hill, and, mutatis mutandis, from a credible alternative into a presidential campaign pledge. Along the way, the approach had been refined, recast, and recombined—often in ways its founders had never envisioned. Within a year, it would be transformed yet again, from a campaign proposal into an ambitious legislative initiative.

CHAPTER 5

The Plan

ALTHOUGH Clinton's victory in the 1992 election was impressive, ending as it did twelve years of Republican occupancy of the White House and ushering in the first period of unified party control since the Carter administration, Clinton entered office facing a very difficult strategic context. First, there was his narrow partisan majority in the Senate, where sixty votes were needed to break a filibuster. If Senate Republicans filibustered legislation, Clinton would need the support of every Democrat plus at least three Republicans (four after Texas Republican Kay Bailey Hutchison won a special Senate race in June) to ensure its passage.

A second difficulty Clinton faced was fiscal. The 1992 election had focused heavily on the federal budget deficit, and many new members of Congress were committed to deficit reduction. Although this created a receptive climate in which Clinton could advance a major deficit-reduction initiative, the focus on the deficit could only make it more difficult to pass legislation that entailed new federal spending. Congressional budget procedures adopted in 1990 placed special hurdles in the path of measures that the Congressional Budget Office (CBO) estimated would increase the deficit.

Finally, there was the equivocal nature of Clinton's electoral mandate and popular support. He had, after all, won the election with only 43 percent of the vote, and in congressional districts where Democrats had won he had usually run behind them. More generally, as chapter 3 noted, Clinton entered office at a time when trust in government was at a historic ebb and politics and political figures were widely reviled. Moreover, the tenor of public debate suggested that Americans were more sharply polarized over the appropriate role of the federal government than at any point in the postwar era.[1]

In short, Clinton was greeted with what would later be judged to be an "extraordinarily resource-poor environment" for a social policy innovation of the magnitude and complexity of comprehensive health care reform.[2] But it did not look that way to the Clinton administration or its opponents in early 1993, nor to most of the journalists, pundits, and even political scientists who offered their forecasts of the road ahead. Instead, imponderably, many thought it would be 1933 all over again. Clinton invoked FDR's hundred days, and favorably compared himself to two other plurality presidents, Abraham Lincoln and Woodrow Wilson. Congressional Democrats counseled Clinton to eschew bipartisanship and rely on his Democratic majorities in the House and Senate. And most, if not all, of the Washington press corps expected that Clinton's first term would be crowned by the passage of major health care reform legislation.

As we review the transformation of the president's campaign proposal into legislation, it is worth keeping in mind the enthusiasm and optimism that characterized the early days of the president's reform effort and that were so quickly forgotten after the defeat of health care reform and the Republican capture of Congress in 1994. Despite the serious obstacles the Clinton administration faced—some recognized, some ignored—the president's reform effort began with the conviction that managed competition within a budget would square the policy circle that past presidents had found politically insoluble.

This chapter follows the president's reform effort from its inception during the presidential transition through its formal launching in the fall of 1993. It begins by exploring the disagreements and deliberations during the transition that cemented Clinton's choice of managed competition within a budget and shaped the future course of the policy development process. The next part of the chapter examines the formal development of the president's plan during the dramatic hundred-day rush to craft a finished legislative proposal. Then the focus shifts to the political assumptions that were embodied in the Clinton reform proposal and to the question of why these assumptions proved far less robust than the advocates of managed competition within a budget had hoped. Finally, the discussion turns to the design and early implementation of the president's campaign to raise public support for his plan. The general weakness of this campaign—and in particular its failure to stem the hemorrhaging of public support for the proposal that followed the president's September speech—appears to have reflected not only the nature of the proposal, but also the assumptions and constraints that shaped the president's communication strategy.

Whether things could have been different is an open question, and one that would take us far afield from the focus of this book. The aim of this chapter is not to present an alternative road map by which the president and his aides could have sidestepped the obstacles they encountered. It is rather to show why managed competition within a budget was far more vulnerable than Clinton and his advisers had believed and, indeed, posed serious risks and challenges that were neither foreseen nor adequately confronted during the campaign and the early months of the new administration. These risks and challenges were partly internal to managed competition and partly a reflection of the unrealistic hopes and assumptions to which it had given rise. Some of them could have been avoided; others may have been inescapable. But all of them helped thwart the rosy forecasts that managed competition within a budget had initially inspired.

THE PRESIDENTIAL TRANSITION

During the transition, health care reform received little attention from the president-elect, who was preoccupied with executive branch appointments and his economic reform package. Nonetheless, the transition advisers on health care reform—led by Judy Feder and Atul Gawande—worked to develop a set of recommendations for the new president. The advisers were divided into three groups: a budget team headed by Kenneth Thorpe; a policy team consisting of Lynn Etheredge and Brandeis University professor Stuart Altman; and a public affairs team with links to Congress, interest groups, and grassroots organizers.[3]

The composition of the transition group—particularly the leadership position of Feder—immediately prompted speculation in the press about the direction that Clinton's reform effort was heading.[4] Feder, after all, was not a strong supporter of the reform framework Clinton had endorsed during the campaign, and neither was Altman or Thorpe. Immediately after the election, in fact, Feder had sent a memorandum to Clinton asking that he abandon the managed-competition design or at least rely much more heavily on rate regulation than he had indicated he would. Feder's suggestion had been rejected before it reached Clinton, but disagreements over the structure of the plan continued. These came to a head later, when Etheredge almost resigned from the transition because he believed Feder was trying to move Clinton away from the core ideas advocated during the campaign.[5] Etheredge complained to a number of people outside the transition—including Paul Starr, Jeremy Rosner of the Progressive Policy Institute, and Representative Jim Cooper—and a string of protests from managed-competition advocates reached Feder, Ira Magaziner, and even Clinton himself. By the middle of December, there was little talk within the transition about abandoning the managed-competition framework.

The initial disagreement over the structure of the plan was soon replaced with a new dispute, this time centering on the question of how quickly Clinton could achieve his goal of providing universal insurance coverage with minimal new taxes and moderate cuts in existing programs. Magaziner emerged as a leading antagonist in the debate, arguing that managed competition combined with strict budgetary limits could squeeze out enough administrative and clinical waste to fund universal coverage. The budget specialists retorted that it would take several years for managed competition to slow the growth in medical costs and that, in any case, most of the savings would accrue to the private sector rather than the federal government. The budget debate culminated in a disastrous meeting in Little Rock in early January between Clinton and his transition advisers. Some members of the transition group later suspected that the meeting, like the August campaign session in Washington, had been set up by Magaziner to criticize the Washington advisers and thereby claim rightful control over the policy development process. Whatever Magaziner's motives, the meeting featured repeated accusations by Magaziner that the estimated cost of the budgetary options was excessive. Clinton was equally unhappy. He had promised during the campaign to achieve universal coverage without significant new taxes or deficit spending and through a reform strategy that relied heavily on managed competition. But the transition team estimates cast those commitments in doubt. The least expensive option presented to Clinton might not have reached universal insurance coverage before the turn of the century and, even then, would have added $22 billion to the deficit in the first five years of operation. The most expensive option would have achieved universal coverage in 1997, but only after adding $215 billion to the deficit in the first five years. If Clinton decided to limit the tax deductibility of employer-provided health insurance, the resulting revenue for the first five years could amount to more than $100 billion. Even with the tax cap, however, tens of billions of dollars would still have to be raised through Medicare cutbacks and sin taxes on tobacco and alcohol.[6]

Although the budgetary estimates received the most attention during the transition, they were not the only materials produced. The policy team headed by Altman and Etheredge also produced its own set of documents, which further developed the reform proposal Clinton had presented during the campaign.[7] The goal of the policy team was to formulate a rough legislative proposal before the inauguration. The team understood that Clinton would have the best opportunity to enact legislation early in his term when public and congressional support was high. Although Clinton had promised during the campaign that he would present his health care reform proposal within a hundred days of taking office, the transition staff hoped to have the program ready in half that time.[8]

These efforts were hindered, however, by two constraints common to presidential transitions. First, because health care reform was overshadowed by the transition scramble over appointments and Clinton's economic program, the policy team received little guidance from Clinton or the advisers close to him. The team identified many of the key policy choices that needed to be made, but no one with the requisite authority was able to review them or locate them within Clinton's broader legislative agenda. Second, the secrecy that characterizes policy formulation during a transition posed particular drawbacks for developing and building support for a proposal whose core elements were relatively unfamiliar and vague. Not only did it complicate the process of consulting outside experts, but it also prevented the policy team from familiarizing congressional leaders, interest groups, and the public with Clinton's distinctive reform design.

With the secrecy of the transition efforts leaving a vacuum of knowledge about the president-elect's intentions, the conference on managed competition that Paul Starr had arranged in 1992 emerged as a critical forum for explaining the rationale behind "competition within a budget." Held in Princeton, New Jersey, in late November, the conference brought together congressional staff and policy experts to discuss different aspects of the managed-competition approach. The papers presented at the conference circulated widely on Capitol Hill, and all but two were later reprinted in a supplementary volume of the health policy quarterly *Health Affairs*. Well into the Clinton administration's first year, the *Health Affairs* articles were the most influential articulation of the policy streams that had fed into the Clinton campaign in 1992.

The Princeton conference was a paradigm example of policy advocacy, redolent of the preinaugural task forces commissioned by President Kennedy but without any official connection to the Clinton transition.[9] Like the Kennedy task forces and unlike the transition group, the Princeton conference produced a set of public documents outlining the policy ideas that might be embodied in a major presidential proposal. These papers were presented and understood as policy options for the incoming administration, and, indeed, ten of the participants in the conference—including Paul Starr, Linda Bergthold, Richard Kronick, and Walter Zelman—would later join the White House effort.[10] The twist was that the conference had been organized by Starr long before Clinton's victory and had no formal relation to the transition. It was an attempt to push Clinton farther down the policy path he had embarked on during the campaign, immensely successful in part because it was treated by the policy analysts and congressional staff who participated in it simply as an extension of the transition efforts.

A few weeks after the conference, Starr wrote Magaziner to request a formal role in the White House effort. The letter detailed all of Starr's considerable efforts to garner support for managed competition and closed with an optimistic forecast of managed competition's prospects. "If the political foundation is laid carefully," Starr wrote, "the reception for a Clinton program could be strongly positive—with a broad consensus on structure. The conflict will then narrow to who will pay for what and how fast—obviously tough [issues] to resolve, but negotiable."[11] The next few months would begin to put Starr's optimism to the test.

THE TASK FORCE

On January 25, 1993, less than a week after the inauguration, President Clinton announced that he was establishing a presidential task force to oversee the development of his health care reform proposal. The twelve-member task force would be composed of senior administration officials, chaired by Mrs. Clinton, and advised by a group of policy experts headed by Ira Magaziner. The advisory group (rarely distinguished from the official task force in press accounts) would eventually include more than five hundred administration officials, congressional staff members, and outside experts organized into more than thirty "working groups" studying various aspects of health care reform.

Although the idea of the task force grew out of conversations between the Clintons and Magaziner that stretched back to the beginning of the transition, the president did not make the final decision to appoint the task force until after the budget fiasco in Little Rock.[12] The obvious precedent for the White House effort was the presidential task forces popularized by President Johnson in 1964.[13] These were small policy planning staffs that operated in secrecy under one of the president's key assistants. Their main benefit for the president was that they reduced his dependency on the departments, the traditional source of presidential proposals. Clinton had a somewhat similar motive: he was reluctant to have the policy-development process handled by the Department of Health and Human Services (HHS) because he did not believe that the new HHS secretary, Donna Shalala, was experienced enough in health policy.[14] Furthermore, Clinton had used the task force device a number of times as governor of Arkansas, most notably in 1983, when he appointed a fifteen-member committee headed by Mrs. Clinton to develop a proposal for reforming the state's education system.[15]

If the official task force had a distinguished lineage in presidential policymaking, the huge advisory body headed by Magaziner was of a scope and design never before seen in the White House. According to Paul Starr, "Magaziner had designed the working group effort on a model taken from his experience as a business consultant. The paradigm was a corporate restructuring or technological innovation that required thinking through innumerable options and suboptions and meshing together previously uncoordinated activities and groups into a coherent plan."[16] The sheer audacity of the effort was symbolized by the periodic "tollgate" meetings that Magaziner convened to review the progress made by the working groups. Held in the majestic Indian Treaty Room of the Old Executive Office Building, the meetings routinely included well over one hundred people. The acoustics of the high-ceilinged room were terrible, and the members of the working groups had to strain to hear the presentations. The meetings could drag on for days, with some sessions starting close to midnight. And presiding over them all was Magaziner.[17]

Magaziner had never envisioned the working group effort as the behemoth it became, but the forces behind its expansion were seemingly inexorable. First, as the working groups came across new subjects that might be relevant to the president's proposal, Magaziner felt compelled to commission separate groups to explore them.[18] Linda Bergthold, who headed a group on benefits coverage, complained that the effort "was a rolling game. New groups were added all through March. . . . The White House honestly didn't know who was involved, there were so many people floating in and out."[19] Second, because the secrecy of the task force had upset many Democratic leaders in Congress, the White House decided to make the working groups as open as possible to Democratic congressional staff.[20] Finally, Mrs. Clinton demanded that more women and minorities be brought into the process to make the groups more representative of society as a whole.[21]

The role of the working groups, as Magaziner explained in a long memo in late January, was to explore all the policy options that were consistent with the reform framework Clinton had articulated during the campaign. Each of the working groups was therefore to begin by considering the full range of policy ideas relevant to its subject area—a process that Magaziner termed "broadening."[22] The broadening process was to be followed by a "narrowing" phase, during which the working group analyses would be distilled down to a list of specific options for President Clinton and his close advisers. The working groups were not to make the final decisions about the structure of the plan, nor were they to concern themselves with the politics of their recommendations. The hard choices about policy and politics would be made by the president and his advisers before the proposal was introduced.

The working group effort quickly proved far too unwieldy to be an effective vehicle for policy formulation. The working groups only analyzed a fragment of the broader proposal. They were generally staffed by people who were interested in and knowledgeable about the specific subject areas under consideration. All the incentives encouraged the members of the working groups to do more analysis and develop more—and more comprehensive—solutions. Although some of the work done by the groups was useful, their main effect was to push the president's proposal in the direction of greater comprehensiveness and detail. The important policy choices were made not by the working groups, but by a smaller collection of advisers centered around Magaziner, including Paul Starr, Richard Kronick, Walter Zelman, and former Zelman aide Larry Levitt. A second coterie of advisers, most with campaign experience, developed a strategy for building public and congressional support for the proposal. A third group—encompassing several departments, the Office of Management and Budget (OMB), and the Council of Economic Advisors (CEA)—was in charge of analyzing the plan's budgetary impact.[23]

Two interrelated subjects dominated deliberations within Magaziner's select circle of advisers: financing and cost containment. Since the campaign, there had been no question that the primary financing mechanism would be mandated payments by workers and their employers. This approach had appealed to Clinton because it built on the existing system of employer-sponsored health insurance and because, properly structured, it obviated the need to raise a large amount of new revenue through the tax code. But Clinton had never set forth the details of the mandate, and it was inevitable that once he took office those details would become the subject of heated debate within the White House.

At the outset, the health policy advisers assumed that Clinton would stick with the straight employer mandate he had endorsed during the campaign, coupled with subsidies for the poor (which would replace Medicaid) and perhaps a cap on the total payments required of an individual or family. But the working group charged with developing the details of the mandate added new features to further reduce its regressivity. The result was an extremely complicated premium scheme that left even the supporters of the model uneasy. In April, Magaziner made a startling suggestion: why not sidestep all of the contortions required to make a mandated premium proportional to income and fund the plan through a tax on payroll? The initial reception to the idea was positive, but soon there were dissenting voices. Starr, supportive of the idea at first, wrote a series of memos to Magaziner stating his unequivocal opposition to a payroll tax.[24] Although many of Starr's arguments involved technical objections to the tax, his main concern was political. A payroll tax, Starr worried in one memo, might "consume the entire debate about health care, and sink the reform." More important, it could "consume the entire administration, and sink the president's popularity."[25]

In the end, Starr and others who opposed the payroll tax prevailed. Instead of a payroll tax, the health policy team settled on a premium scheme that closely resembled one ("a payroll tax dressed up as a premium," as Starr had called it in one of his memos).[26] The contributions required of employers and workers would be based on premium levels, but total payments by employers and workers would be limited to a fixed percentage of payroll and family income, respectively. To complicate matters further, the policy team had the caps for businesses with seventy-five or fewer employees vary on a sliding scale, so that small, low-wage firms would pay a smaller percentage of payroll than large firms and small, high-wage firms. These provisions would later cause considerable consternation among health policy experts, who alternately criticized them for being too generous, too complicated, poorly targeted, or potentially distortionary (leading employers to create or farm out work to small, low-wage firms, for example). Yet Clinton's advisers felt that the subsidy scheme was necessary to reduce the opposition of small firms, and they rejected other subsidy schemes that might have been less distortionary (such as subsidizing all low-wage firms regardless of employment size) because the cost was too high.

A mandate on employers and individuals to contribute to the cost of insurance was not, however, the only source of financing for the proposal. Depending on the structure of the plan, an additional $30 to $90 billion in new federal health care spending would be needed to pay for new benefits and to fund subsidies for individuals and small firms. Since the campaign, Clinton and his advisers had stood firm on two other sources of funds: cuts in the rate of growth in Medicare spending and an increase in federal taxation of tobacco. A more controversial funding source was a limit on tax-free employer payments for health insurance. Unlike the founders of managed competition, Clinton's advisers did not view the tax cap as essential to encouraging cost-consciousness, but they did see it as a potential revenue source. The difficulty with the tax cap was that it was opposed by organized labor and by leading members of Congress. There were also outstanding questions about where to set the cap. It could be set at the price of the lowest-cost plan contracting with the local HIPC, which would vary from region, thus making the cap virtually impossible to administer; or at some uniform national level, which would not allow for regional variation in premiums, thus contradicting the basic theory of managed competition.[27] As it became apparent how difficult the implementation and administration of the tax cap would be, the advisers began to lean against it. In April, Magaziner hinted that it would not be a "significant" source of funding for the plan, although a month later he wrote to Enthoven to get his suggestions about possible ways to structure a tax cap.[28] The task force disbanded without a final decision on the tax cap (or many other critical subjects), but by then it seemed clear that despite the theoretical virtues of the cap, the practical and political barriers to its passage, implementation, and administration argued strongly for its exclusion from the president's proposal.

Other sources of financing considered by Clinton's advisers included a tax on providers (to offset the new revenues they would receive under universal insurance coverage), a small increase in the federal unemployment tax, and even a national value-added tax on consumption goods.[29] Besides the provider tax, however, none of these ideas received serious consideration. An untimely mention of the value-added tax by Donna Shalala set off a media feeding frenzy on tax day, April 15.[30] Leaks to the press about other taxes being considered threatened passage of legislation pending in Congress. When it was revealed that the White House was considering a tax on wine and other alcoholic beverages, for example, the California congressional delegation sent a letter to the White House warning that it might block Clinton's budget package.[31]

The second major subject Magaziner and his advisers struggled over during the spring of 1993 was cost containment. Near the end of the presidential campaign, in part to appease the *New York Times*, Clinton had characterized his proposal to restrict the rate of growth in health insurance premiums as a secondary measure that would only take effect if competition failed to contain costs. It soon became clear, however, that premium regulation would assume a more prominent position in the president's reform proposal. In early February, the Congressional Budget Office estimated that the Conservative Democratic Forum's managed-competition bill would lead to sizable deficit spending and have little effect on medical inflation.[32] The estimate made it clear that the CBO was not willing to attribute the kind of savings to managed competition that would be needed to simultaneously guarantee universal coverage and meet Clinton's budget goals. In addition, Clinton's advisers were concerned that in the absence of stringent premium regulation, providers and insurers would pocket the new revenues they received under universal coverage. Without a requirement that providers and insurers cut their rates to reflect the reduction in unpaid medical bills, the federal government might end up underwriting a costly windfall to the medical sector.

So worried were Clinton's health policy advisers about the impact of health care costs on the deficit and the inflationary effects of expanding coverage that they seriously considered imposing short-term controls on wages, prices, and revenues in the medical sector. A working group was chartered by Magaziner to study the possibility. In early February, Starr suggested that Clinton request authority to impose across-the-board price controls on the medical sector, to be invoked only if medical inflation continued unabated or if Congress failed to pass a reform proposal in 1993.[33] Magaziner and Mrs. Clinton were supportive of stringent payment controls, but the idea faced sharp resistance among Clinton's economic advisers and budget officials. Even if the economic advisers had been more receptive, however, it would probably have been too late to develop the necessary provisions to include them in Clinton's budget package.[34]

The schism between Clinton's health policy advisers and his economic advisers over short-term price controls would reemerge on other subjects. Many of the economic advisers, for example, supported a relatively "bare-bones" package of health benefits with high cost-sharing requirements. The health policy advisers, in contrast, wanted a more comprehensive package with limited cost-sharing. The economic advisers argued that subsidies to fund universal coverage would burden the budget and hence should be phased in slowly, while the health policy advisers supported a shorter phase-in period.[35] On both these issues, the Clintons ultimately sided with their health policy staff.

Compared with the amount of intellectual energy Clinton's advisers devoted to the subjects of financing and cost containment, the administrative architecture of the plan received scant attention. Although there was some analysis of the role and structure of the purchasing cooperatives, the basic institutional configuration of the proposal elicited little scrutiny or debate. The health policy advisers could not, of course, avoid making many important decisions about administrative structure. Yet these decisions were usually a by-product of other strategic choices. In fact, the most common pattern of institutional design was for the health policy advisers to identify a problem and then simply structure the institutions to solve it. Surprisingly few of them asked the broader question of whether such institutions could actually be created or expected to operate effectively.

This pattern of institutional design was particularly evident in working group deliberations over the size of the purchasing cooperatives. The advisers recognized that the purchasing cooperatives would be vulnerable if they included only small employers. First, smaller purchasing cooperatives would be composed disproportionately of low-income Americans, whose medical costs were higher than average. This would mean that firms outside the HIPCs would be freed of the burden of subsidizing coverage for the poor while smaller firms, forced to buy coverage through the HIPCs, would not. It would also raise the budgetary cost of the subsidies, since the plans contracting with the HIPCs would charge higher premiums. Second, if larger firms were allowed to join the HIPCs at their discretion, the likelihood of adverse selection would be very high, as high-cost firms joined the cooperatives and low-cost firms stayed out. Finally, the advisers wanted the HIPCs to include most employers because that would give cooperatives greater ability to restrain premiums, regulate the practices of health plans and employers, and provide Americans with equal access to health plans.

The solution the health policy advisers arrived at was to set the size threshold for the cooperatives very high, requiring that all employers with fewer than five thousand employees join the HIPCs. Firms above the size threshold would have to meet federally imposed budget limits and

offer a range of health plans, as well as comply with other costly requirements. All in all, it was an effective solution to some worrisome policy
problems. But what is striking is how little consideration was given to
other concerns—such as the political feasibility of the cooperatives, their
ability to fulfill their mandate, and the administrative infrastructure in
which they would be embedded.

A similar type of reasoning led the advisers to reject a far more significant structural alteration in the proposal—making Medicare available to
the nonelderly through the HIPCs. As Clinton's reform initiative began to
take shape, several congressional leaders and outside policy experts suggested that the proposal include Medicare in the roster of plans offered by
the purchasing cooperatives. Medicare, after all, was a highly popular
program with a well-developed institutional infrastructure. Its administrative costs were low, it already had a system of payment regulation in
place, and it paid providers far less than private insurers. Allowing the
nonelderly to enroll in Medicare through the purchasing cooperatives
would effectively guarantee that all Americans had access to a relatively
inexpensive fee-for-service plan. Yet Clinton's policy advisers were extremely hostile to the idea. Paul Starr launched a strident assault on Medicare, claiming that its inclusion in the plan would be "an exceptionally
clever way of undermining the entire strategy." Starr's complaint was
that Medicare was incompatible with managed competition. Its fee-for-
service reimbursement system encouraged high-cost services and undermined the incentives for people to join alternative systems. "Medicare's
entire history," Starr contended, "should be a lesson on how not to structure a national health program."[36]

Starr won the argument easily: the policy planners agreed that Medicare was a route foreclosed. But the "lesson" that Starr had drawn from
Medicare's history was not the only one available. For all its imperfec-
tions, Medicare was the largest and most popular federal health program
and the only one whose infrastructure could credibly form the basis of a
broader public system. Starr's critique of Medicare made no mention of
these administrative advantages, nor did it take into consideration the
political advantages of ensuring that people would be able to purchase an
inexpensive fee-for-service plan. Instead, Starr and others in the White
House dismissed Medicare because it did not fit into the carefully balanced framework of incentives that they envisioned. As with the architecture of the purchasing cooperatives, the decision to rule out Medicare
reflected a stubborn absence of attention to the problems of administrative and structural design.

Clinton had convened the task force with the promise that it would
have legislation ready by the end of May. In early April, however, the
White House announced that the plan would not be released until at least

the middle of June. By June the task force had expired, the members of the working groups had dispersed, and the date of introduction had been pushed back to July. The core of the White House effort—Magaziner and his close advisers, the political strategy team, and the economic analysts—confronted the difficult task of drafting the proposal and developing a strategy for passing it.

POLITICS, PRESSURE, AND THE PLAN

Although the primary focus of the health policy advisers was the structure and detail of the proposal, they realized that the plan could not be passed without constructing a congressional coalition and building public support. Recent accounts of President Clinton's reform effort have suggested that the health policy team never really developed a strategy for passing the president's plan, preferring instead to immerse themselves in "the arcana of systems analysis."[37] While this indictment contains a kernel of truth, it does not capture the complexity of the president's strategic difficulties. The president and his advisers did not ignore the politics of passing the proposal; they misunderstood the politics. The problem was not that they had no strategy for enacting reform; indeed, the reform proposal they developed was based on a very specific set of strategic assumptions. The problem was the strategy itself. Criticizing the president and his advisers for their political naïveté will therefore only take us so far. We need to understand what exactly about the strategy undergirding the president's reform effort was politically naive. And we cannot answer that question without analyzing the strategy itself and linking it to the reform approach that President Clinton proposed.

The president's strategy for passing reform focused on three main areas: timing, coalition building, and public relations. Each of these areas granted President Clinton different degrees of latitude, and each was influenced in different ways by his endorsement of managed competition within a budget. This section examines important features of the president's strategy concerning timing and coalition building. The next discusses the design of the president's campaign to raise public support for reform. My aim is not to provide a catalogue of the strategic choices made by President Clinton and his aides. That would require another book motivated by a different set of empirical and theoretical concerns. Rather, my purpose is to explain some of the most significant of those strategic choices and show how they relate to the political processes that moved managed competition onto the government agenda.

President Clinton initially considered including health care reform in his budget package. Doing so would have eliminated the threat of filibuster, since Congress considers the budget under special rules limiting debate and amendment, and it would have allowed health care reform to piggyback on a major deficit-reduction initiative. Furthermore, it would have ensured that the proposal was considered in 1993, before the congressional agenda grew crowded and the "honeymoon" period that presidents typically enjoy immediately after taking office came to an end.[38] For Clinton, the potential for legislative backlog was acute. He was pressing an ambitious roster of initiatives, and Congress was considering several major legislative items from the last Congress. If the White House put health care reform off until after the budget passed, Congress would probably not have sufficient time to debate and vote on the bill before the end of 1993.

In addition to being extremely risky, the strategy of including health care reform in the budget reconciliation process faced a major hurdle in the personage of Senator Robert Byrd of West Virginia.[39] Byrd, the custodian of the Senate rules, was the architect of a rule designed to stop just the sort of procedural opportunism the Clinton administration was contemplating. The so-called Byrd rule limited the items that could be considered under the expedited procedures of the reconciliation process. Although Senate Majority Leader George Mitchell begged Byrd to stretch the rule, Byrd refused to sanction the inclusion of health care reform in the budget process. The president's initial strategy for introducing his proposal was thus effectively foreclosed.[40]

Clinton was caught in a bind. His leading legislative priorities for his first year were his economic program and health care reform. Unfortunately, both were large and controversial initiatives that had to pass through many of the same congressional committees. Clinton and his congressional allies worried that Congress would not be able to act on two such weighty initiatives at once. Moreover, Clinton was reluctant to put off the smaller items on his legislative agenda, including his economic stimulus package and national service bill.

The Clinton administration's worst fears about the filibuster were confirmed in March, when Senate Democrats were forced to dramatically scale back a voter registration bill supported by Clinton to break a Republican filibuster. Clinton suffered a far larger defeat the next month. Under a withering assault by Republicans, his economic stimulus package was killed in the Senate by a filibuster led by Senate Minority Leader Bob Dole. The action by Dole had not been expected, in part because the filibuster has traditionally been used by disgruntled minority factions in the Senate rather than the minority party itself. Dole had taken extraordinary steps to defeat the bill, invoking a parliamentary action that made it impossible for Republicans to amend the bill and thereby assuring unified Republican opposition.[41] Clinton's inability to peel off enough Republican senators to end the filibuster augured poorly for his other legislative initiatives. And in fact the president would be forced by a Republican filibuster to all but gut his national service bill to push it through the Senate in August.

Clinton nonetheless continued to maintain that he would introduce his proposal sometime near his May deadline, while the budget was still being considered. The health policy advisers had originally planned to present a less detailed blueprint of the proposal and allow Congress to fill in the legislative specifics. But this minimalist approach was undermined by the political insularity of the working group effort and congressional demands for a more detailed bill. As the debate over the budget dragged on through the summer, the health policy advisers who had stayed on when the task force disbanded found themselves caught between escalating congressional demands for a detailed bill and growing worries that the details of the bill would spark a congressional revolt over the budget. With media reports about possible new taxes in Clinton's proposal endangering swing votes on the budget, the health policy team ceased virtually all its activities through much of the summer, undermining the minimalist approach and any other approach the White House might have wished to pursue.[42] By the time the budget squeaked through the Senate in early August, Clinton arguably had little choice but to introduce a detailed reform proposal.

From the first days of the White House effort on health care reform, the main outside influence on Clinton and his advisers was the Democratic leadership in Congress. This is to be expected. Presidential reliance on Congress is deeply embedded in the American political system, with its "separated institutions *sharing* powers."[43] But Clinton's interest in accommodating the congressional leadership went beyond the dyadic nature of the legislative process. Clinton harbored particular concern about his relations with congressional Democrats because he feared repeating the mistakes of the last southern Democratic governor to reach the White House, Jimmy Carter.[44] Furthermore, Clinton recognized that health care reform was a goal for which many top members of Congress had been fighting their entire careers. He wanted these members to have a stake in the proposal he was advocating, especially since his bill would have to pass through the committees they chaired.

The problem was that the congressional leaders whose advice and support Clinton sought were generally skeptical of the reform proposal Clinton advocated. None of the major committee chairs was a proponent of managed competition, and one of the most powerful—Pete Stark, the chair of the House Ways and Means Health Subcommittee—was a vocal critic. On the other hand, the members of Congress who might have been more natural allies of Clinton, such as Representative Jim Cooper, did not occupy influential positions within the congressional hierarchy. Cooper was a poor negotiating partner for other reasons as well. He had no particular sway over the other conservative Democrats who had signed onto the CDF bill. He was posturing for the media to attract campaign donations for his 1994 Senate campaign. (In the first six months of 1993 alone, Cooper received more than $160,000 from health and insurance political action committees—more than any other member of the House.)[45] Most important, Cooper did not share Clinton's goal of universal coverage: by the CBO's estimate, the CDF bill would have covered less than half the uninsured.[46]

Clinton and his advisers were thus placed in the difficult position of trying to gain the support of the powerful committee chairs who distrusted managed competition while not alienating the congressional moderates whose votes would be needed to pass any proposal. The strategy they adopted was to remain true to the reform framework Clinton had outlined during the campaign but to include within it provisions that would appeal to the congressional leadership, such as larger purchasing cooperatives and more generous benefits. This was a strategy of accretion: Clinton would build up the proposal until he had the support of the leadership and then scale back the proposal to gain the votes of congressional moderates.

The difficulty with this approach was that it did not win Clinton the committed support of either group. The committee chairs still looked skeptically on managed competition, and the moderates attacked Clinton for abandoning the middle path he had taken during the campaign. Neither side showed the slightest interest in crossing the "bridge to compromise" that Starr and Zelman had hoped to build by combining managed competition and global budgeting.[47]

Starr has since argued that the Clinton administration made the mistake of tracking to the "left" between the inauguration and the release of the plan.[48] Yet Starr's account begs the question: *Left from where?* Clinton's campaign pronouncements were cryptic enough to be consistent with a number of different approaches; he never clearly resolved the tensions that had surfaced during the campaign among the different views of managed competition. The legislative details that Starr describes as a bow to the left were the very ones that the architects of the liberal synthesis had left unaddressed. The real problem was not that Clinton tracked left, but that there was not a significant constituency for the compromise approach he supported. This unfortunate truth had been obscured during the campaign and the early days of the new administration by the vagueness of Clinton's position on reform. The appearance of unstoppable momentum behind managed competition was a mirage that was bound to fade as Clinton grappled with the divisive issues that had been sidestepped during the campaign.

Clinton and his advisers had to walk the same tightrope in their dealings with the interest-group community, and they adopted much the same strategy with much the same result. Although Clinton never endorsed the Jackson Hole proposal or the CDF bill, there is no question that part of what attracted him to the managed-competition approach was the prospect of garnering support from the business community and medical interests. As in his negotiations with Congress, however, the most immediate pressure on Clinton came from the committed supporters of reform—organized labor, the American Association of Retired Persons (AARP), and citizen groups. None of these organized constituencies strongly supported managed competition. Labor was opposed to the tax cap and to the option of allowing large firms to remain outside the HIPCs. The AARP was concerned about the Medicare cuts Clinton had proposed to fund reform and about the potential integration of Medicare into a managed-competition framework. And many of the citizen groups that supported reform were demanding nothing short of a single-payer system.

The administration's approach to these groups was roughly the same as its approach to the congressional leadership: it made concessions, some quite costly, without backing away from the core policies advocated during the campaign. The desire to attract the enthusiastic support of organized labor and single-payer supporters was one of the reasons the health policy team pushed for larger purchasing cooperatives and more comprehensive benefits. The administration would also eventually back away from the tax cap, in part to appease organized labor. The most visible concessions, however, were two expensive new benefits added to the proposal to garner the support of the elderly: a prescription drug benefit under Medicare and a new program of home-based care.

Again, however, the administration's strategy of accretion won neither the loyalty of proreform groups nor the grudging acceptance of groups that supported the Jackson Hole and CDF proposals. Instead, the former concentrated on the provisions of the proposal they found distasteful and the latter accused the administration of abandoning its commitment to managed competition. The reasons why Clinton's coalition-building strategy failed to have the desired effect in this case were almost exactly the same as in his negotiations with congressional Democrats, and it is worth reviewing them in somewhat greater depth.

First, the hope that had animated the architects of the liberal synthesis was that a middle ground could be found between conservatives who proclaimed the virtues of competition and liberals who were enamored of other countries' social insurance programs. As the White House's policy-development effort unfolded, however, it became apparent that the middle ground it so eagerly sought was a chimera. The rhetoric of competition notwithstanding, there were many aspects of Clinton's blueprint for reform that supporters of the Jackson Hole model refused to even consider. Despite Clinton's commitment to universal comprehensive insurance and a national health budget, liberals were not eager to squander their last best hope for national health insurance on an untested scheme associated with health economists, conservative Democrats, and medical interests. The political presumption undergirding the liberal synthesis was that these two camps would accept a policy package that they viewed as less than ideal because it contained the critical elements each supported. But neither side saw such a compromise as desirable or even possible. It was not simply that the two sides were advancing nonnegotiable demands, but that they saw no reason to negotiate. Why negotiate, after all, toward a middle ground whose existence they doubted?

Paradoxically, Clinton's campaign embrace of "competition within a budget" may have actually complicated the already-Herculean task of building a majority coalition. However strongly Clinton expressed his support for universal coverage and global budgeting, liberals identified his approach with the Jackson Hole Group and conservative Democrats. Even before the inauguration, Walter Zelman wrote a memo to Ira Magaziner in which he lamented the misconceptions liberal Democrats had about managed competition. "Many Democrats are alarmed," Zelman wrote, "over the ascendancy of managed competition as a reform concept. This alarm, I believe, springs . . . from the reality that many of the early and still most visible advocates of managed competition are viewed—properly in most cases—as conservatives who distrust government and have little interest in dramatically expanding access to health care."[49] Liberal suspicion of the president's proposal was further fueled by Clinton's ambiguous campaign pronouncements, by media reports that described the Jackson Hole Group as the progenitor of Clinton's reform ideas, and by Magaziner's attendance at a Jackson Hole conference in May 1993. Everything that liberals saw in the Clinton proposal, even those elements that they most cherished, was colored by their negative attitudes toward managed competition and its supporters.

The supporters of managed competition likewise did not view Clinton's half-turn toward competition during the campaign as a sign that they should compromise. Instead, Clinton's endorsement of managed competition was a vindication of their reform philosophy and approach. A conference held by the Jackson Hole Group shortly after the election was filled with an air of expectation and a sense of triumph.[50] As the details of the Clinton proposal came into view, the Jackson Hole principals wrote plaintive and increasingly bitter letters to Ira Magaziner criticizing the administration's departure from their approach and denouncing the president's proposal as a "single-payer system in Jackson Hole clothing."[51] Although Magaziner traveled to Jackson Hole in May to try to assuage their concerns, nothing less than total victory would appease them now. Paul Ellwood informed Magaziner that the Jackson Hole Group would only support the president's proposal if it eschewed binding budget constraints and limited the ability of states to design their own systems.[52] Although these were measures that the president had supported since the campaign, the members of the Jackson Hole Group were convinced that Clinton was abandoning his commitment to managed competition by endorsing them.

Business leaders, too, saw in Clinton's campaign statements a more modest and procompetitive proposal than Clinton and his advisers envisioned. And like the Jackson Hole Group, they soon expressed surprise and anger at Clinton's "movement" away from managed competition. The Chamber of Commerce wrote Magaziner in early May stating its "grave concern over what seems to be a movement toward a government financed and controlled system." "We are frankly astonished," the Chamber blustered, "that, at this late date, you could be moving toward a single payer system. . . . Make no mistake, the business community does not support a single payer system, even one which purports in the short run to cost business less than current premiums."[53] There was of course no way to avoid business opposition to aspects of Clinton's proposal. What Clinton meant when he spoke about managed competition was very different from what business leaders saw in the concept. The irony is that Clinton's partial embrace of policy ideas with which business leaders identified fostered an even greater sense of betrayal in the business community than might have surfaced otherwise. After all, corporate America's almost comically overwrought denunciation of the Clinton proposal as a heavy-handed government program just short of national socialism was the very charge that Clinton had hoped to avoid by siding with managed competition.

A second basic problem with the Clinton administration's coalition-building strategy was that it relied on promises that Clinton had neither the will nor the ability to fulfill. Paul Starr has described the administration's accretionary strategy as a "bargaining chip" or "onion" theory of bargaining in which the administration would "go to Congress with a big program intentionally including elements that [it] would have to bargain away later." The model for the strategy, according to Starr, was a complex negotiation in which each side came to the table demanding more than it expected to eventually receive.[54] The problem with this analogy is that it ignores the first rule of negotiation: that participants will try to assess what their counterparts are planning and craft their strategies accordingly. This is the difficulty Clinton faced with liberals in Congress and the interest-group community. They knew Clinton would need to scale back his proposal to gain the votes of moderates in Congress, and they knew Clinton had every intention of forfeiting the very features of the proposal—large alliances, generous coverage, the special benefits for the elderly—they most strongly supported. It should come as no surprise, then, that these provisions attracted less support for the Clinton proposal than the administration had anticipated.

Likewise, Clinton's overtures to business were viewed with skepticism and even outright disbelief by corporate leaders. Anticipating business opposition, Clinton's policy advisers included in the plan provisions designed to mute business opposition and attract the support of specific sectors of the business community. The proposed subsidies to the smallest of firms, for example, were a top demand of business leaders. The proposal also included a costly provision to relieve large corporations of much of the expense of health benefits they had promised to early retirees. But business was not consoled by these strategic concessions. It simply did not believe that Clinton was committed to fighting for them, that Congress would enact them, or that fiscal realities would permit them. Business skepticism was further compounded by the basic distrust corporate leaders feel toward government. Clinton's grand promises were bound to sound hollow to a segment of American society "whose most characteristic, distinctive, and persistent belief . . . is an underlying suspicion and mistrust of government."[55]

A third and final difficulty with the administration's coalition-building strategy—the most fundamental of the three—was that it was based on a crude political logic that placed inordinate emphasis on the president's proposal and far too little on the political and institutional context in which that proposal would be debated, attacked, and perhaps enacted. The logic had been outlined by Starr and Zelman in 1992: the debate had grown stale; people were locked into old ideas and terminology; a new proposal combining elements of what each side in the debate wanted would free the combatants from their fixed positions, realign them, and create a critical base of support for a new reform approach. It was the proposal that would break the logjam, the proposal that would serve as a bridge to compromise, the proposal that would find the critical common ground between the antagonists and finally draw them together. In March, Zelman proclaimed in a memo: "We have found a unique blend of approaches that is better than the competing models. . . . It is not a low-level compromise, a product of political give and take, but a genuinely higher synthesis. . . . We have something . . . we can really be proud of—a true political breakthrough, and [a] new possibility of achieving the kind of consensus we've never gotten to before."[56] The proposal was the political breakthrough.

For reasons already discussed, the conviction that managed competition within a budget represented a unique middle ground toward which disparate interests would naturally converge was politically implausible.

Not only that, it manifested an excessive faith in the ability of new policy ideas—or rather new combinations of familiar ideas—to make old political trade-offs obsolete. As the Clinton administration quickly discovered, there are no elegant new solutions to the political dilemmas that have bedeviled reformers in the past. Nor is there some "higher synthesis" of regulation and competition that provides the advantages of both and the political liabilities of neither. In fact, the subtle, responsive regulation that managed competition requires is at least as difficult to construct properly and package appealingly as the straightforward controls that most other advanced nations have adopted.[57]

Most important, the idea that the liberal synthesis was itself the compromise that reformers had so long sought was dangerous. It made the crafting of a perfectly calibrated proposal the focal point of the administration's reform effort. It made the task of passing reform a problem of policy analysis rather than one of values, interests, institutions, and strategies. In the end, Clinton's advisers approached political strategy in the same way they approached policy. The delicately balanced structure of the proposal was matched only by the delicately balanced political strategy it embodied. The bargains had already been made, the concessions already included. The politics, like the proposal, simply awaited implementation.

The fixation on the proposal is the common thread running through nearly all the strategic mistakes that friends and foes of the Clinton administration have blamed for the political weakness of the Clinton plan. The decision to develop a presidential proposal rather than embrace legislation on Capitol Hill, the scope and detail of the bill, the failure of the administration to negotiate with Republicans or negotiate early and seriously enough with Democrats, the benefits given to constituencies in the absence of reciprocal pledges of support—all these alleged strategic errors can be linked to the conflation of the proposal with its politics. The decision to develop the proposal in the White House, never seriously questioned, ensured that the administration's delicate compromise would not be jeopardized by (or credited to) Congress. The scope and detail of the bill sewed up the bargain, guaranteeing the proper alignment of politics and policy. The Republicans were tangential: the proposal was perfectly poised to unite Democrats, leaving at most a few Senate Republicans to convert. The Democrats were tangential: the proposal was perfectly poised to unite them, leaving at most a few liberal committee chairs to appease. The concessions to critical constituencies were preemptive—an attempt to shore up the dazzling political structure that the architects of the proposal had constructed.

Each of these much-criticized mistakes was a symptom rather than a cause of the Clinton administration's troubles. The fundamental problem was that the administration was carrying on a political dialogue largely with itself. If the proposal was the politics, the political negotiation that would lead to reform needed only to be made within the confines of the proposal. A wonderfully revealing White House memo authored by Starr describes the "conundrum" that the administration confronted in its effort to construct a support coalition. The preface to the memo states: "One or more of the following premises has to be wrong, or has to give." Starr proceeded to tick off each of the major interests the proposal needed to appease: "the elderly," "unions," "governors," "providers," "reform advocates," "the average employee," "big corporations," "small employers," "moderate and conservative Democrats." Next to each interest Starr listed the many conflicting policy provisions that would be required to get it "on board." The "moral of the story," Starr concluded, was that the administration could "get so many people on board that our boat may sink from its own weight."[58] The more fitting moral might have been that the administration was building a boat for people who had not yet bought a ticket.

THE PUBLIC CAMPAIGN

There was one element of the administration's strategy that was not closely tied to the specifics of the proposal, and that was its campaign to attract public support for the plan. The main reason that the public campaign did not hinge on the structure of the proposal was that the supporters of managed competition had never given much thought to the way in which the public would react to the approach. As previous chapters have shown, managed competition developed within a community of experts and advocates. The arguments used to explain and defend the approach were aimed at elites, not the general public. Indeed, the rationale behind the liberal synthesis was that it would resolve elite-level disagreements over the appropriate framework for health care reform.

As a president advancing a key initiative, however, Clinton could not rely on the diffuse public support he had enjoyed during the campaign. To attract and maintain congressional allies, Clinton would need to raise public support for at least the broad outlines of his proposal. In addition to its coalition-building strategy, therefore, the White House developed a plan for bypassing Washington elites and taking the proposal directly to the public. The public relations effort was overseen by Bob Boorstin, a key figure in Clinton's campaign, and by White House pollster Stan Greenberg. Although most of the advisers involved were former campaign staff with no prior experience in health policy, Magaziner and a few other members of the health policy team were also prominent participants.

The advisers who were in charge of developing the president's public campaign recognized that the administration proposal contained many elements that were popular with the public, such as universal coverage, strict insurance regulations, controls on premiums, and modest new taxes. Nonetheless, the mechanics of the proposal were complex, many of the institutions it envisioned were unfamiliar, and some of its provisions threatened to raise public fears. Moreover, because very little intellectual energy had been devoted to the development of straightforward ways to explain the approach, there was not a readily available fund of rhetoric on which the President's advisers could draw. How would the HIPCs be explained to the public, for example? What was the best way to present a national health budget or the incentives for people to choose less expensive health plans? These were questions with which the architects of managed competition had never really grappled.

The public relations advisers finally decided on a two-pronged campaign. The first prong was to distill the president's proposal down to a few key principles backed up by appealing but vague rhetoric. All the policy slogans that had dominated the debate—managed competition, global budgets, managed care—would be avoided, replaced with promises of "health security" and "health care that can never be taken away." One memo to the White House staff warned: "Do not use terms like 'managed competition,' 'single payer' and the like. . . . Whatever you do, don't get caught up in the details of the policy."[59]

The second prong of the public relations effort was to take the administration's new message to the public. This would be done mainly through public pronouncements by the president, Mrs. Clinton, and other administration figures, as well as by members of Congress who supported the president. In addition, a more limited paid advertising campaign would be run by the Democratic National Committee (DNC) and by interest groups that supported reform. Initially, Clinton and his advisers had hoped to run the bulk of the paid advertising campaign as a nonpartisan effort eligible for special tax treatment, but legal attacks forced them to transfer the project to the DNC.[60] The paid promotional campaign was further hindered by the continued refusal of key proreform groups such as the AARP to move from general expressions of support to targeted endorsements of Clinton's proposal.

The organization of the administration's public relations strategy was influenced by several considerations. The first and most important was the continuing public confusion and ambivalence about the major alternatives in the reform debate. By March 1993, fewer than a quarter of Americans even knew what "managed competition" meant; fewer still understood other common reform concepts, such as single payer or play-or-pay.[61] Polls and focus groups conducted by the White House showed that the public neither understood nor liked the terms that policy experts had been using to explain the Clinton proposal. Thus the public relations advisers proposed a completely new terminology for talking about the plan. "Managed competition" was shunned; now the proposal was simply a "uniquely American solution to an American problem." The term "health insurance purchasing cooperatives" was replaced with the less technical but less precise "Health Alliances." The new theme was "health security," a phrase that spoke to people's concerns about losing insurance coverage. "Universal coverage" was dropped because the public might associate universalization with coverage of the poor.[62]

The public relations staff also advised the president and other administration officials to stop talking about aspects of the proposal that might be unpopular. Polls showed, for example, that most of the public remained wary of HMOs and other health plans that restrict patients' choice of physicians. Most also did not believe the United States spent too much on medical care.[63] The costs that Americans were alarmed by were the visible personal and family expenses not directly paid by employers, insurers, or the government. Few people realized the extent to which they paid for health care indirectly through general taxes and forgone cash wages. Since managed competition aims to make people more conscious of the true relative cost of different types of health plans, it could very well raise visible personal expenses even while slowing the growth in national costs. Thus the public relations advisers counseled against making any mention of the consumer incentives established by the president's proposal. Also to be avoided was an emphasis on HMOs and other organized delivery systems (instead, the proposal would simply give "everyone a choice of health plans"). Even the HIPCs from which people would obtain coverage should not be emphasized because they might be perceived as bureaucratic. "Whenever possible," the strategy memo read, "health alliances should be downplayed, because they add to the illusion of more complexity in the system."[64]

A second reason that the public relations staff chose a streamlined strategy based on vague, appealing rhetoric was that the administration faced significant constraints in transmitting its message to the public. The Democratic party, as Theda Skocpol notes, "no longer has a nationally widespread, locally rooted infrastructure of loyal local organizations and allied groups (such as labor unions) through which it can run grassroots political campaigns."[65] Although the White House sought to cultivate a grassroots effort among interest-group supporters of health care reform, even the groups most closely allied with the administration were only willing to endorse the broad principles of the president's proposal. Paid advertising was an option, but the resources that the White House could invest in the effort were minuscule in comparison with the resources of the opposition. That left the normal channels of the news media as the main vehicle by which the president and his allies could explain the proposal to the public.

However, the media were a poor vehicle for conveying any consistent message to the public, much less the core dimensions of a detailed reform proposal. Even as presidents have become the focal point of political reporting, the press has grown less deferential in its coverage of their actions.[66] Clinton's relationship with the Washington press corps was particularly strained, in part because of White House attempts to keep the task force and working group effort secret. More important, the news media did not reveal themselves to be capable of thoughtfully analyzing the problems in American medical care or explaining the merits and demerits of competing reform approaches. Instead, as two careful content analyses of media coverage in 1993 show, news stories focused disproportionately on the politics of health care reform and, to a lesser extent, on the systemic impact of reform proposals.[67] Very little coverage explored the effects of reform on the public or explained the policy options before Congress. Most of the stories on health care reform originated in Washington and were written by reporters whose background was in campaign journalism and general political reporting. The overwhelming focus was on political strategy, the balance of power between contestants in the "game," and the ulterior motives of leading political figures. As one journalist who covered the debate explained: "You always look for some way to be slightly more cutting edge—and sometimes more cutting—to find a critique that nobody else has thought of, to expose the seamy underbelly of politics, to show you're in the know. . . . Some of that ended up playing out like 'gotcha' journalism, looking for the hidden pork in all the bills, looking for the miscalculations and mistakes, leaving the impression that everyone was a bungler or on the take."[68]

The main result of this hyperpolitical style of coverage, according to surveys and focus groups, was continuing public confusion about the potential impact of reform and deepening public cynicism about the true intentions of reformers.[69] From the vantage point of Clinton's public relations advisers, both trends represented serious obstacles to building public support for the policy changes contained in the president's proposal. Given the limits of the news media as a means of communication, a highly simplified public relations strategy based on catchy slogans and comforting terminology must have seemed all but unavoidable to the president's advisers.

Finally, the shape of the public relations effort was influenced by the experience and orientation of the advisers who headed it. These were not policy experts but people who had cut their teeth in campaigns and political consulting. Their expertise was in developing short but powerful messages that cast their clients in the best possible light (or cast their clients' opponents in the worst possible light). The natural analogy was marketing. The politician was a product; the voter, a consumer. The goal of the consultant was to help craft a persona and thematic agenda for the politician that convinced the voter that the politician was worth supporting—that the consultant's "product" was better than the competing alternatives. This marketing mind-set transferred naturally over to policy promotion. The president's proposal needed to be "sold" to the public. The best way to sell the proposal was to use simple and appealing slogans. A fairly benign example of the marketing strategy was the use of focus groups to develop new terms to describe the proposal. A more troubling example was the decision to simply avoid explaining integral elements of the proposal that might evoke public mistrust or fear.

The Clinton administration's strategy for passing its reform proposal was thus marked by a core disjunction. The structural details of the proposal were central to—indeed, I have argued, the embodiment of—the administration's strategy for navigating the institutional labyrinth of Congress and hammering out a compromise among established interests. The administration's campaign to raise public support for the proposal, however, was radically disconnected from these very same structural details. The health insurance purchasing cooperatives were on the one hand the "pivot" of the proposal and on the other an additional "complexity" that should be downplayed at all costs. Capitated health plans were on the one hand an engine of cost control, and on the other an incidental feature of the proposal that would only elicit public concern. The proposal understood by elites rested on a fundamental reorganization of government's role in the regulation and finance of medical care. The proposal presented to the public had no apparent government role and promised only greater "choice," "security," "simplicity," and "savings."

UNVEILING THE PLAN

On September 22, President Clinton delivered a resonant speech to a joint session of Congress about the reform proposal he would soon formally introduce. Talking past the political leaders assembled in the House chamber to the millions of Americans watching him on television, Clinton praised the efforts of the task force and outlined the fundamental principles that had guided its deliberations. The speech was peppered with anecdotes about ordinary Americans who had suffered because of the cost and instability of health insurance, and filled with compelling arguments about the need for reform. President Clinton closed the speech by linking national health care reform to the establishment of Social Security more than a half century ago. Just as Americans could no longer conceive of a time when "retirement was nearly synonymous with poverty," they would soon "find it unthinkable that there was a time in this country when hardworking families lost their homes, their savings, their businesses—lost everything simply because their children got sick or because they had to change jobs."[70]

The speech was a stirring articulation of the president's vision and an unqualified rhetorical triumph. National polls released in the aftermath of the president's address showed public support for the plan outstripping public opposition by a 2-to-1 margin, with roughly 60 percent of the public expressing support.[71] White House surveys conducted the night of the speech showed even stronger public approval.[72] Although Senate Minority Leader Bob Dole pledged that Senate Republicans would introduce a proposal "dramatically different from the administration's," many congressional Republicans expressed willingness to help the president achieve his goals.[73] When Mrs. Clinton toured Capitol Hill the following week to explain the proposal before congressional committees, the New York Times declared that the President's plan was "Alive on Arrival."[74]

Nonetheless, the initial public enthusiasm about the Clinton plan belied the fairly shallow understanding most Americans had of the Clinton proposal and the reform debate of which it was part. In a poll conducted by the Harvard School of Public Health during the first week of October, for example, 42 percent of respondents felt they knew nothing or very little about health care reform, 49 percent believed they knew a fair amount, and 9 percent thought they knew a great deal. Clinton's proposal was the subject of greater public confusion. Almost half of those surveyed admitted that they either did not understand the proposal well or did not understand it at all. Only 22 percent of respondents claimed to know what a "consumer purchasing cooperative" or "health alliance" was. Thirty-seven percent of those surveyed either did not know or did not believe that the Clinton proposal promised universal health insurance, and nearly half did not know or believe that the proposal would guarantee coverage if workers left their jobs.[75]

Likewise, the conciliatory remarks made by members of Congress in the immediate aftermath of the president's speech merely represented opening gambits. Given the heightened media attention to health care reform and the positive public reception to the president's speech, many members of Congress who were hostile to the White House effort withheld their more caustic criticisms and proclaimed their general support for reform. Yet these pronouncements were largely symbolic. Under conditions of relative uncertainty, members of Congress are inclined to take ambiguous positions and wait until the political costs and benefits come into clearer view. They are aided in this task by American political institutions, which provide numerous opportunities for delay and few mechanisms for enforcing past commitments. President Clinton could not, therefore, expect members of Congress to seriously pursue a legislative compromise in the absence of strong public support for the means as well as the ends of his proposal.

Accordingly, Clinton's September speech to Congress and the nation needed to be followed by the first salvo in the president's public campaign. But the salvo was never fired, for immediately after the speech a series of foreign crises in Somalia, Russia, and Haiti demanded the president's attention. Then the president was further distracted by the difficult task of rounding up enough votes in Congress to ratify the North American Free Trade Agreement (NAFTA), a regional trade pact negotiated by the Bush administration that Clinton had embraced as part of his general commitment to free trade. The debate over NAFTA not only required that President Clinton and Vice President Al Gore engage in the kind of concerted public campaign that was sorely lacking on health care reform, explaining to Americans the provisions and benefits of the trade agreement and effectively answering the charges of its noisy critics; it also pitted the Clinton administration against the congressional liberals and labor leaders whom the president counted as his strongest allies on health care reform. The Democratic leadership in the House split over the trade pact, with the Democratic whip (the member of Congress responsible for rounding up votes for party causes) leading the campaign *against* the White House. And the AFL-CIO repeatedly warned Clinton that his decision to side with Republicans and the business community on NAFTA would cost him labor support on health care reform.

Stepping back from these immediate events, it becomes clear that the weakness of the president's public campaign was a result not just of the cross-cutting pressures on the president or the failure of the public relations advisers to tackle public concerns directly. Rather, the weakness of the campaign appears inextricably bound up with the broader political logic embodied in the plan itself. That logic, we have seen, elevated the proposal—and the concessions and compromises made within it—above the messy political struggle that would lead to its enactment. It promised a world in which political differences would narrow to "who will pay for what and how fast" and in which policy mechanisms, rather than basic principles, would be at stake. It promised a world, that is, in which the president would need to do *little more* than market his plan to a receptive public and enact the interest-group deals that the proposal already incorporated.

To be sure, the vacuum of communication and negotiation that followed the president's September speech may also have reflected the general political inexperience of the president and his aides. Yet there seems to have been more at work than this—a method to the madness, so to speak. After all, the president had shown himself to be a consummate legislative horse-trader during the debates over the budget and NAFTA. He had not only used his own considerable powers of persuasion, but had also brought in skilled political operatives and even established a campaign-style war room from which to orchestrate his efforts. On health care reform, by contrast, the president did not even have a prominent political adviser until early 1994 (when the New York political hand Harold Ickes assumed the reins), and for most of 1993 only a few junior political advisers were devoted full time to the president's reform effort. The White House did not just bungle the politics—it failed to take any real action to speak of. Paul Starr complains that "the administration had gone to the trouble of writing a bill and then left it like a foundling on the doorstep of Congress."[76] Theda Skocpol notes that "for many months there was a remarkable vacuum of top-level White House leadership for the politics of health reform."[77] James Fallows observes that "even flatly untrue attacks on the health plan went unanswered."[78] Given this stark reality, it is hard to escape the unsettling conclusion that the president and his advisers did not initially launch a full-scale effort on behalf of the Clinton plan because they did not think they had to.

Meanwhile, the opponents of the president's proposal wasted no time in explaining how *they* believed it would impact the American public. The most prominent effort was a $10.5 million advertising campaign launched by the Health Insurance Association of America (HIAA) even before the president's September speech. The HIAA advertisements featured a young couple—known as "Harry and Louise," though the ads make no mention of their names—criticizing aspects of the president's proposal and urging viewers to call a toll-free hot line to "know the facts." The ads did not have much direct effect on public opinion. They were not aired on the three major national networks, but on the cable news network CNN and in local markets where they might affect swing members of Congress. Focus groups conducted by the Annenberg Public Policy Center revealed that the ads were neither very effective in conveying the HIAA's core message nor very memorable. The actual public response to the ads was in fact costly and slight: the Annenberg researchers estimated that each call to the HIAA's toll-free hot line cost the Association forty dollars.[79] Nonetheless, the ads proved to be a public relations triumph for the HIAA. The White House and leading members of Congress criticized the ads, elevating Harry and Louise to "the status of cultural icons" among Washingtonians.[80] In the press, the HIAA ads became a symbol of public and interest-group opposition to the Clinton proposal and a reference point for interpreting the actions of the White House, congressional leaders, and other interest groups running ads for or against the Clinton proposal. In a pattern that would recur throughout the debate, media coverage of the ads was both uncritical and sensational, giving the HIAA far more—and far more positive—exposure than the association could have expected from the advertisements themselves.

Furthermore, press attention to the Clinton proposal grew more negative and more politically oriented in the weeks following the president's speech. Although more than half of newspaper and television stories on the proposal were neutral about the likelihood of its passage, unbalanced coverage was more than twice as likely to be negative, and the ratio increased between September and December. Negative editorials also outweighed positive editorials during this period, by a margin of 3 to 2. The politics of reform was the subject of only about one-fifth of media coverage in the first week of September. By the end of October, however, politically oriented stories represented 49 percent of media coverage.[81]

The change in media tenor and focus reflected not only the advertising campaigns against the Clinton proposal, but also the rising cries of anger and impatience emanating from Congress. Although a rough draft of the administration's proposal had been circulated on Capitol Hill (and then leaked to the press to become the most widely distributed version of the proposal), administration lawyers along with the legislative counsel of the House were drafting the actual bill well into October.[82] In the meantime, Republican leaders loudly accused the administration of trying to deceive the public, while Democrats complained that the president had failed to consult with them adequately before the initial draft had leaked. And both sides criticized Clinton for not introducing his proposal close on the heels of the September address.

In step with the shifting pattern of media coverage, the public's perception of the Clinton proposal grew increasingly negative. One survey showed a roughly 20 percentage point drop in public support for the proposal (from 67 percent approval to 48 percent approval) between Clinton's speech and the beginning of 1994.[83] As if to underscore the administration's inability to convey its message to the public, the proportion of Americans who claimed they understood Clinton's proposal fairly well or better was exactly the same in December as it had been in September—47 percent. Public understanding of key provisions of the proposal actually dropped between September and December. In September, for example, 64 percent of Americans knew that Clinton's proposal achieved universal coverage. By December only 54 percent understood this. Likewise, in September 54 percent of Americans correctly stated that the plan would guarantee coverage to people who lost or quit their jobs. By December only 44 percent thought this was a provision of the proposal.[84]

It is hard to know what to make of the rapid decline in public approval of the Clinton plan. Some analysts have suggested that support for the proposal was dragged down by President Clinton's poor standing with the electorate. Paul Starr argues, for instance, that "when polls asked for opinions about 'Clinton's health plan,' they tapped into general feelings of confidence in President Clinton rather than preferences about the specifics of health policy."[85] One piece of evidence that seems to bear out this relationship is the coexistence of dwindling public support for the Clinton proposal with strong and stable public support for two of its key features: universal coverage and an employer mandate. Whatever was causing Americans to turn against the Clinton proposal in those early months, it was not measurably affecting public support for the essential goals the proposal sought to achieve.

The difficulty with the argument that Clinton's general unpopularity with the public rubbed off on his reform proposal, however, is that Clinton's overall approval rating did not drop in the immediate aftermath of his September speech. In fact, Clinton's approval rating in November was the highest it had been since June. Moreover, the percentage of Americans who approved of Clinton's handling of health care was much higher than the percentage who approved of his handling of other policy areas.[86] If Clinton's unpopularity decreased public support for his policies, therefore, it did so less on health care reform than on other policy issues. More to the point, if Clinton's unpopularity was the reason public approval of his reform proposal dropped in the last three months of 1993, then this public dissatisfaction was of a sort that did not affect his overall approval rating—which, if anything, rose slightly. Public disapproval of President Clinton no doubt shaped the political response to his proposal, but it does not appear to explain the hemorrhaging of public support that occurred in the aftermath of Clinton's September address.

A more probable explanation of the decline in public support for the Clinton proposal highlights the dynamic interaction among the public, the opponents of the proposal, and the media. This account begins with the president's September speech and an initially positive public reception to the proposal. Most Americans were enthusiastic about the proposal. They shared the president's goals, and they saw much to like in the president's appealing description of the plan. Yet public support was shallow. People did not feel they knew much about the proposal or its alternatives. Before reaching any final judgment, they wanted more information about the main features of the proposal and their likely effect.

The first shift occurred not in public opinion, but in elite opinion. The opposition started running advertisements against the proposal. Republicans began to attack it on Capitol Hill. Members of Congress grumbled about the lack of presidential legislation. The opposition did not go after the features of the president's proposal that had broad public appeal, but instead targeted its criticisms on the nasty bureaucratic details the president had allegedly neglected to mention. The media devoted much of their attention to the claims and counterclaims surrounding the plan, since conflict is the staple of their reporting. Many opinion leaders in the media themselves began to have second thoughts about the proposal, the criticism of which confirmed their suspicion that the Clinton presidency was a sinking ship. News stories about the Clinton proposal grew more negative and more divorced from the concerns of the public.

Here is where President Clinton might have interceded to defend the proposal and explain the features under attack. But the proposal did not lend itself to easy defense or explanation, and the White House had not in any case developed a compelling, easily understood rationale for the besieged features of the plan. Besides, President Clinton was consumed by the task at hand: trying to ratify a trade pact supported by the harshest critics of his proposal and opposed by the strongest supporters. In the absence of a concerted presidential effort to maintain public support for the proposal, the accusations against it further confused Americans and began to color their perception of the plan. People began to wonder if Clinton's proposal might not be an overbearing government program poised to destroy their own health care arrangements, which they by and large liked. They grew angry at the press for not providing the information they needed to make such a weighty judgment. The proportion of the public that believed the media was doing a good job addressing their concerns fell steadily.[87]

The opponents of the proposal smelled blood in the continuing public ambivalence, and they stepped up their attacks on the proposal. The media covered these attacks, adding some of its own. Public confusion and cynicism rose. Fewer people could remember the good aspects of the proposal mentioned in the president's speech. Some become aware of aspects of the proposal they did not like—possible restrictions on their choice of doctor, for example. For the most part, however, public distrust of the proposal remained nonspecific. Support for the proposal waned not because of its key features, which remained popular, but because of a general fear among Americans that the proposal would make them worse off. Although the paucity of support for President Clinton meant that fewer people were willing to give him the benefit of the doubt, the decline in support for the proposal occurred without a fundamental change in the public's assessment of the president's performance.

Not all the data necessary to evaluate the foregoing explanation can be obtained, but this explanation has the virtue of fitting the available evidence very well. What is more, the process just described is a paradigm example of the positive-feedback dynamic mentioned in the first chapter (although in this case it hurt the prospects for reform rather than helped them). It is also consistent with the corollary argument advanced in that chapter: that the media play a critical role in the process by which political leaders interpret and shape public opinion. Indeed, the point of this account is that the shift in public opinion that followed the president's speech did not occur in a vacuum. The public response to the Clinton proposal was shaped by elite attacks on the plan and by the character of press attention to the reform debate. Without an effective presidential countercampaign to explain the proposal to the public in the critical months following the September speech, Americans grew steadily more confused and skeptical about the president's plan. The fall in public support for the proposal emboldened the opponents of the plan, which in turn influenced the tenor of media stories on the proposal, which in turn further depressed public approval. An agenda-setting scholar would be hard pressed to find a more rapid and politically devastating instance of positive feedback.[88]

CONCLUSION

Into this worsening political climate, President Clinton finally introduced the legislative text of his Health Security Act in a Capitol Hill ceremony on October 27.[89] The introduction of the bill was marked by sharp contrasts. The president presented a mammoth, intricately detailed legislative proposal to Congress with the claim that he had "no pride of authorship." Echoing the president, Mrs. Clinton contended that the White House had "literally no pride of authorship on many of the details and technical aspects of the bill." But the bill, not the president or his wife, was the focus of the ceremony. House Majority Leader Richard Gephardt described the proposal as the "most complete work product" he had ever seen. Representative Charles Stenholm, a leader of the Conservative Democratic Forum, complained that the bill "was a little more expensive and a little more government than the American people can get excited about." The Republican leadership ridiculed the bill as "government-run medicine" and an attempt to turn over "one-seventh of [the] economy to the United States government."[90] All but one Republican had declared their opposition to the plan.

Although Republicans and conservative Democrats criticized the president for forsaking his pledge to propose a middle-of-the-road plan, the bill was in fact almost wholly consistent with Clinton's campaign statements, as well as with the reform framework advocated by Starr and others during the campaign. It was based on private insurance plans. Health plans would contract with regional insurance purchasing cooperatives. Different types of plans would be offered through the cooperatives, including at least one fee-for-service plan. Plans would offer almost identical benefit packages (cost sharing would differ somewhat among plan types) and would be required to abide by strict limits on their under-writing, enrollment, and marketing practices. People who chose plans whose premium rates were above average would pay more. Workers and employers would be required to contribute to the cost of insurance. Subsidies—in the form of caps on premium contributions—would be provided to low-income Americans and small firms. Employers with five thousand or more workers would be allowed to opt out of the purchasing coopera-tives, but only if they paid an assessment on payroll, offered a choice of health plans, and kept the growth rate of their premiums under federally established limits. The entire system would operate within the constraints of a national health budget, which would be enforced by the purchasing cooperatives through caps on the premiums of capitated health plans and through rate-setting for fee-for-service providers.

The proposal did not include a central aspect of managed competition advocated by the Jackson Hole Group as well as supporters of the liberal synthesis: a limit on tax-free employer contributions. (The plan would not even tax employer payments for *supplemental* coverage until the year 2003.) Yet Clinton had never publicly endorsed the tax cap because he worried that it would be perceived as a tax hike. This fear, along with the opposition of organized labor and serious outstanding questions about implementation, prompted the administration to leave the tax treatment of employer contributions essentially unchanged.

The proposal clearly required far more government regulation than the Jackson Hole Group and conservative Democrats wanted. But Clinton had never supported the Jackson Hole proposal or the CDF bill. More-over, many of the regulatory features of the bill were required by the president's adoption of a managed-competition structure—to prevent health plans from selecting risk, for example, and to ensure that all cur-rent spending on medical care was tapped.[91] The national health budget and inclusive purchasing cooperatives were the core elements of the lib-eral synthesis and had been supported by Clinton since the campaign. The tightness of the national health budget was necessary to hold down the federal budgetary cost of the proposal and fulfill the president's pledge to achieve universal coverage without significant new taxes. In short, with few exceptions, the Health Security Act was remarkably true to the re-form framework articulated by Starr and Zelman, and by Clinton him-self, during the campaign.

What had changed in the twelve months between Clinton's election and the introduction of the bill was not the reform approach that Clinton advocated, but the political context and degree of detail in which he pre-sented it. When Clinton had seized on managed competition within a budget during the campaign, it had appeared to be the perfect compro-mise—between liberals and conservatives, between traditional Democrats and New Democrats, between advocates of reform and stakeholders in the medial sector. Crafting a compromise, however, proved more difficult than declaring one. As the president and his advisers struggled to draft a proposal and build a support coalition, all the thorny questions left unanswered by the advocates of managed competition came rushing to the fore. In the process of answering them, the Clinton administration lost valuable time and tracked increasingly afield from the hopeful centrist vision that Starr and others had envisaged during the campaign. The proposal grew more intricate. The criticisms mounted from both left and right. By the time the proposal was introduced, the political climate had changed appreciably. The economic recession had dampened, the sentiment in favor of action had eroded, and Republicans had reassessed the electoral landscape. Instead of building a bridge to compromise, the president had burned the bridges behind him. He had a bill but no coalition to defend it. He had avoided the "big government" solutions of the past, but his plan was condemned as such nonetheless. He had responded to the deepest concerns of the American people, but he could not tell them how.

THE GENESIS and defeat of President Clinton's health care reform proposal was a remarkable interlude in American politics, and no more so than for those involved in its development. Whipsawed by the stunning defeat of the president's reform effort and the equally stunning triumph of congressional Republicans in the 1994 elections, many of those involved in the development of the Clinton plan now portray themselves as victims of a bitter, misleading campaign by interest groups and congressional Republicans. Some blame defeat on delays in forwarding the proposal; others point to the president's low approval rating, the deficiencies of media coverage, and the abatement of public concerns. Some have even endorsed the view, held by many political historians, that comprehensive health care reform was doomed from the start.

This pessimism and gloom contrasts sharply with the triumphalism that accompanied President Clinton into office in 1993. Then, the widely expected outcome was not resounding defeat or the painful whittling away of reform aspirations but far-reaching reforms that would control costs, cover everyone, and revive public faith in government. And a crucial reason for this optimism was the belief of many reformers, particularly those who were part of the president's effort, that managed competition within a budget was poised to break the political stalemate that had blocked health care reform so many times before.

We know now that this belief was sadly misplaced. Managed competition within a budget came no closer to passage than the other failed health care reform proposals that litter the landscape of reform efforts past. Surely this disjunction—between the rosy expectations of reformers and the bitter defeat they experienced—deserves reflection. If the received wisdom in the wake of Clinton's victory was that *reform* was inevitable, today's commentators are equally certain that *defeat* was inevitable. Yet neither view captures the complexities of what happened between 1991 and 1994. To understand why the reform debate took the course that it did, it is necessary to understand why Clinton and his advisers believed so strongly—and wrongly—that managed competition within a budget would finally overcome the formidable obstacles to national reform.

I return, then, to the question explored throughout this book: Why did managed competition emerge so dramatically onto the government agenda in the early 1990s? In the next three sections, I suggest three different types of explanations, each focusing on a distinct aspect of agenda setting: the power of vested interests, the diffusion of ideas, and the force of leadership.

POWER AND THE PUBLIC AGENDA

The earliest studies of the government agenda took it as given that power was central to the agenda-setting process. These studies documented the remarkable ability of elites to dominate policymaking by limiting the formal agenda to "safe issues." Contemporary agenda-setting research, however, has abandoned this preoccupation with power, focusing instead on the role of ideas and strategic entrepreneurs in the process of policy innovation. In these analyses, the power of vested interests to affect the agenda of government appears considerably more circumscribed.

This shift parallels a more general movement in American political science away from group theories of the political process. In recent decades, destabilizing changes in the political system and interest-group environment have eroded the explanatory power of interest-group liberalism, the view that politics is essentially a struggle among competing particularistic groups.[1] These changes—the growth in the number of competing interest sectors in Washington, the diffusion of power in Congress, the more individualized and entrepreneurial style of electoral politics, and the more centralized control of the executive branch—have made it extremely difficult for a small number of interests to dominate policymaking in a given policy area. Although the number of groups trying to influence policy has exploded, their ability to dictate policy has declined. This is what Robert Salisbury calls "the paradox of interest groups in Washington:" there are "more groups," but they have "less clout."[2]

The way in which the health policy domain has changed over the last quarter-century is representative of these trends. The institutional reforms of the 1970s tore apart the cozy little triangles that linked congressional committees with the organized opponents of comprehensive health care reform. Rising health care costs fragmented the previously unified antireform alliance of medical groups, insurers, and business, and the members of this once-hegemonic alliance faced growing opposition from a shifting coalition of health-oriented citizen and public interest groups—almost half of which came into existence after 1970.[3] By the early 1990s, the major stakeholders in the health policy domain were more fragmented and divided than at any time in the recent past.

And yet many of these stakeholders were able to play a critical role in the emergence of the managed-competition model onto the public agenda. In particular, the large private insurers that have invested billions of dollars in managed care over the last decade—such as Blue Cross/Blue Shield, Prudential, Metropolitan Life, Cigna, and Aetna—were crucial to the development and advocacy of the approach. Many large employers, which had increasingly turned to managed care during the 1980s, also offered their initial support for the proposal. And although medical provider groups were less prominent participants in the Jackson Hole Group, they too left their imprint on the design of the plan.

How were these groups—considerably less cohesive and politically secure than in the past—able to affect the government agenda? Rather than rushing to Capitol Hill and pressing their demands on policymakers, they contributed their expertise and political support to a set of policy ideas that would come to dominate the reform debate. This set of ideas, in turn, allowed these groups to identify their own interests and forge a political alliance in support of managed competition.

The interests of managed-care insurers, large employers, and provider groups are not unambiguous. The leaders of these groups know what they are against, namely a government monopoly of health insurance, but they are far from certain of what they support. Indeed, they may not even have a clear idea of what is in their group's "interest," especially when the prospect of government intervention remains uncertain. This view clearly runs counter to a major strand in the literature on corporate involvement in public policy. A dominant theme of this literature is that the preferences of producer groups are objective and self-evident.[4] Ideas, if they enter into these analyses at all, are portrayed as instruments of economic interests and thereby take on the character of epiphenomena.

Yet scholars who adopt the economic approach fail to acknowledge the critical role played by ideas, and the institutions and social networks through which they are disseminated, in the definition and articulation of interests and the formation of political alliances.[5] Managed competition provided the medical industry leaders in the Jackson Hole Group with a set of policy ideas that legitimated their activities and gave them a central role in the process of reform. To be sure, these ideas had been formulated by individuals who were sympathetic to the prerogatives of the private medical industry, but it would be a mistake to assume that the policy ideas that grew out of the neoclassical critique and the work of Enthoven, Ellwood, and Etheredge simply reflected the objective preferences of the groups that would eventually come to embrace them. In fact, the reform concepts that would evolve into managed competition received only luke-warm support from the business community and were stalwartly rejected by the insurance industry and medical providers when they first received national attention in the early 1980s.[6] Far from serving as proxies for various private-sector interests, these policy ideas and the individuals who produced them played an important independent role.

At the same time, ideas themselves do not create policy change. They must be supported by individuals with the capacity to transform them into public policy. When numerous ideas are competing for the scarce attention of policymakers, political actors who want to secure a place on the public agenda for their policy ideas need to build a support coalition that will keep those ideas in the spotlight and protect them from political attack.[7] Thus the policy experts who presented their ideas to the Jackson Hole Group sought to enlist the support of key actors within American medicine. They recognized that without the backing of these groups it was extremely unlikely that policymakers in Washington would take notice of a reform approach that had not yet been seriously considered. As Lynn Etheredge put it: "It is absolutely essential for any market or private-sector reform that the major private-sector interests support it. If we came out with a proposal that included complete, radical reform of the insurance industry and restructuring of the delivery system, and the physician groups and all the insurance groups said, 'We hate this and it will never work,' it would get published in the *New England Journal [of Medicine]* or something, but it wouldn't go anywhere. Part of the real impetus for this, the source of its credibility, is that major actors who will have to be involved in it support it."[8]

Etheredge describes what might be characterized as a "transactional relationship" between the intellectual leaders of the Jackson Hole Group and the groups that comprised it.[9] Each set of actors—the theorists of managed competition and the industry leaders who supported them—had something the other needed. The policy specialists brought to the group their knowledge and expertise, as well as their influence within a vast interpersonal network of policy analysts and health services researchers in academia, private research institutions, and government. The private sector brought the economic resources and political clout that were needed to draw attention to a relatively obscure policy approach, as well as an informal network of communication with other industry leaders and large employers. Together, these two sets of political actors played a pivotal role in bringing managed competition to the forefront of the reform debate.

IDEAS AND POLICY COMMUNITIES

Attention to agenda setting highlights the crucial importance of ideas in the process of defining social problems and formulating policies to address them. Although the raw power of interest groups undoubtedly shapes the agenda of government, agenda setting is also a process of argumentation, in which persuasion can be as important as pressure.[10] At the heart of this argumentative process are competing ideas about the causes of social problems and the appropriate ways to mitigate them—what Deborah Stone refers to as "causal stories."[11]

But where do policy ideas come from? It should be clear from the preceding chapters that most of the policy ideas discussed in this study were developed by policy specialists or public officials working closely with them. In health care, as in other policy areas, there exists a loosely knit community of professionals engaged in studying the politics and procedure of government policy. Such "policy communities" involve a wide range of actors both inside and outside government who share a common interest in a given policy area and who, despite sometimes bitter partisan or ideological differences, agree on a collection of central norms and understandings that facilitate discussion and bargaining within the community.[12] In his research on agenda setting, for example, John Kingdon found that people active in health policy used a common language to describe the problems in health care, spontaneously producing "an explicitly common paradigm, using exactly the same terminology."[13] This language is in evidence at almost every meeting of health policy experts, who are infamous for speaking with one another in a lingua franca of obscure acronyms and technical jargon. Indeed, Kingdon concluded that one of the main obstacles to national health insurance in the 1970s was the widespread acceptance within the health policy community of the economic theory of health insurance.[14] Because members of the policy community accepted the view that insurance reduces the marginal cost of medical care and thereby leads consumers—or physicians acting as their agents—to demand "excess" care, they were extremely reluctant to champion an extension of health insurance to the remaining uninsured.

Kingdon's conclusion underscores the fact that the accepted norms of a policy community have a political bias. In the health policy community, the most influential ideas have been associated with economists. For nearly two decades, the neoclassical critique described in the first chapter of this work has enjoyed a privileged position within health policy circles. It is clearly more than coincidence that many of the people who have promoted managed competition—from Alain Enthoven to Michael Weinstein—are economists by training. Managed competition evolved out of the neoclassical critique, and it incorporated many of its key tenets. The importance of the neoclassical critique to the prevailing intellectual framework of the health policy community helps explain the level of acceptance that has greeted the managed-competition approach.

Managed competition has also benefited from a closely allied but broader current of American thought that contrasts the freedom of private initiative with the heavy hand of government regulation. In the health policy community, this basic dichotomy is referred to as the "competition-regulation debate," and it has assumed an importance among health policy specialists grossly incommensurate with its utility for clarifying the differences among health care reform proposals. Nearly all the policymakers with whom I spoke credited the rise of managed competition to its unique position in the competition-regulation debate, whether that position be squarely between the two contending camps or safely on the side of competition. And almost all used the same basic antonyms—competition versus regulation, market versus government, private versus public—to describe the primordial divide that the Clinton proposal attempted to straddle.

As a rough guide to the variation among comprehensive reform proposals, the competition-regulation dichotomy is highly misleading. It ignores, first, the extensive private regulation that already takes place in the medical sector, where hundreds of private insurers entangle hospitals and doctors in an increasingly intricate web of rules, requirements, and restrictions. Second, the competition-regulation dichotomy ignores the fact that all comprehensive reform proposals—even the most procompetitive—require a framework of government regulation to work properly, indeed to work at all. Finally, the competition-regulation dichotomy ignores the considerable evidence that countries in which government sponsors or directly provides insurance regulate the provision of care much less extensively and directly than do most managed-care insurers in the United States. Put simply, government as a bill payer has relied on forms of cost control (global fee schedules, hospital operating budgets, and so on) that are much less intrusive, burdensome, and distortionary than is the norm for the managed-care plans that procompetitive reform proposals aim to encourage.

But criticisms like these are probably immaterial. The power of the competition-regulation dichotomy stems not from its descriptive accuracy, but from the underlying ideological current on which it feeds. In American politics, the authority of the state to assume new roles and commitments is always suspect. This creates a powerful motive for politicians to search for alternative sources of legitimacy when government action is demanded.[15] Perhaps the most attractive of such sources is the private market. The market

> works automatically and is self-regulating. It is part of the American dogma
> that government relies on the "heavy hands of bureaucrats" whose decisions
> are arbitrary and may be inequitable unless they are constrained by ever
> more detailed legal constructs, rules, and regulations that, in turn, inhibit
> change, reduce flexibility, and freeze the existing system. Similarly, it is part
> of a deep-seated belief that there is an alternative to government, an alterna-
> tive that contains costs, reduces misallocations, maximizes consumer (pa-
> tient) and producer (health professional) freedom, allows for diversity, re-
> sponds to new discoveries, and encourages change.[16]

In reality, of course, the regulation necessary to make managed competition work is of a scope and complexity that would test even the most skillful public bureaucracy. Furthermore, managed competition does not so much obviate the need for regulation as place regulatory functions and authority in private hands. Nonetheless, the rhetoric and claims associated with managed competition, even the term *managed competition* itself, all had particular appeal to the American antistatist ideology. The alternatives to managed competition were "regulation," "rationing," and "extensive government controls." Managed competition would require only a narrowly tailored set of public requirements—"a procompetitive regulatory framework"—within which the private sector would operate. It would place responsibility for the delivery and organization of medical care in the hands of competent private managers instead of insular government bureaucrats.

Finally, the general intellectual acceptance of managed competition reflects the fact that the ideas embodied in it have developed over a fairly long period of time. For a proposal to be taken seriously, its advocates generally need to build acceptance for it within policy circles. Kingdon calls this process "softening up"; Nelson Polsby refers to it as "policy incubation."[17] Its purpose is to ensure that policy ideas are firmly embedded in the consciousness of policy professionals and public officials when an opportunity to push them emerges. One Hill staff member described the process in evolutionary terms: "I think these ideas don't ever really completely die. They are reborn and they are advanced by some of the same people who were gurus in their era, people like Enthoven. Obviously, Enthoven wouldn't want [the original Consumer Choice Health Plan] to die. He just keeps reshaping it to fit the times or his evolving thinking."[18]

Another staff member active in health policy expressed a similar view: "I think that [the Consumer Choice Health Plan] played a pretty strong role, just because it's an idea that has been out there for a long time, and Enthoven keeps bringing it back up. So people, at least the health policy people, had some conception of what this plan was and how it could work. It wasn't something completely new or different. If Enthoven had not been out there . . . it would have been harder to explain what managed competition is, at least in terms of the initial reaction of the health policy community."[19]

The process of incubation does not guarantee acceptance, of course. Nor does it ensure that policy ideas will be fully worked out or substantively sound by the time they come to policymakers' attention. Polsby argues that policy innovations that develop over time (such as Medicare) differ from rapid innovations (such as the Community Action Program) in that competing "alternatives are systematically justified by recourse to formally assembled facts and figures."[20] But this distinction obscures the extent to which long-incubated policies can experience sudden shifts in emphasis or direction. Proposals for national health care reform have circulated in the policy community for more than half a century, but the managed-competition approach emerged from relative obscurity to become a leading framework for reform in less than two years. The approach was not well understood even by many policy experts, it had not been widely applied or rigorously evaluated in the United States or abroad, and few of the politicians who embraced it had a clear idea of how it would work—or whether it would work at all. In this respect, the sudden turn toward managed competition in 1992 more closely resembles the Johnson administration's development of the hazily defined Community Action Program than it does the dogged, deliberate development of the Medicare proposal under the Truman, Kennedy, and Johnson administrations.

More important, in determining whether systematic research will guide policymakers in their choice of policy alternatives, one cannot ignore the *demand* for policy research. After all, politicians do not choose policy alternatives simply because they are substantively sound but also because they meet perceived political needs. And these needs do not necessarily coincide with the motives and methodologies that animate policy research.[21] The reasons that politicians embraced managed competition were in fact quite distinct from the criteria used by health policy analysts to study and evaluate reform proposals. Politicians were attracted to the market symbolism of managed competition and to its veneer of freshness and originality. The aspects of managed competition they found most appealing—the promise of painless reform, the ambiguous role of government, the reliance on private managerial expertise—were the very aspects that elicited skepticism among many policy experts. Whether policy research will prove important, therefore, hinges crucially on the degree to which it can be cloaked in compelling symbolism and rhetoric and linked to the constraints and opportunities that government officials face. Although a long period of policy gestation may be a prerequisite for systematic research, such research is not likely to influence politicians unless it is considered relevant to their own political fortunes.

Policy incubation is thus an active process in which advocates of a proposal attempt to educate other members of the policy community about the value of their ideas, constantly reshaping those ideas so that they address currently recognized political problems and are appealing to the audience whose support they seek. As Walker emphasizes: "*The energy supplied by a policy entrepreneur who makes . . . proposals and engineers their acceptance is an essential ingredient in the process of social learning.* The circumstances must be ripe for change before knowledge can be translated into concrete policy, but the crucial matching of problems and solutions is almost always the result of the drive and imagination of a gifted leader."[22]

But there are many policy entrepreneurs who wish to see their pet so-lution attached to a political problem. Why are some successful while others fail? Answering this question requires a closer examination of the characteristics and strategies of leadership.

LEADERSHIP AND POLITICAL INNOVATION

It is only recently that political scientists have attempted to formulate theoretical models of leadership behavior.[23] As Richard Neustadt argues, leadership "is among the most challenging of human activities, stirring ambition, exciting admiration, arousing fear and pity (to one's taste), in-spiring the dramatists since literature began, ignored by almost nobody in all of human history—until the coming of American political science."[24] The reason why leadership has fared poorly in political science is not hard to fathom. Political analysts strive to create general models of explainable regularities in the political process. The problem faced by students of American politics who wish to tackle the subject of leadership is that they "continue to have inadequate indicators for determining when leadership matters, and rather poor measures of leadership's contribution to out-comes when it does matter. . . . [W]ithout the undergirding of formal models or concrete empirics, [they] are afraid to speak about something so amorphous as leadership."[25]

While the difficulties are real, recent studies of the characteristics and strategies of leadership have yielded important insights. That many of these studies have focused on the agenda-setting process suggests that leadership opportunities may be more pronounced here than at other stages of policymaking. Agenda setting is more fluid and less bound by institutional and political constraints than the decision stage of policy-making. It comes closest, perhaps, to resembling the indeterminate "orga-nized anarchies" that have been described by Michael Cohen, James March, and Johan Olsen.[26] This is the realm of policy entrepreneurs, indi-viduals whose "defining characteristic, much as in the case of a business entrepreneur, is their willingness to invest their resources—time, energy, reputation, and sometimes money—in the hope of future return."[27]

Several scholars have attempted to parse out the specific strategies used by policy entrepreneurs. William Riker has invented the term "heresthet-ics" to refer to the efforts of strategic entrepreneurs to manipulate the environment to their advantage. By using skillfully crafted rhetoric that recasts the terms of a debate, a policy entrepreneur can redefine "the po-litical situation so that formerly unsympathetic competitors wish to stand with the erstwhile disadvantaged."[28] Frank Baumgartner extends Riker's analysis to incorporate E. E. Schattschneider's notion of the scope of conflict. Baumgartner argues that strategic entrepreneurs manipulate the terms of a debate to expand or contract the scope of conflict surrounding an issue, with those wishing to expand the conflict using broad, emotional symbols and those wishing to contain it using technically complex terms.[29] Finally, Frank Baumgartner and Bryan Jones add another element to this model—"venue shopping by strategically minded political actors." They claim that the options open to policy entrepreneurs are not limited to expanding or contracting the scope of conflict. In addition, entrepreneurs "may identify particular venues, such as congressional committees, state government organizations, courts, private businesses, or any other relevant institution, in their search for allies."[30]

Policy entrepreneurship thus involves two distinct types of entrepreneurial activity.[31] The first is the actual development and promotion of policy ideas. This notion of policy entrepreneurship is well established in the agenda-setting literature, and its importance is widely recognized. The second type of entrepreneurial activity is that described by Riker, Baumgartner, and Jones—strategic manipulation of the dimensions of a debate. This second notion of policy entrepreneurship is less clearly understood than the first, although its impact on policymaking is arguably much greater. When opportunities for political innovation arise, policy entrepreneurs of this second type attempt to match politics and policy. They not only remain poised to take advantage of a propitious moment for pushing the policy ideas they favor; they also reshape their ideas to fit the constraints of the moment. These entrepreneurs use carefully crafted rhetoric to convince others that their assessment of the situation is correct and to attract the attention of a receptive institutional venue.

These leadership functions may be joined in a single entrepreneur. Alain Enthoven, for instance, performed both leadership activities. He played an instrumental role in the development of managed competition, as well as in convincing medical industry leaders and policymakers that it was suited to the political exigencies of the moment. The hallmarks of a gifted policy entrepreneur who performs both entrepreneurial activities are flexibility and persistence. Those who remain wedded to an approach that does not meet the requirements of the day or who quit when the chips are down will rarely be successful. Enthoven constantly adapted managed competition to address critics of the approach and to fit the model to the changing structure of American medicine and the shifting political environment. And he suffered through almost two decades of rejection before his policy ideas received committed support from industry actors or political leaders.

More often, however, strategic manipulation is performed by policy entrepreneurs who assimilate existing policy ideas and present them in a new way. Michael Weinstein transformed the abstruse prose of the

Jackson Hole proposal into a set of clear and simple principles that appealed to policymakers who were searching for a comprehensive market approach to health care reform. Walter Zelman and Paul Starr took the idea of managed competition and recast it so that it would attract reform-minded liberals who supported the single-payer concept but worried about its political viability. These policy entrepreneurs are less likely to press for the same set of policy ideas for many years. Rather, they may jump from one set of ideas to another, based on their perception of which are advantaged at any given moment. They are "battlefield strategists," searching for the combination of policy ideas that will attract the most political support.[32]

These three conceptual themes—interests, ideas, and leadership—lead back to the puzzle that has animated this study: how managed competition moved so rapidly onto the national political agenda. In the next part of this chapter, I apply the conceptual themes I have just developed to the history presented in chapters 2 through 5 to better explain the emergence of managed competition as a leading paradigm for national health care reform.

THE JACKSON HOLE PROPOSAL AND THE RISE OF A
CREDIBLE ALTERNATIVE

The main purpose of the Jackson Hole proposal was to lend legitimacy to the role of the private sector—and, in particular, the managed-care industry—within American medicine. In the proposal and the promotional efforts surrounding it, the Jackson Hole Group sought to weaken their opponents' claims that the government had the ability and authority to assume a more active role in medical financing. First, they identified fee-for-service medicine as the primary cause of health care inflation. Since reformers have generally assumed that a national health plan will employ a fee-for-service payment system, and since the two largest public health programs—Medicare and Medicaid—primarily reimburse practitioners on a fee-for-service basis, the Jackson Hole Group's indictment of fee-for-service called into question the general efficacy of a government solution.

Second, and more important, the group attempted to shift the focus of debate from the financing structure of a reform plan to the configuration of the delivery system. By identifying the delivery system as the most important target of health care reform, they portrayed health care reform as a policy issue best handled by private-sector organizations, in particular managed-care plans. With the exception of a scattered set of public-sector programs for Native Americans, underserved populations, veterans, and military personnel, the federal government has little experience managing the direct provision of care. By arguing that reform should be aimed at improving the management of care rather than its financing, the Jackson Hole Group attempted to shift the issue of health care reform into an arena in which the scope of legitimate government involvement remains greatly circumscribed.

This also helped the Jackson Hole Group gain the support of business leaders. On a practical level, many large employers have worked to put in place innovative managed-care plans and are firmly committed to an aggressive private purchasing strategy. On a more symbolic level, the portrayal of managed competition as a mechanism for injecting managerial expertise and market forces into the medical sector made the approach philosophically attractive to corporate leaders. Etheredge admitted that "the major thing [the Jackson Hole Group has] done is co-opt the two correct words: management and competition. If there is one thing that readers of *Fortune* believe produces all good things in this world, it's management and competition."[33] Indeed, a March 1992 article in *Fortune* endorsing managed competition reiterated these same themes. "For all its lifesaving miracles," contended the article, "most of the $800-billion-a-year U.S. medical system is as wasteful and managerially backward as Detroit before Henry Ford."[34]

Yet the most difficult challenge faced by the members of the Jackson Hole Group was not to attract business support for their proposal. It was to enlist federal policymakers to their cause. As it happened, two factors beyond their immediate control intersected with their efforts and thrust the Jackson Hole model onto the national political agenda. The first was Michael Weinstein's ringing endorsement of managed competition in the *New York Times*. The second was Pennsylvania's Senate race and its reverberations in Washington.

The instrumental role played by Weinstein in the process by which managed competition emerged onto the government agenda does not square with the findings of other agenda-setting studies. Kingdon, for example, concludes that the media has little effect on the agenda of government, beyond magnifying movements that have already started elsewhere.[35] Although communications scholars who have studied media agenda setting have focused primarily on the effect of the media on the issue priorities of the public, those who have examined the media's effect on policy elites have concluded that their issue priorities are largely unaffected by the news media.[36] Thus the question naturally arises as to whether Weinstein's active role in the policy process was simply an anomaly or represents a more general pattern of interaction between journalists and policymakers.

There are several reasons to think that this case is not anomalous. For one, it is important to distinguish between setting the agenda and affecting the way in which policymakers perceive an issue. Members of a policy community largely ignore periods of sensationalist coverage, knowing full well that the popular media will turn to another issue in short time.[37] Once an issue is on the public agenda, however, policymakers pay close attention to the media, looking for stories on issues with which they are actively involved to keep abreast of what other political actors are doing. Indeed, the media serves as a crucial channel of communication between members of a policy community.[38]

For another, many scholars have noted an emerging symbiotic relationship between journalists and policymakers.[39] Baumgartner and Jones, for example, argue that a crucial strategy of policy entrepreneurs is to appeal to journalists who share their concerns. They note that strategically minded policymakers attempting to redefine an issue often seek out ideologically like-minded people in the media. "In seeking to appeal to a new audience," Baumgartner and Jones point out, "one of the most important allies ... may be a sympathetic reporter who shares the source's interest in generating some new controversy where previously there had been little attention."[40]

The leadership of the *New York Times* in publicizing managed competition is also consistent with academic and popular portrayals of the newspaper as a powerful setter of the media agenda. Stephen Reese and Lucig Danielian, for instance, found that the *New York Times* led the way in covering the problem of cocaine abuse in the mid-1980s, when the topic was high on the national political agenda. It was only after the *New York Times* began to focus on the problem that other national newspapers—as well as *Time*, *Newsweek*, and the three major television networks—picked up the story.[41] Other scholars in the communications field have described a dissemination process known as "pack journalism," in which journalists take cues from one another about which events and ideas are newsworthy and how they should be interpreted. The views promoted by elite newspapers such as the *New York Times* play a dominant role in this process, since smaller media outlets generally do not have the journalistic staff, the access to government officials, or the visibility and prestige to influence the media agenda themselves.[42]

I have argued that the effect of Weinstein's editorials was greatly magnified by the outcome of Pennsylvania's Senate race. In Kingdon's phraseology, Wofford's victory was a critical "focusing event," promoting an abrupt redefinition of the political risks and benefits of national health care reform. Suddenly, politicians who had not been active on the issue recognized that they needed to stake out their position. But the complexity of health care reform and the well-developed roster of available policy alternatives precluded designing an original reform plan. Instead, politicians and their staffs scanned the alternatives already under consideration, searching for ones that appealed to their political instinct and philosophy. As an aide to a Senator who endorsed managed competition explained: "[The Senator] was interested in the debate and looking for an opportunity that coincided with his basic philosophy of government. And that's what my job is, to look for those opportunities."[43]

At the crucial moment of Wofford's victory, the concept of managed competition was spreading through the health policy community, pushed by the Jackson Hole Group and the *New York Times*. Both the group and Michael Weinstein portrayed the approach in a way that appealed to conservative Democrats and to members of the Bush administration. When key members of the CDF began to take an interest in managed competition, the leadership of the Jackson Hole Group campaigned hard to ensure that they would adopt the approach. By linking managed competition to symbols to which the CDF members were receptive—such as competition, individual responsibility, and limited government—the Jackson Hole Group was successful in bringing managed competition to Capitol Hill.

THE LIBERAL SYNTHESIS

The second policy stream that I have described in this work resulted in what I have called the "liberal synthesis." The political dynamic animating this stream was far different from that played out in the formation of the Jackson Hole model. The architects of the liberal synthesis deeply believed in national health insurance, in the ideology of social insurance, in an activist role for government in the health system—but they were concerned about the political viability of a single-payer plan. As I argued in chapter 3, the reasons for this concern were manifold; they ranged from the weakness of organized labor to the perceived antitax, antigovernment sentiments of the public. This concern also reflected an awareness that the structure of American medicine was very different in the early 1990s than it had been just a decade before. The 1980s had spawned a diverse array of new managed-care organizations, all prepared to fight against a reform plan in which they were not accommodated.

The fundamental innovation that led to the liberal synthesis was the realization among reformers who were uncomfortable with the pure single-payer concept that capitated payments to private health plans could be a powerful cost-control mechanism. This new policy understanding was embodied in Senator Kerrey's plan, which combined the unitary financing structure of the single-payer plan with a pluralistic system of competing public and private health plans. The Kerrey plan also shifted the burden of administering the public plan to the states—with the hope that this would create a more flexible and decentralized system that would be more acceptable to the public.

The Garamendi plan built upon the Kerrey plan, but it also borrowed much more explicitly from managed competition. The advisory panel that developed the Garamendi plan was familiar with Enthoven's recent work on health insurance purchasing cooperatives, and it came to see the cooperatives as a vehicle for melding the single-payer approach with managed competition. The plan that was introduced by Garamendi in early 1992 recast the idea of purchasing cooperatives to bring it closer to a single payer, transforming the cooperatives from a limited initiative de signed to remedy the deficiencies of the small group market into a single sponsor that would cover all Californians. Through the payroll tax-based financing system, moreover, the Garamendi plan included a budget for state health care spending that would be enforced solely through capitated payments to private health plans, rather than the all-payer rate regulation endorsed by Kerrey.

Finally, Paul Starr expanded the Garamendi plan into a national proposal. He kept most of the key features of the Garamendi plan—the inclusive HIPC, the individual incentives to choose low-cost plans, and the global budget—but he suggested that the plan could be funded through employment-based premiums rather than a payroll tax. Starr also emphasized that the states should be able to experiment within a framework of minimum federal criteria, adapting the single-sponsor approach to suit local circumstances.

Starr and the architects of the Garamendi plan explicitly framed the liberal synthesis as a compromise approach. By compromise, they did not mean simply that it would please both liberals and conservatives (although they believed it would), but also that it represented a way to achieve many of the ends of a single-payer plan without government health insurance, significant new taxes, or comprehensive regulation of provider rates—in short, without those aspects of a single-payer plan that they believed would doom it to political failure. This argument won them a small audience on Capitol Hill among the handful of senators whose health policy staffs were already developing similar approaches. Its greatest effect, however, was on the Clinton campaign.

THE CLINTON PLAN

I have argued that it was Clinton's embrace of "competition within a budget" in September 1992 and his subsequent electoral victory that transformed the approach into the leading alternative for national health care reform. Why did the Clinton campaign move toward managed competition as it backed away from play-or-pay?

The first and most obvious reason was ideological. Clinton was running as a New Democrat who had cast off the philosophical shackles of his old-style "tax-and-spend" brethren. Even before he endorsed managed competition within a budget, Clinton had promised that his reform plan would build on the employment-based system of health insurance and impose minimal new taxes. As the campaign progressed, however, the Bush administration linked Clinton's vague play-or-pay plan with damaging symbols—taxation, job loss, heavy-handed regulation—symbols that called into question Clinton's centrism. In this context, endorsing a plan that incorporated elements of managed competition was a way for Clinton to deflect the challenge from the Bush campaign while reaffirming his commitment to the New Democratic philosophy. According to Atul Gawande, the campaign's policy shift was concordant with Clinton's own philosophy of government—with his "attraction to policies that involve a partnership between the public and private sector, his concern about a government takeover of the private health care system, his not being allergic at all to the involvement of the market."[44]

But the view that the Clinton campaign embraced managed competition within a budget because it was consistent with Clinton's political ideology—true enough as a description of what happened—does not address the prior question of why the approach was in a position to be adopted by the campaign. Nor does this view explain why Clinton and his advisers perceived the approach in the terms that they did. To the Clinton campaign, managed competition within a budget certainly seemed like a unique middle road to health care reform in 1992. But to understand why it seemed so we need to consider the actors and ideas that intersected during the presidential race. On one side, the Jackson Hole Group, the *New York Times*, the CDF, and key figures in the Democratic Leadership Council were lobbying in support of a "pure" version of managed competition without expenditure limits or rate regulation. On the other side, policy advocates like Garamendi, Zelman, and Paul Starr were suggesting that Clinton could attract the support of liberal reform advocates as well as the proponents of managed competition by embracing a reform approach that coupled managed competition with a national health budget. In this context, facing this specific constellation of forces, Clinton and his campaign advisers naturally saw managed competition as a centrist approach that would place Clinton squarely between the contending camps in the national reform debate.

Managed competition within a budget served the immediate purpose of freeing Clinton from the political burdens of the payroll tax and all-payer rate regulation that were associated with play-or-pay. The straight employer mandate obviated the need for a payroll tax, and the HIPCs and subsidies for small firms mitigated the negative impact of a straight mandate on small firms and low-wage workers. Although the campaign retained the national budget, it shifted the focus of budgetary control from provider reimbursement rates to capitated payments to health plans. And by making state flexibility a centerpiece of the plan, Clinton left the door open for individual states to experiment with alternative approaches, such as a single payer.

The campaign's shift to managed competition within a budget was not simply a change in policy, however; it was also a change in language. The rhetoric the Clinton campaign used to explain and justify the approach was crafted to appeal to both sides of the managed-competition spectrum—to the supporters of the Jackson Hole model as well as the proponents of the liberal synthesis. As a staff director of a Senate committee said of the Clinton proposal, "There was a certain amorphous quality to it that allowed people to read into it what they wanted."[45] The inchoate nature of the proposal reflected its delicate balance between the two views of managed competition. On the one hand, the campaign stressed that the Clinton proposal would encourage people to enroll in private managed-care plans and utilize market forces to hold down costs. On the other, it drew attention to the national health budget and universal insurance coverage. As a Senate staff member put it, "People saw a lot of what they wanted in managed competition, and people who in the past had wanted less government control or less financing through the government saw that, whereas people who wanted more regulation saw the budget."[46]

The ambiguity of managed competition made it a compelling campaign proposal. Clinton's embrace of the approach allowed him to attract support from disparate quarters in the final stretch of the campaign, and it left the Bush campaign without a coherent message on health care reform. But precisely because of the positive initial response to the proposal, Clinton and his advisers never fully appreciated the risks of the approach. The perception that managed competition was sweeping the policy community obscured some deeper and more troubling realities.

The first of these was that the breadth of support for managed competition was far narrower than it had appeared from the vantage point of the campaign. Although the membership of the Jackson Hole Group was impressive on paper, the strongest support for the Jackson Hole proposal came from just a handful of large insurance companies. Likewise, the CDF included a sizable number of House Democrats, but few of them truly understood or were committed to the CDF bill (which in any case fell far short of Clinton's goal of universal health insurance). On the other side of the spectrum, the proponents of the liberal synthesis represented an even smaller group of supporters. They included policy advisers who had helped develop the Garamendi plan, several left-leaning senators, and a few prominent policy specialists. This was a committed band of advocates, but it was far from a formidable alliance.

Even if the base of support for managed competition had been as broad as it had appeared to Clinton's advisers during the campaign, there still remained the problem of finding common ground among the self-proclaimed advocates of managed competition. The initial enthusiasm that greeted Clinton's campaign proposal fed the illusion that there was a groundswell of support for a specific compromise proposal. In fact, however, it was the slogan of managed competition that had widespread appeal; at the level of policy, the differences between the conflicting views of managed competition remained sharp. As one House staff member put it: "For a while, [managed competition] got everybody using the same language and coalescing and not using the same old language to describe policies that various coalitions had already said that they would never support. . . . I think that there was this tolerable but relatively brief period during which groups were able to be supportive because the details had not been hammered out."[47]

Of course, shallow support and disagreement on details were not difficulties unique to the managed-competition approach. No policy proposal in the fractious reform debate had yet to overcome these hurdles. But the belief that managed competition was the elusive compromise that past reformers had failed to discover posed a particular danger. It led Clinton's advisers to treat their "bridge to compromise" as an accomplishment rather than an aspiration. It made the structure of the president's proposal the overriding focus of the administration's reform effort. The resulting strategic myopia, I have argued, contributed to a number of the most prominent mistakes made by Clinton and his advisers during the early months of the new administration.

Finally, because of the narrow circle of participants involved and the quickness with which the process occurred, managed competition's movement onto the national political agenda took place without due attention to the challenge of building public support for the approach. From the earliest agenda-setting studies, scholars have viewed the formation of government agendas and the specification of policy alternatives as stages of policymaking that occur in relative exclusion from the currents of public sentiment. Kingdon argues, for example, that public opinion "may set limits on the possibilities and may affect an agenda of subjects in a general way, but the general public opinion is rarely well enough formed to directly affect an involved debate among policy specialists over which alternatives should be seriously considered."[48] My account of the emergence of managed competition confirms Kingdon's observation that the influence of public opinion on debates within policy communities can be fairly limited (although, contrary to Kingdon, I have argued that public opinion played an important role in the rise of health care reform on the government agenda and the narrowing of the acceptable range of policy options). But my account also highlights some of the dangers that are posed by the insulation of policy communities from public opinion. These include a widening gap between public and elite understandings of policy issues, a tendency for policymakers to design policies on the basis of specialized expertise and then market them to the public using vague rhetorical appeals, and a concomitant syndrome of public confusion, disenchantment, and cynicism.[49] It seems clear that the insularity of the health policy community was one reason why proponents of managed competition failed to anticipate public concerns and prepare a compelling set of arguments with which to justify and defend the approach.

Hence a bitter irony lies at the heart of the story I have told. The recent agenda-setting scholarship points to the forces that promote rapid change within the American polity. Focusing events pry open windows of opportunity and promote new understandings of policy issues. Policy entrepreneurs struggle among themselves to win political approval of their pet solutions. A solution is attached to a problem and both then move to the stage of decision making. The process can be fluid, unpredictable, and powerful. Forces of change sweep through the political system, allowing well-positioned political leaders to overcome the institutional deadlock and cozy arrangements that might otherwise obstruct fundamental policy change.

Of course, agendas can be set without action. A solution may not be ready when a problem comes into view, or a policy window may close before a compromise is reached. But nothing in the agenda-setting scholarship suggests that the dynamics of agenda setting might actually create barriers to policy change. Nothing in this scholarship suggests that the process of agenda setting might prevent policy advocates from fully comprehending and preparing for the political and institutional obstacles they face. Agenda-setting theorists do not claim that decisions will always follow on the heels of agenda setting. Yet they also do not claim that the process by which problems and solutions reach the government agenda will complicate the task of reaching meaningful compromise. In the concluding sections of this book, I look at some of the reasons why agenda setting failed to produce policy change in this case, and I suggest what this failure tells us about the promise and the limits of American politics.

THE FAILURE OF REFORM

National health care reform has risen on the political agenda a half-dozen times in this century. Each time, the pressures for reform have either dissipated or, in the case of Medicare and Medicaid, culminated in partial steps toward national health insurance. In at least two periods when reform failed—the Progressive Era and the 1970s—reformers were absolutely convinced that they were on the verge of fundamental reform. The Progressive activist Isaac Rubinow wrote ruefully in 1931 that the reform movement had grown "intoxicated" by its early successes and failed "to appreciate the strength of the enemy."[50] The economist (and later Clinton budget official) Alice Rivlin summed up the conventional wisdom in 1974 by heading an article on health care reform "Agreed: Here Comes National Health Insurance."[51] Yet national health insurance did not arrive—not in the Progressive Era or the 1970s; not during the New Deal, the Fair Deal, or the Great Society; and not, most recently, with the unprecedented leadership efforts of President Clinton. In each case, the liberal ideal slipped out of reach, leaving reformers to wonder why they had been so confident that national health legislation was finally at hand.

The repeated demise of national health care reform in the United States cautions against placing too much blame for the defeat of reform on the Clinton administration, its reform proposal, or even the strength of its opponents. Thus far we have examined President Clinton's reform effort from the perspective of agenda setting. Obviously, however, agenda setting is only part of the legislative process. Although problems and proposals must reach the agenda of government before a shift in policy can occur, a shift in policy does not always follow from a change in the agenda. Indeed, most scholars of American health politics agree that despite the recurrent attention to health care reform in the United States, there has never been any period when universal health insurance was close to passage. Focusing on the recent debate, most scholars have argued that the obstacles faced by Clinton were so formidable that it would have taken amazing luck and strategic acumen to pass any reform proposal. Some have even contended that comprehensive reform would have been defeated whatever Clinton proposed.

The view that the passage of the Clinton proposal—or any comprehensive reform proposal—was highly problematic is not in any way inconsistent with the historical and conceptual account I have presented in this book. As I have argued, the genesis of the Clinton proposal cannot be understood without an appreciation of the political, institutional, and cultural barriers to universal health insurance that reformers confronted in the early 1990s. From the intellectual principals of the Jackson Hole Group to the advisers who headed the White House effort, the policy advocates who developed and promoted the policy ideas embodied in the Clinton proposal were all cognizant of, if not fully prepared for, the daunting roadblocks that lay in their path. Indeed, Clinton and his advisers embraced managed competition within a budget precisely because they believed that it stood a better chance than other comprehensive reform proposals of surviving the American political gauntlet.

The view that the defeat of reform was inevitable, however, does pose something of a challenge to the argument of this book. For if defeat was inevitable, the genesis of the Clinton proposal and the strategies to which it gave rise—though interesting in their own right—do not help us assess why reform failed. We are left with a case study of agenda setting and an analysis of presidential policy development, intriguing to scholars perhaps but irrelevant to the basic question of why agenda setting and presidential leadership did not result in the passage of reform legislation.

For a number of reasons, however, I do not believe the argument that defeat was inevitable can be sustained. Meaningful reform legislation might have been passed in the early 1990s, and it may still be passed in the future. To argue otherwise is to transform enduring constraints on policy change into immutable and insurmountable barriers—and, in doing so, to misunderstand the significance and the lessons of the recent health care reform debate. Although it would be wrong to attribute the defeat of reform solely to the strategies of reformers and their opponents or to the policy alternative that President Clinton proposed, it would also be wrong to argue that these did not matter. The death of reform can only be understood if we consider both the constraints reformers confronted and the strategies they chose.

Perhaps the leading version of the "defeat was inevitable" argument is the claim that America's fragmented constitutional structure kills major social reforms of any kind (or at least, major reforms that benefit the many and hurt the few). Compared with most parliamentary systems, for example, American government sharply divides executive and legislative power. Executive officials are not drawn from the legislature, legislators are not significantly constrained from amending and proposing legislation, and the executive and legislative branches are not necessarily controlled by the same party. Furthermore, the fragmentation of government power, the relative weakness of American political parties, and the organization of American elections promotes a highly individualized and entrepreneurial style of politics—a style further encouraged by the relatively freewheeling and decentralized committee system in Congress. Add to this federalism, the regional malapportionment of the Senate, and the power of the filibuster and one has a political system in which significant policy departures require an exceedingly high level of agreement and coordination among political leaders.

The institutional explanation of health care reform's failure has been most clearly articulated in a recent article by Sven Steinmo and Jon Watts. They argue that Clinton's attempt at reform, like all previous attempts, was defeated by America's fragmented political institutions. "The failure of the president's health care reform plan," they contend, "is neither a failure of this president nor a failure of his specific plan. Rather it is a failure of American political institutions with which he has been forced to work and through which the plan had to be passed."[52]

This explanation of health care reform's failure is not without its difficulties. Steinmo and Watts ignore, for example, considerable evidence suggesting that congressional power has grown *less* fragmented over the last decade, and they stretch the definition of political institutions so far as to include nearly every obstacle to health care reform under the institutional rubric.[53] Nonetheless, the core argument made by Steinmo and Watts is undoubtedly correct. American political institutions do make major reforms extremely difficult to win. Government authority is fragmented, and integrative mechanisms (such as political parties) are comparatively weak. Numerous "veto points" allow politicians and organized interests to stall or halt policy changes they oppose.[54] Without a high level of agreement among political actors or strong public pressure for policy change, significant proposals can easily die a death of a thousand paper cuts in the Byzantine legislative process.

The crucial issue, then, is not whether American political institutions create barriers to significant policy change but how fixed those barriers are. Consumerism, environmentalism, and deregulation were all policy movements that pitted powerful private interests against the broader public interest—but which were nonetheless favorably acted on by Congress and the president. Reagan's 1981 budget, the Tax Reform Act of 1986, and Clinton's 1993 deficit-reduction package all involved changes in government spending that were comparable in magnitude to the new expenditures demanded by Clinton's health care reform proposal. Yet each was passed under institutional conditions that were arguably as onerous as those faced by President Clinton in 1993 and 1994. An agenda-setting framework helps us understand how such major initiatives are able to surmount the normal institutional barriers to policy change. In each case, electoral incentives, changing understandings of policy, and competition among entrepreneurs allowed adept political leaders to overcome the fragmentation of American political institutions and pass significant reforms. This suggests that the structure of American government is only part of the story behind policy failure or success. Another critical part is the strategies that political leaders adopt to navigate the institutional constraints they face. Whether efforts at policy change fail or succeed is usually a product not of institutions alone, but of the "fit" between the strategies reformers employ and the institutional structures through which they must pursue their goals.[55]

The focus on reform strategies directs our attention to another, more simple "defeat was inevitable" argument—that Clinton did not have the votes to pass his proposal. To succeed, Clinton needed the support of a majority of legislators in the House and, given the filibuster, perhaps as many as sixty votes in the Senate. But the Clinton proposal stood no chance of capturing the breadth of congressional support it needed. The proposal included a requirement that employers contribute to the cost of health insurance and a budget on national health spending—two measures that most conservative legislators opposed. As a result, it never had more than thirty Senate votes firmly on its side.[56] Since the Clinton proposal was the central alternative in the reform debate, its defeat effectively killed the prospects for legislative compromise.

David Brady and Kara Buckley have advanced the most sophisticated version of this straightforward argument. Relying on a simple median voter model in which policies are located on a single ideological dimension and politicians vote for the policy closest to their own ideological preference, Brady and Buckley argue that the Clinton proposal was too far to the left of the median voter in the Senate to win majority support, much less to gain the sixty votes needed to ensure passage. Even the CDF bill (which was not considered in the Senate) would have been too liberal for more than a majority of senators. In fact, according to Brady and Buckley, the choice to not take action at all was preferred by more than forty senators, making the passage of health care reform all but impossible given the Senate filibuster. "Considering both the preferences of legislators and the super-majority institutional arrangements in the Senate," Brady and Buckley conclude, "the Clinton plan was doomed from the start."[57]

In one sense this pessimistic analysis cannot be wrong. The Clinton plan never gained majority support in either house of Congress, and the 103rd Congress closed in 1994 without taking any action on health care reform. Yet those who endorse the view that the preferences of the 103rd Congress prevented reform are not making the truistic claim that Congress did not pass comprehensive reform because there was not sufficient congressional support for comprehensive reform. Rather, their argument is that by looking at the ideological composition of the 103rd Congress, one could have predicted in advance that reform would not pass in 1993 or 1994. It is here that the invocation of congressional preferences becomes more problematic.

The first problem that attends any analysis of this sort is deciding how to conceptualize the preferences of politicians. One approach—the one taken by Brady and Buckley—is to assume that conflict over policy only involves a single ideological dimension and that politicians cannot introduce cross-cutting issues into policy debates. Neither assumption seems plausible in the case of health care reform. Including multiple dimensions makes the analysis more realistic, yet then it generally becomes impossible to pinpoint the equilibrium outcome, since numerous majority coalitions could form cutting different ways across the different dimensions.

Another problem is determining where policy options and the preferences of politicians are located ideologically. Even if one accepts, for instance, that a single dimension captures most of the variation in policy proposals or politicians' positions, one must still determine where a proposal or position falls on this ideological spectrum.

As serious as these problems are, there is an even deeper difficulty with the argument that the preferences of members of Congress doomed health care reform from the start. To sustain this argument, one must assume that both legislators' ideological positions and the location of policy options on the ideological continuum are fixed. It would not have made any difference, in other words, if the various policy options that were debated through 1994 were voted on in 1993—or in 1991 or 1992, for that matter—as long as the same legislators were involved. In fact, the positions of members of Congress could have been adduced as soon as one knew the features of the relevant policy options. Those positions would have remained constant regardless of the arguments made for and against the competing options and regardless of the political strategies used by the opponents and proponents of each option (unless, of course, those strategies somehow changed the rules of voting).

If these assumptions appear deeply implausible, that is because they are. Such an argument completely ignores the enormous changes in legislators' positions that occurred during the course of the health care reform debate. To take an extreme example, Senate Minority Leader Bob Dole first supported a relatively comprehensive bill, then abandoned that bill and embraced a more modest proposal, then abandoned *that* bill and became an all-out opponent of reform. Between 1992 and 1994, Senator Bob Kerrey repudiated the single-sponsor, tax-financed reform initiative that had been the centerpiece of his presidential campaign and came out against the Clinton proposal and the employer mandate. And these highly visible apostasies were only the tip of the iceberg. After the Pennsylvania election, no fewer than twenty-four Republican senators signed onto a fairly comprehensive reform bill; by the end of the debate, support among Republicans for any compromise had all but evaporated.

Why did so many members of Congress abandon the cause of health care reform between 1991 and 1994? Part of the reason, no doubt, is that their earlier positions were not entirely sincere. But that merely raises the further question: Why did members of Congress feel compelled to assure the public they supported reform? The answer, of course, is that they believed there were political benefits inherent in supporting reform and political risks inherent in opposing it. I explained in the first chapter how the Pennsylvania election transformed health care reform into a policy issue of particular electoral significance. By 1993, however, members of Congress had started to reevaluate the lessons they had taken away from

Wofford's victory. Republicans in particular began to conclude that public support for reform was more shallow than they had earlier supposed and that defeating President Clinton's reform proposal might actually help them at the polls. This reevaluation was spearheaded by conservative strategists like William Kristol, who warned Republicans in December 1993 that passage of the Clinton plan would "revive the reputation of . . . the Democrats . . . as the generous protector of middle-class interests."[58] Republican pollster Bill McInturff advised congressional Republicans before the 1994 midterm election that "one of the most important predicates for Republican success is not having health care pass."[59]

The median voter explanation advanced by Brady and Buckley says nothing about the relationship between public opinion and congressional action. Brady and Buckley acknowledge that legislators' positions may be influenced by their constituents, but argue that, for their purposes, "it does no matter if the members' preferences . . . are induced by constituents or are the members' own preferences."[60] To the contrary, it matters a great deal. If members of Congress believe that their constituents will punish them if legislative action is not taken, then they will be more willing to work toward a legislative compromise and more willing to support a departure from the status quo.[61]

Like the institutional explanation, however, the median voter explanation of the failure of reform does contain an important element of truth. The composition of the 103rd Congress clearly did represent a serious obstacle to the passage of meaningful reform legislation, and by 1994 the Clinton plan was obviously too far to the left of swing voters in Congress to be passed intact. But like the institutional explanation, the median voter argument is too deterministic in its prediction of failure. It portrays the obstacles to reform as objective, immutable, and insurmountable while at the same time overlooking the importance of strategic action within those constraints. Moreover, it raises an obvious question: Why did President Clinton propose a reform plan that was so far to the left of the congressional median? Indeed, the puzzle holds more generally: Why did such a broad range of political actors and observers believe that national health care reform would finally be enacted? In short, why did so many politicians misread the political environment and propose policies that stood little chance of enactment?

The agenda-setting framework helps us see these misplaced expectations as a characteristic response to the forces that push policy issues onto the agenda of government. By creating a rapid rise in attention to an issue, the positive-feedback dynamic can foster the perception that policy change is inevitable. Wofford's victory in the Pennsylvania election alerted members of Congress and presidential aspirants to the surprising electoral appeal of national health care reform. Almost immediately, members of Congress were scrambling to "make pleasing judgmental statements" about health care reform and to sponsor and cosponsor legislation that displayed their commitment to the cause.[62] The heightened media attention to health care reform that followed on the heels of the Pennsylvania election further increased the incentives for congressional position taking, as well as the level of public attention to the subject. Bill Clinton responded to these cues and made national health care reform a centerpiece of his presidential campaign and then his presidency. In this environment it was easy for reformers to see the opportunities for fundamental change as greater than they actually were.

Since the demise of health care reform in the 103rd Congress, advocates and analysts have trotted out a long list of alternative proposals that President Clinton would have been better served to embrace. Some have argued, for instance, that a Canadian-style single-payer system would have been easier to explain and rally support behind, especially if Clinton had launched a concerted campaign against the health insurance industry. But a single-payer plan would have been subject to the same attacks that helped kill the Health Security Act, and it is extremely unlikely that such a plan would have garnered strong enough public support to overcome the frenetic opposition it would have provoked. Other analysts, such as Theda Skocpol, have argued that Clinton should have proposed a managed-competition or play-or-pay bill with loose payment regulation and large initial subsidies so as to lessen interest-group opposition and alleviate public fears.[63] However, any such proposal would have run afoul of fiscal constraints and congressional procedures designed to limit deficit spending. Other commentators have suggested that an expansion of Medicare or a decentralized approach based on state experimentation within minimum federal criteria would have been politically viable. Yet these proposals would have faced serious obstacles of their own. A less than universal Medicare expansion, for example, would have been virtually impossible to sustain without measures to prevent employers from dumping workers into the public system.

It is difficult to conclude which, if any, of these proposals would have stood a better chance of passage than the Clinton proposal all else being equal, because all else would not have been equal. In criticizing the president's reform strategy, I am not claiming that another policy proposal would have tipped the balance in the Clinton administration's favor. First it is unclear whether *any* comparably comprehensive reform proposal could have been passed, given the constraints Clinton faced. But second, and more to the point, the policy proposal itself was less important than the assumptions it embodied and the strategies to which it gave rise. If we are to understand why the Clinton proposal was defeated so resoundingly, contributing not only to the crippling of Clinton's domestic agenda but also to the conservative countermobilization that set the stage for the 1994 elections, we need to understand why Clinton and his aides were so certain that managed competition within a budget would allow them to succeed where past reformers had not.

The belief of Clinton's policy planners that managed competition would break the stalemate over health care reform can only be understood in historical context. Clinton and his advisers understood the managed-competition approach in the terms that they did because of the specific forces that intersected during the campaign. They believed the approach would be a vehicle to compromise because they saw the divisions among reformers as differences of policy that could be resolved through adjustments in policy. Managed competition within a budget, they assumed, would split the differences among competing advocates of health care reform and, at the same time, capitalize on the gathering momentum of the managed-competition design. But the differences among reform advocates proved more intractable than Clinton's advisers had expected, and the apparent enthusiasm for managed competition obscured the deep differences between its proponents and the superficiality of its appeal. Ironically, Clinton's policy planners crafted their entire policy strategy with the hope of capturing the median voter in Congress, only to find that the middle ground they so assiduously sought had shifted out from under them.

The search for that elusive middle ground defined the Clinton administration's reform effort, just as it has defined the Clinton presidency. Linda Bergthold remembered the heady early days of the working group effort, when "there was real excitement that [managed competition within a budget] was . . . an idea that could really draw in the middle."[64] The search for the center was a constant preoccupation of Clinton's reform team. The policy advisers who labored on the plan now berate themselves for tracking to the left or straying from the center or failing to capture the middle. The fundamental problem with the White House effort, however, was not which way Clinton and his policy team tracked or even where they started; it was the conception of politics on which their reform strategy was based. For despite the impressive intellectual energy devoted to the Clinton proposal, the underlying political logic was remarkably crude. The president and his advisers sought a massive transformation of the role of government in the finance and delivery of medical care. But they built their proposal on a foundation of ideas and rhetoric that embodied an extremely negative view of government and government capacity. They championed reforms in response to the deeply felt concerns of the American public. But they designed a reform proposal that they were neither willing nor able to explain to the citizens whose support they needed. Perhaps most important, they treated the task of coalition-building as a problem of policy analysis rather than one of political bargaining. They sized up the political landscape, adduced the preferences of the relevant actors, and then assumed that they could split and recombine those preferences at will. A compromise would be reached when all of the critical provisions that each side wanted were included in a policy package that all sides would support. The proposal became so central to the entire strategy that the Clinton health care team never truly grasped that the opportunities for reform were slipping away.

If there is a single cautionary lesson that emerges from the defeat of the Clinton plan, it is that policy analysis is a flawed mechanism for achieving political compromise. The policy-analytic methodology has much to recommend it. It imposes order and discipline on what can be a staggering array of data. It creates a framework for understanding and clarifying the relationship between policy instruments and objectives. Yet the methodology of policy analysis has come to embody an emaciated conception of politics and policymaking. It is fixated on policy solutions, with solutions understood as rational choices to achieve given objectives within fixed constraints. This exclusive preoccupation with solutions prevents a full realization of the political, institutional, and cultural context in which policy ideas must be justified, debated, enacted, and implemented. More important, it pushes policy analysts to conceive of politics and institutions in purely instrumental terms, as means to the policy objectives they have specified. This view misses the dynamic, deliberative, and expressive character of politics. It leads policy advocates to believe that it is sufficient to specify ends and means and identify possible constraints without developing strategies for justifying and promoting their ideas within the realm of public discourse. It is in short a view of politics that systematically underappreciates "the role of justification, communication, and persuasion in the formation and development of public policy."[65]

This is the most troubling aspect of the policy-analytic perspective—the lack of room it leaves for democratic deliberation and debate. Once the objectives of government policy are delineated, they can be pursued most efficiently by a benevolent dictator (or a benevolent policy analyst) armed with the relevant information and empowered to create the necessary institutions. As a problem solver, government is no different than a consumer choosing among products or an entrepreneur seeking to maximize profits; it simply chooses the most efficient means to a given end. Yet this view misses the very essence of politics. In politics, ends are not given and differences are not only about means but also about the relative merit of competing values, interests, and understandings. In politics, existing policies and institutional legacies constrain government in ways that may prevent the pursuit of otherwise "optimal" solutions. And most important, in politics arguments and ideas are not mere rationalizations of fixed and objective preferences but a central means by which democratic societies resolve disagreements and overcome collective problems.

THE PROMISE AND THE LIMITS OF AMERICAN POLITICS

Amid the ubiquitous laments that American government can no longer govern, the recent scholarship on agenda setting presents a more sanguine portrait of the possibilities for policy change in American politics.[66] The theme of this scholarship is that the government can indeed govern, at least some of the time and under certain conditions. The forces that promote change—ideas, leadership, competition among institutional venues—are sometimes strong enough to allow reformers to overcome the power of vested interests and the inertial tendencies of American political institutions. As Baumgartner and Jones declare, "In the long sweep of American politics, one is less tempted to claim that cozy arrangements between politicians, interest groups, and the media prevent change and more likely to ask when and how new policy arrangements will emerge, sweeping away those currently in place."[67]

But perhaps the new breed of scholars who study agenda change are too quick to declare victory for the American political system. In studying the dynamics of agenda setting or the instances of successful reform, it is easy to overlook the many pressing policy issues such as health care reform that emerge onto the government agenda without precipitating fundamental policy change. It is easy to overlook the hopes and expectations that are raised each time the forces of agenda change are unleashed and then dashed each time America's enduring constraints on policy change kick in. It is easy to overlook, that is, the persistent tension between the promise of American democracy and the limits of American government.

This is a tension inherent in the very structure of American government: the institutions that cultivate the promise of democracy make its complete fulfillment impossible. Powerful and frequent electoral pressures push politicians to identify with social movements and interest groups and to champion new programs and policies. Electoral cycles and demands "routinely create needs and tensions that . . . are resolved by recourse to the policy innovation process."[68] Moreover, the competing branches and levels of government offer multiple points of access for citizens seeking representation or hoping to promote new understandings of policy. As David Vogel notes, it is the very fragmentation of American political institutions that has allowed American government to respond more promptly and permanently to diffuse interests such as environmental organizations than many parliamentary systems have.[69]

And yet the most frequent result of the constitutional routines that incite pressures for reform is political stalemate. Reforms are left "sprawling helplessly in a scrum of competing interests."[70] Vested interests in society find other institutional venues from which they can slow or halt the progress of change. Even when they do not, the legitimacy of government action is itself suspect, leading to the sputtering pattern of administrative development that James Morone aptly describes as "roundabout state-building."[71] The administrative apparatus that springs up when change is won pleases neither reformers nor their opponents; indeed, frequently it can scarcely operate at all.[72] Conservatives attack a liberal welfare state; liberals hardly consider it a state.

Over the past decade, the constraints have only grown more onerous. The looming public debt that is a principal legacy of the Reagan era makes new government commitments all but unthinkable. New budget rules make them all but impossible. The Senate is now so malapportioned that senators representing just a tenth of the U.S. population can sustain a filibuster. And twenty years of stagnating real wages, rising economic inequality, and changing demographics have helped to exacerbate many of the deepest fault lines in American society.

All this is not likely to change with Republican control of Congress or even if Republicans recapture the White House. The Republicans have their own demands to meet. Already, a long roster of interests—the religious right, small business leaders, property-rights advocates—have lined up outside Capitol Hill to demand repayment for their electoral support. Devolving federal responsibilities to the states, or dissolving them altogether, will not make the promise of American democracy any less attractive. Despite the current antipathy toward government, most Americans still believe that government has a role to play in tempering the vicissitudes of the market. They still believe that it is the responsibility of government to help Americans in their old age, to protect the least advantaged, to increase access to medical care. What may change is the ability of government to act on these expectations and, more important, to help Americans see their common interests in the challenges that will inevitably confront them. In attempting to tear down the old order, Republicans may well end up further crippling the capacity of American government to respond to the common aspirations to which it gives rise.

National health care reform represented an unprecedented opportunity to respond to those aspirations, and its defeat will shape the contours of American politics—and Americans' perception of government—for many years to come. As in past debates, the defeat of reform has prompted recriminations and lamentations among advocates of reform. Many reformers now proclaim that 1994 marked the passing of the last great opportunity to achieve universal health insurance or substantial progress toward it. Perhaps this is true, but it does not seem likely. If the story I have told offers any lesson, it is that the right combination of interests, ideas, and leadership can create possibilities for policy innovation where reformers once thought none existed. If America's health insurance arrangements continue to deteriorate, if the tattered medical safety net continues to fray, and if the dictates of leadership come together with the enlightened self-interest of citizens and organized interests, then American health care reformers may well have new opportunities to pursue their vision of a good society. It is acting on those opportunities that will be difficult.

Methodology

THE RESEARCH for this book employed several methods, including interviews with people in and around government, analysis of original memoranda and policy documents, and examination of such measures of agenda status as media coverage, legislative activity, and congressional hearings. The interviews and primary sources proved especially crucial in tracking the actions and interactions that helped move managed competition onto the government agenda.

Of particular interest to political historians will be the thousands of policy documents released by the White House in 1994 in response to a lawsuit against President Clinton's task force.[1] These documents—which include briefing books, materials prepared for "tollgate" meetings, internal memoranda, and correspondence between task force members and outside experts and groups—have been housed at the National Archives since September 1994. I reviewed many of them while researching this book, but their sheer volume and haphazard organization prevented a full review. Most of the documents are papers (or computer files) retained by the roughly six hundred participants in the working groups that advised the official task force. (However, many of the participants, particularly congressional staff, did not keep or turn over any documents.) The papers are grouped by participant and contain a mixture of dry policy papers and routine but sometimes revealing memoranda. I focused on the papers of people who occupied leadership positions or who were involved most deeply in the development of the proposal. Although much of the information contained in these papers is already public record and I came across no startling new insights, the materials did provide a fuller picture of the internal debates and deliberations that shaped the Clinton proposal.

I conducted thirty-four interviews for this book, half in person and half by phone. I did not attempt to select a sample of respondents that was somehow representative of the health policy community as a whole, but instead focused on individuals who had worked on or were knowledgeable about the Clinton proposal or the reform plans that fed into it. More than half the respondents had been part of the White House working groups, about half were current or recent congressional aides, roughly one-third had advised the campaign or transition, and a little more than a quarter had been directly involved in the development of the CDF/

TABLE A.1

The Interviews

	Involvement[a]	Interview Date(s)
Senate Staff Member	1, 3, 5	11 August 1993
House Staff Member 1	1, 3	17 August 1993
House Staff Member 2	1, 3	10 August 1993
House Staff Member 3	1, 3	10 August 1993
Bergthold, Linda	1, 6	6 December 1994[b]
Cohen, Rima	1, 3	12 August 1993
Ebeler, Jack	2	27 October 1993[b]
England, Mary Jane	4, 5	18 August 1993
Enthoven, Alain	4, 5	21 December 1994[b]
Etheredge, Lynn	2, 4, 5	6 August 1993
		17 May 1995[b]
Fiske, Mary Beth	1, 3	17 August 1993
Fried, Bruce	2	27 October 1993[b]
Gawande, Atul	1, 2, 3	1 September 1993[b]
		25 October 1993[b]
		17 May 1995[b]
Kaplan, Gabe	3	17 August 1993
Kosterlitz, Julie	7	18 October 1994
Magaziner, Ira	1, 2	21 October 1994
Nexon, David	1, 3	12 August 1993
Nix, Shiela	1, 3	10 August 1993
Pollack, Ron	2	3 November 1994[b]
Raman, Anand	3, 5	2 September 1993[b]
Rosenthal, Jack	7	3 April 1995[b]
Schulke, David	1, 3	26 August 1993
Singh, Rakesh	3	17 August 1993
Sossaman, Mendi	3	29 July 1993
Starr, Paul	1, 2	15 February 1995[b]
		17 May 1995[b]
Thorpe, Kenneth	1, 2	28 October 1994[b]
Wiener, Joshua	1, 2	19 October 1994
Weinstein, Michael	7	8 September 1993[b]
Zelman, Walter	1, 2, 6	2 September 1993[b]
		20 October 1994

[a] 1 = participant in White House effort; 2 = participant in campaign or transition; 3 = congressional staff member; 4 = helped develop Jackson Hole proposal; 5 = helped develop CDF/Boren-Breaux proposal; 6 = helped develop Garamendi plan; 7 = other.

[b] Phone interview.

Boren-Breaux bill, the Jackson Hole proposal, or the Garamendi plan. (The total exceeds 100 percent because many of the respondents were involved in several capacities.) Table A.1 lists the respondents, the capacity (or capacities) in which they were involved, and the date (or dates) on which I interviewed them. Some of the congressional staff members offered information only on the condition that I not cite them by name.

The interviews ranged in length from thirty minutes to more than two hours. I chose a semi-structured interview method that allowed respondents to guide the interview in a direction of interest to them. In most cases, I began by asking informants a set of uniform questions and then tailored the interview to focus on their particular role in the policy process. At each interview, I also requested the names of several additional individuals with whom the respondent felt I should speak. By the last several interviews, I had spoken with the majority of the people who had been cited as important in the course of my interviews. This suggests that I interviewed at least the core group of individuals who were actively involved in the process of bringing managed competition to the political forefront.

Jackson Hole Participants, 1990–1992

John R. Ball, M.D., J.D.
Executive Vice President
American College of Physicians

James Bentley
Senior Vice President
American Hospital Association

John B. Crosby
Senior Vice President
American Medical Association

Rick Curtis
Director of Public Policy
Health Insurance Association
of America

The Honorable David Durenberger
United States Senate

David M. Eddy, M.D., Ph.D.
Jackson, Wyoming

Paul M. Ellwood, M.D.
President and CEO
InterStudy

Mary Jane England, M.D.
President
Washington Business Group
on Health

Alain C. Enthoven, Ph.D.
Stanford University

Lynn M. Etheredge
Chevy Chase, Maryland

Donald W. Fisher, Ph.D.
Executive Vice President
American Group Practice
Association

Paul Freiman
Chairman and CEO
Syntex Corporation

Jerome Grossman, M.D.
President
New England Medical Center

John Iglehart
Editor
Health Affairs

Henry M. Kaiser
San Francisco, California

Edmund F. Kelly
President
Employee Benefits Division
Aetna Life & Casualty

The Honorable John Kitzhaber, M.D.
President
Oregon State Senate

Kermit Knudsen, M.D.
President
Scott & White Clinic

Richard Kronick, Ph.D.
University of California, San Diego

Thomas W. Langfitt, M.D.
President
Pew Charitable Trusts

David Lawrence, M.D.
President and CEO
Kaiser Foundation Health
Plan, Inc.

Maurice Lazarus
Boston, Massachusetts

Thomas A. Levin
President and CEO
Blue Cross and Blue Shield—
Colorado

William P. Link
Executive Vice President
Prudential

Alan Maltz
Vice President and Actuary
Aetna Life and Casualty

Albert R. Martin, M.D.
President and CEO
InterPractice Systems

Kevin Moley
Deputy Secretary
Department of Health and Human
Services

Edmond C. Moy
Director
Office of Prepaid Health Care
Health Care Financing Administration

John Moynahan, Jr.
Executive Vice President
Metropolitan Life Insurance

Marilyn Carlson Nelson
Senior Vice President
Carlson Holdings

G. Robert O'Brien
Executive Vice President
CIGNA Corporation

David Ottensmeyer, M.D.
President
Lovelace Medical Foundation

Douglas Peters
President
Main Line Health

Thomas O. Pyle
Former President and CEO
Harvard Community Health Plan

Dan Roble
Ropes & Gray
Boston, Massachsetts

William L. Roper, M.D.
Director
Centers for Disease Control

William R. Roy, M.D., J.D.
Topeka, Kansas

Ray Scheppach, Ph.D.
Executive Director
National Governors' Association

Carl Schramm
President
Health Insurance Association of
America

Thomas A. Scully
Office of Management and Budget

Richard S. Sharpe
Program Director
The John A. Hartford
Foundation

Deborah Steelman, Esq.
Washington, D.C.

Seymour Sternberg
Executive Vice President
New York Life Insurance

Michael Stocker, M.D.
Executive Vice President
U.S. Healthcare

James Strain, M.D.
Executive Director
American Academy of Pediatrics

Barney Tresnowski
President
Blue Cross and Blue Shield Association

John F. Troy
Vice President
The Travelers

Ronald Van Horssen
  President and CEO
  Mobile Technology

Robert Waller, M.D.
  Chairman of the Board
  Mayo Foundation

Winston R. Wallin
  Chairman of the Board
  Medtronic, Inc.

Michael M. Weinstein, Ph.D.
  Editorial Board
  New York Times

California Insurance Commissioner's Health Care Advisory Committee

Linda A. Bergthold, Ph.D.
William Mercer Incorporated

Andrew Bindman, M.D.
Institute for Health Policy Studies
University of California, San
Francisco

David Carlisle, M.D.
University of California, Los
Angeles
Rand Corporation

Geraldine Dallek, M.P.H.
Executive Director
Medicare Advocacy Project

Lynn Dorsey, M.B.A.
McKinsey & Company

Kenneth W. Drummer
Partner
Coopers & Lybrand

Paul Feldstein, Ph.D.
Graduate School of Management
University of California, Irvine

Mark Finucane
Director
Contra Costa County Health
Services Department

Fernando Torres-Gil, Ph.D.
University of California,
Los Angeles
University of Southern California

Lucy Johns, M.P.H.
Consultant
Health Care Planning & Policy

Richard Kronick, Ph.D.
Department of Community and
Family Medicine
University of California, San Diego

Diana Mellon Lacey
Research Associate
California Healthcare in the 21st
Century Project

Larry Levitt, M.P.P.
Special Assistant
California Healthcare in the 21st
Century Project

Roland Lowe, M.D.
Chinese Hospital

John M. Luce, M.D.
University of California, San
Francisco

Elizabeth A. McGlynn, Ph.D.
Rand Corporation

Kathleen Morrison
Research Associate
California Health Care in the 21st
Century Project

Mary Pittman, Ph.D.
President and CEO

California Association of Public
Hospitals

Patricia E. Powers
Executive Director
Bay Area Business Group on Health

James C. Robinson, Ph.D.
Associate Professor of Health,
Economics and Policy
University of California, Berkeley

Jacque J. Sokolov, M.D.
Vice President and Medical Director
Southern California Edison
Company

Julia Thomas
Chairman and CEO
Bobrow/Thomas and Associates

Joan B. Trauner, Ph.D.
Principal
Coopers & Lybrand

Richard Trogman, M.S.
Research Associate
California Health Care in the 21st
Century Project

Robert Valdez, Ph.D.
University of California, Los
Angeles
Rand Corporation

Walter Zelman, Ph.D.
Special Deputy for
Health Insurance
California Health Care in the 21st
Century Project

Notes

Preface

1. "The Bush-Clinton Health Reform," *New York Times*, 10 Oct. 1992, A20.
2. John W. Kingdon, *Agendas, Alternatives, and Public Policies* (New York: HarperCollins, 1984).
3. Frank R. Baumgartner and Bryan D. Jones, *Agendas and Instability in American Politics* (Chicago: University of Chicago Press, 1993).

Introduction

1. See in particular Frank R. Baumgartner and Bryan D. Jones, *Agendas and Instability in American Politics* (Chicago: University of Chicago Press, 1993); William H. Riker, ed., *Agenda Formation* (Ann Arbor: University of Michigan Press, 1993); Frank R. Baumgartner, *Conflict and Rhetoric in French Policymaking* (Pittsburgh: University of Pittsburgh Press, 1989); Deborah A. Stone, "Causal Stories and the Formation of Policy Agendas," *Political Science Quarterly* 104 (1989): 281–300; Nelson W. Polsby, *Political Innovation in America: The Politics of Policy Initiation* (New Haven: Yale University Press, 1984); John W. Kingdon, *Agendas, Alternatives, and Public Policies* (New York: HarperCollins, 1984); Barbara J. Nelson, *Making an Issue of Child Abuse* (Chicago: University of Chicago Press, 1984); Roger W. Cobb and Charles D. Elder, *Participation in American Politics: The Dynamics of Agenda-Building*, 2d ed. (Baltimore: Johns Hopkins University Press, 1983); Jack L. Walker, "Setting the Agenda in the U.S. Senate: A Theory of Problem Selection," *British Journal of Political Science* 7 (1977): 423–45; Roger Cobb, Jennie-Keith Ross, and Mark Howard Ross, "Agenda Building as a Comparative Political Process," *American Political Science Review* 70 (1976): 126–38; Anthony Downs, "Up and Down with Ecology—The 'Issue Attention Cycle,'" *Public Interest* 28 (1972): 38–50; Mathew A. Crenson, *The Un-Politics of Air Pollution* (Baltimore: Johns Hopkins University Press, 1971); Peter Bachrach and Morton S. Baratz, *Power and Poverty: Theory and Practice* (New York: Oxford University Press, 1970); and E. E. Schattschneider, *The Semi-Sovereign People: A Realist's View of Democracy in America* (New York: Holt, Rinehart, and Winston, 1960).
2. Hugh Heclo, "Issue Networks in the Executive Establishment," in *The New American Political System*, ed. Anthony King (Washington, D.C.: American Enterprise Institute, 1978), 102.

Chapter 1

1. Quoted in Larry Reynolds, "Healthcare Options in an Election Year," *Management Review* 81 (1992): 10.
2. Gabe Kaplan, interview by author, 17 Aug. 1993.

3. Robert J. Blendon, et al., "The 1991 Pennsylvania Senate Race and National Health Insurance," *American Health Policy* 2 (1992): 21–24.

4. Pierce Lewis, "Anatomy of an Upset," *American Demographics* (June 1992): 52–56.

5. Medicare is a federal program that provides hospital insurance (Part A) and coverage for physician services (Part B) to the elderly and persons with advanced kidney disease. Medicaid is a joint federal-state program that covers low-income families on public assistance, the disabled, and, increasingly, elderly residents of nursing homes.

6. Congressional Budget Office, *Projections of National Health Expenditures* (Washington, D.C.: CBO, 1992), 5.

7. Linda Bergthold, *Purchasing Power in Health: Business, the State, and Health Care Politics* (New Brunswick, N.J.: Rutgers University Press, 1990), 34.

8. For a more detailed exposition of this point, see Deborah A. Stone, "AIDS and the Moral Economy of Insurance," *American Prospect* 1 (spring 1990): 62–73.

9. Kenneth E. Thorpe, "Expanding Employment-Based Health Insurance: Is Small Group Reform the Answer?" *Inquiry* 29 (summer 1992): 129.

10. Karl Polzer and Judith Miller Jones, "Risk Pools, Reinsurance, and Subsidies: Reforming the Small Group Market for Health Insurance" (Issue Brief No. 596 for the National Health Policy Forum, George Washington University, Washington, D.C., 1992), 4.

11. Paul Starr, "The Undelivered Health System," *Public Interest* 42 (winter 1976): 75.

12. Ibid., 75.

13. Mark Merlis, *Health Care Reform: Managed Competition*, CRS Issue Brief IB93008 (Washington, D.C.: Congressional Research Service, 4 June 1993), 2.

14. For evidence on HMO savings, see Joseph P. Newhouse, "Controlled Experimentation in Research Policy," *Health Services Research: Accomplishments and Potential*, ed. Eli Ginzberg (Cambridge: Harvard University Press, 1991), 161–94; Joseph P. Newhouse, et al., "Are Fee-for-Service Costs Increasing Faster than HMO Costs?" *Medical Care* 23 (August 1985): 960–66; and Willard G. Manning, et al., "A Controlled Trial of the Effect of Prepaid Group Practice on Use of Services," *New England Journal of Medicine* 310 (7 June 1984): 1505–10. Little research has been done on the savings, if any, achieved by PPOs and POS plans. Since PPOs and POS plans negotiate discounts with providers, at least some shift costs onto payers that do not receive discounts. However, the extent to which cost-shifting occurs is a subject of considerable debate. See Employee Benefit Research Institute, *Hospital Pricing: Cost Shifting and Competition* (Washington, D.C.: EBRI, 1993).

15. Foster Higgins, *1992 Health Care Benefits Survey* (Princeton, N.J.: Foster Higgins, 1992), 8.

16. One study of the effect of utilization review estimated that groups adopting it experienced a one-time savings of 8.3 percent of total medical expenditures. Paul J. Feldstein, Thomas M. Wickizer, and John R. C. Wheeler, "Private Cost Containment: The Effects of Utilization Review on Health Care Use and Expenditures," *New England Journal of Medicine* 318 (19 May 1988): 1310–14. Foster

Higgins's 1992 health care survey suggests that the savings is more on the order of 4 percent. Both figures are small in relation to the recent double-digit annual increases in the cost of conventional insurance. Perhaps this is why Foster Higgins finds that 71 percent of employers do not know if their utilization review programs lower costs, while only 21 percent feel they have. Foster Higgins, *1992 Health Care Benefits Survey*, 18.

17. Paul Starr, *The Logic of Health Care Reform* (Knoxville, Tenn.: Whittle Direct Books, 1992), 41.

18. Employee Benefit Research Institute, *Sources of Health Insurance and Characteristics of the Uninsured: Analysis of the March 1992 Current Population Survey* (Washington, D.C.: EBRI, 1993), 4.

19. Paul Starr, "The Middle Class and National Health Reform," *American Prospect* 6 (summer 1991): 7–12.

20. Gabe Kaplan, interview by author, 17 Aug. 1993.

21. Rosita M. Thomas, *Health Care in America: An Analysis of Public Opinion*, CRS Report for Congress 92–769 GOV (Washington, D.C.: Congressional Research Service, 26 Oct. 1992), 10.

22. On the general stability of public views about major policy issues, see Benjamin I. Page and Robert Y. Shapiro, *The Rational Public: 50 Years of Trends in Americans' Policy Preferences* (Chicago: University of Chicago Press, 1992); and James A. Stimson, *Public Opinion in America: Moods, Cycles, and Swings* (Boulder, Colo.: Westview Press, 1991).

23. Mark Schlesinger and Taeku Lee, "Is Health Care Different? Popular Support of Federal Health and Social Policies," in *The Politics of Health Care Reform: Lessons from the Past, Prospects for the Future*, ed. James A. Morone and Gary S. Belkin (Durham, N.C.: Duke University Press, 1994), 315.

24. Ibid., 315–17.

25. Although these figures certainly suggest an impressive rise in public support, there are several reasons to be cautious about drawing sweeping conclusions. First, the survey question asked respondents whether they supported health care reform in general rather than specific reform measures, so the results obscure substantive disagreement over the direction reform should take. Second, the survey results do not indicate the *depth* of support for reform, that is, how willing Americans were to make sacrifices to enable reform. Finally, the question did not allow respondents to express support for the status quo (although other opinion surveys suggest that the proportion of Americans who prefer no change is extremely small—around 3 percent).

26. See Page and Shapiro, *Rational Public*.

27. I am aware that economists locate the official beginning of the national economic recession—defined as six months or longer of contracting domestic economic output—between June and September 1990. Yet sluggish economic growth began before 1990, and in many regions of the country including Pennsylvania, the economic downturn started earlier and accelerated faster than it did at the national level. Louis Uchitelle, "Data Verify Economy's Malaise: 16 States in or Near Recession," *New York Times*, 16 July 1990, A1.

28. Schlesinger and Lee, "Is Health Care Different?" 364.

29. See the nuanced analysis in Lawrence R. Jacobs, "The Politics of American

Ambivalence toward Government," in *The Politics of Health Care Reform: Lessons from the Past, Prospects for the Future*, ed. James A. Morone and Gary S. Belkin (Durham, N.C.: Duke University Press, 1994), 375–401.

30. Daniel Yankelovich, *Coming to Public Judgment: Making Democracy Work in a Complex World* (Syracuse: Syracuse University Press, 1991).

31. McCombs and Shaw's study is the *locus classicus* of the field. Maxwell E. McCombs and Donald L. Shaw, "The Agenda-Setting Function of Mass Media," *Public Opinion Quarterly* 36 (1972): 176–87. For a review of the wider communications literature on agenda setting, see McCombs and Shaw, "The Evolution of Agenda-Setting Research: Twenty-Five Years in the Marketplace of Ideas," *Journal of Communications* 43 (spring 1993): 58–67.

32. In a carefully designed experiment, Fay Lomax Cook and colleagues found that news media presentations affected policymakers' perceptions of public concern about an issue—in this case, fraud and abuse in home health care—but not their own judgment of the issue's importance. "Media and Agenda Setting: Effects on the Public, Interest Group Leaders, Policy Makers, and Policy," *Public Opinion Quarterly* 47 (1983): 16–35.

33. David L. Protess and Maxwell McCombs, "The Public Agenda," in *Agenda Setting: Readings on Media, Public Opinion, and Policymaking*, ed. David L. Protess and Maxwell McCombs (Hillsdale, N.J.: Lawrence Erlbaum Associates, 1991), 2.

34. This would confirm the results of other media agenda-setting studies that have found that the media's effect on public opinion varies in accordance with the "obtrusiveness" of an issue, with media presentations having greater impact the less directly the public is affected by an issue. See Harold G. Zucker, "The Variable Nature of News-Media Influence," *Communication Yearbook 2*, ed. Brent D. Ruben (New Brunswick, N.J.: Transaction Books, 1978), 225–45. For a dissenting view, see Lutz Erbring and Edie N. Goldenberg, "Front-Page News and Real-World Cues: A New Look at Agenda-Setting by the Media," *American Journal of Political Science* 24 (1980): 16–49.

35. Everett M. Rogers and James W. Dearing, "Agenda-Setting Research: Where is it Going?" *Communication Yearbook 11*, ed. James A. Anderson (Beverley Hills, Calif.: Sage Publications, 1988), 571.

36. For evidence of the former proposition, see Herbert J. Gans, *Deciding What's News: A Study of* CBS Evening News, NBC Nightly News, Newsweek, *and* Time (New York: Pantheon Books, 1979). For a discussion of the latter, see Jack L. Walker, "Setting the Agenda in the U.S. Senate: A Theory of Problem Selection," *British Journal of Political Science* 7 (1977): 423–45.

37. The notion of journalists as "stand-ins" is presented by Gans in *Deciding What's News,* 292. The concept of "national moods" is developed by John W. Kingdon in *Agendas, Alternatives, and Public Policies* (New York: Harper-Collins, 1984), 153–57.

38. Kim A. Smith, "Newspaper Coverage and Public Concern about Community Issues," in *Agenda Setting: Readings on Media, Public Opinion, and Policymaking*, ed. David L. Protess and Maxwell McCombs (Hillsdale, N.J.: Lawrence Erlbaum Associates, 1991), 52.

39. Mark A. Peterson, "Report from Congress: Momentum toward Health Care Reform in the U.S. Senate," *Journal of Health Politics, Policy, and Law* 17 (fall 1992): 553–54.

40. Russo worked closely with the advocacy group Citizen Action in drafting the bill, which garnered seventy cosponsors in the House.

41. I am not claiming here that committee hearings are a *cause* of the congressional agenda, only that there is a correlation between the agenda of Congress and the agenda of committee hearings. For a theoretical exploration of the ways in which committees set the congressional agenda, see Barbara Sinclair, "The Role of Committees in Agenda Setting in the U.S. Congress," *Legislative Studies Quarterly* 11 (1986): 35–45.

42. These figures on congressional hearings and all that follow were graciously provided to me by Frank R. Baumgartner, Bryan D. Jones, and Jeffery C. Talbert, who compiled them as part of their exhaustive ongoing study of all congressional hearings from 1945 to 1993. All of the data are from National Science Foundation project number SBR-9320922; Frank R. Baumgartner and Bryan D. Jones, principal investigators.

43. Indeed, health care was the fifth most frequent topic of congressional hearings over this period, with 1,408 hearings in total. Foreign affairs and foreign aid was the fourth with 1,491 hearings; banking, finance, and domestic commerce the third with 1,757; defense the second with 1,909; and government operations the first with 2,490. In contrast, the total number of hearings on education over this twelve-year period was 669. Frank R. Baumgartner, et al., "Committee Jurisdictions in Congress, 1980–91" (paper prepared for the annual meeting of the American Political Science Association, New York, September 1994).

44. The health care subtopics eliminated from consideration include the National Institutes of Health, Medicare/Medicaid, drugs and the Food and Drug Administration, medical facilities and nursing homes, medical education, mental illness, fraud and malpractice, long-term care and the elderly, women's health, abortion, veterans' and military health, research and development, AIDS, cancer, heart and lung disease, Alzheimer's disease, and various other diseases.

45. As with congressional hearings, the number of bills introduced in Congress does not provide a precise measure of legislative activity, but it can reveal general trends in an issue's agenda status. The number of bills introduced in Congress has special problems as an indicator, though, because of increases in the number of noncontroversial "commemorative" resolutions introduced in Congress, changes in the rules of cosponsorship in the House, and increasing recourse to the budget reconciliation process, where large numbers of separate policy decisions are packaged together in mammoth omnibus measures.

46. The figures were assembled through computerized searches on the LegiSlate database using preset subject codes. For the 96th and 97th Congresses, the subject code was "national health care." For all other Congresses, it was "national health (insurance) care." I chose to eliminate commemorative resolutions from the figures, but including them does not appreciably change the results.

47. I first eliminated from the totals all bills that dealt with the MCCA, except for the original legislation and the bill that repealed it. I then eliminated all bills

that solely addressed specific programs (for example, the Indian Health Service or Medicare). Finally, I eliminated all bills that dealt only with medical research. As in my earlier tabulations, I did not include commemorative resolutions.

48. In 1990 and 1991, for example, federal Medicaid spending grew by 21 percent and 29 percent, respectively. In 1992 the Congressional Budget Office (CBO) estimated that without measures to check medical inflation, spending for Medicare and Medicaid would account for almost a quarter of the federal budget by the turn of the century. Congressional Budget Office, *Projections of National Health Expenditures* (Washington, D.C.: CBO, October 1992), 6, 41, 45.

49. The sudden emergence of catastrophic health insurance as a policy issue in 1986 illustrates well the instability of the government agenda. As Beth C. Fuchs and John F. Hoadley observed in 1987, "The new drive by the administration and Congress to fill this particular gap in health care coverage is more an accident of politics than the product of any new-found consensus about unmet national needs." "Reflections from Inside the Beltway: How Congress and the President Grapple with Health Policy," *PS* 20 (spring 1987): 212–20. Indeed, Reagan's rambling comments about a possible administration proposal were in response to a question almost completely unrelated to catastrophic health insurance for the elderly (ibid., 213).

50. See, for example, David W. Rohde, *Parties and Leaders in the Postreform House* (Chicago: University of Chicago Press, 1991); Lawrence C. Dodd and Bruce I. Oppenheimer, "Consolidating Power in the House: The Rise of a New Oligarchy," in *Congress Reconsidered*, 4th ed., ed. Lawrence C. Dodd and Bruce I. Oppenheimer (Washington, D.C.: CQ Press, 1989), 39–64; and Roger H. Davidson, "The New Centralization on Capitol Hill," *Review of Politics* 50 (1988): 345–64.

51. James S. Todd, et al., "Health Access America—Strengthening the US Health Care System," *Journal of the American Medical Association* 265 (15 May 1991): 2503–6.

52. Lawrence D. Brown, "National Health Reform: An Idea Whose Political Time Has Come?" *PS: Political Science & Politics* 27 (June 1994): 199.

53. Mark A. Peterson, "Congress in the 1990s: The Change from Iron Triangles to Policy Networks," in *The Politics of Health Care Reform: Lessons from the Past, Prospects for the Future*, ed. James A Morone and Gary S. Belkin (Durham, N.C.: Duke University Press), 103–47.

54. Theodore R. Marmor, *The Politics of Medicare* (Chicago: Aldine, 1973), 108.

55. Peterson, "Congress in the 1990s," 121–25. The figures are from Jack L. Walker's study of interest groups in America. See the posthumous collection of his work, *Mobilizing Interest Groups in America: Patrons, Professions, and Social Movements* (Ann Arbor: University of Michigan Press, 1991).

56. The figures are calculated from the *Encyclopedia of Associations* by Frank R. Baumgartner and Jeffery C. Talbert, and are presented in their article, "From Setting a National Agenda on Health Care to Making Decisions in Congress," *Journal of Health Politics, Policy, and Law* 20 (summer 1995): 438.

57. The relevant committees and their chairs were the Senate Finance Subcommittee on Medicare and Long-Term Care, chaired by Senator Jay Rockefeller; the Senate Labor and Human Resources Committee, chaired by Senator Ted

Kennedy; the House Ways and Means Committee, chaired by Representative Dan Rostenkowski; the House Ways and Means Subcommittee on Health, chaired by Representative Pete Stark; the House Energy and Commerce Committee, chaired by Representative John Dingell; and, finally, the House Health and the Environment Subcommittee, chaired by Representative Henry Waxman. The last holdout was the powerful Senate Finance Committee, chaired by Senator Lloyd Bentsen.

58. Baumgartner and Talbert, "From Setting a National Agenda on Health Care to Making Decisions in Congress," 4–5.

59. Anthony King has argued, for example, that these changes contributed to the "atomization" of the American polity, making leadership more difficult by forcing politicians to build "coalitions in the sand." "The American Polity in the Late 1970s: Building Coalitions in the Sand," in *The New American Political System*, ed. Anthony King (Washington, D.C.: American Enterprise Institute, 1978), 371–95. Even with the growth in the leadership's power in the 1980s, Democratic leaders still find it difficult to act when party members disagree. Indeed, much of the Democratic leadership's renewed effectiveness stemmed not from a more aggressive use of its leadership powers, but from the increasing homogeneity of congressional Democrats. As David Rohde notes, the pattern of Democratic leadership was not of "leaders initiating retaliation against defecting members," but of "a relatively cohesive membership pressuring reluctant party leaders to threaten and impose a range of sanctions against deviating Democrats." In the absence of such cohesion, leadership has proven more elusive. *Parties and Leaders in the Postreform House*, 81.

60. For a discussion of congressional policy expertise in the context of health policymaking, see Mark A. Peterson, "Health Policy Making in the Information Age: Is Congress Better Informed than the President?" Center for American Political Studies Occasional Paper 92–97, Harvard University, August 1992.

61. Kingdon, *Agendas, Alternatives, and Public Policies*, 99–105, 177–78.

62. Ibid., 65–68.

63. John R. Alford and David W. Brady, "Personal and Partisan Advantage in U.S. Congressional Elections, 1846–1990," in *Congress Reconsidered*, 5th ed., ed. Lawrence C. Dodd and Bruce I. Oppenheimer (Washington, D.C.: Congressional Quarterly Press, 1993), 141–57. The article that first sparked extensive scholarly interest in incumbency advantage was David R. Mayhew, "Congressional Elections: The Case of the Vanishing Marginals," *Polity* 6 (1974): 295–317.

64. See the evidence presented in Gary C. Jacobson, *The Politics of Congressional Elections*, 2d. ed. (Boston: Little Brown, 1987), 125–39.

65. Ian Brodie, "Bush Calls Off Overseas Tour after Poll Blow," *Daily Telegraph*, 7 Nov. 1991, 10.

66. Gary C. Jacobson, "The Marginals Never Vanished: Incumbency and Competition in Elections to the U.S. House of Representatives, 1952–82," *American Journal of Political Science* 31 (1987): 126–41.

67. Stephen Ansolabehere, David Brady, and Morris Fiorina, "The Vanishing Marginals and Electoral Responsiveness," *British Journal of Political Science* 22 (1992): 21–38.

68. Keith Krehbiel, *Information and Legislative Organization* (Ann Arbor: University of Michigan Press, 1991), 62.

69. Walker, "Setting the Agenda in the U.S. Senate," 430.

70. House Staff Member 1, interview by author, 17 Aug. 1993.

71. For typical scholarly skepticism, see Robert A. Dahl, "Myth of the Presidential Mandate," *Political Science Quarterly* 105 (1990): 355–72.

72. David R. Mayhew, *Congress: The Electoral Connection* (New Haven: Yale University Press, 1974), 71.

73. Marjorie Randon Hershey, "The Constructed Explanation: Interpreting Election Results in the 1984 Presidential Race," *Journal of Politics* 54 (1992): 943–76.

74. Ibid., 946.

75. Like Hershey, I focused on election coverage in major daily newspapers. Three of the newspapers were from the Northeast (the *Boston Globe, New York Times,* and *Washington Post*). An additional newspaper was chosen from each remaining region of the nation: the South (the *Atlanta Journal*), the Midwest (the *Chicago Tribune*), and the West (the *Los Angeles Times*). Hershey includes these newspapers plus ten others that are not available on the Nexis database and two "black-oriented" newspapers that I chose not to include. Hershey's study examined coverage appearing during two periods: immediately after the election and in the weeks following the presidential inauguration. Since there was no event comparable to a presidential inauguration following the Pennsylvania election, I did not break up the postelection coverage into two discrete periods. Instead, I examined a somewhat longer period after the election than studied by Hershey.

76. By "number of explanations," I mean the number of times a given explanation was cited during the period under consideration, Nov. 6–30, 1991. This is to be contrasted with the "number of different explanations," which is the number of *distinct* explanations of the election that appeared during this period. The former measure tells us which explanations were most prominent in postelection coverage; the latter tells us something about the *diversity* of explanations.

77. Charles Krauthammer, ". . . And the Perils of Populism," *Washington Post*, 8 Nov. 1991, A25.

78. "The Nation: Highlights of Last Week's Elections," *New York Times*, 10 Nov. 1991, sec. 4, p. 3.

79. G. Terry Madonna quoted in Dale Russakoff, " 'The Right to See a Doctor When You're Sick': Wofford's Appeal for Access to Medical Care Creates 'Wildfire' in Senate Race in Pennsylvania," *Washington Post*, 19 Nov. 1991, Z9.

80. Hershey, "Constructed Explanation," 945.

81. Quoted in Dan Balz and Thomas B. Edsall, "In Virginia and Nation, Voters Register Their Discontent," *Washington Post*, 7 Nov. 1991, A1.

82. Quoted in Maralee Schwartz and David Von Drehle, "After Thornburgh's Defeat, Sen. Gramm Again Shifts View of GOP Senate Prospects," *Washington Post*, 17 Nov. 1991, A22.

83. Quoted in Robert Shogan, "Wofford Wins Easily in Pennsylvania Upset," *Los Angeles Times*, 6 Nov. 1991, A1.

84. Quoted in Larry Lipman, "Republicans Unveil Proposal to Widen Health-Care Coverage," *Atlanta Constitution/Journal*, 8 Nov. 1991, A4.

85. Quoted in "Bush: Voter Anger Comes in Loud, Clear; Americans Want Health Care and Economic Relief, He Says; Thornburgh's Pa. Loss Called a Tough Blow," *Atlanta Constitution/Journal*, 6 Nov. 1991, A1.

86. "Here's the Beef," *Washington Post*, 7 Nov. 1991, A22.

87. Of course, the survey results may have been used by journalists without citation. It is very difficult to test this proposition, just as it is difficult to know whether journalists' views of an election are their own or those of an unattributed source. Hershey found that exit polls were "a surprisingly underutilized resource" in newspaper analyses of the 1984 election. My findings, however tentative, support that claim. Hershey, "Constructed Explanation," 965.

88. "Senate GOP Task Force Unveils Health Care Plan," *Houston Chronicle*, 8 Nov. 1991, A8.

89. Julie Kosterlitz, "A Sick System," *National Journal*, 15 Feb. 1992, 376.

90. This adds a further wrinkle to Hershey's argument. Hershey claims that the force of current political events and the struggle among activists to promote their explanations of election results are *separate* influences on the process by which the conventional wisdom about an election develops. In most cases, however, one would expect events and interpretations to be interdependent and mutually reinforcing. If certain explanations are favored, and if politicians use these explanations to craft their political strategies, then political events will reflect widely held presumptions about election results. Moreover, if journalists gravitate toward explanations that are relevant to current events, they will further reinforce these dominant explanations. Whatever the source of consensus explanations, therefore, the interaction between media coverage and political action will tend to increase their credence and impact.

91. For a discussion of positive-feedback effects, see Frank R. Baumgartner and Bryan D. Jones, *Agendas and Instability in American Politics* (Chicago: University of Chicago Press, 1993), 16–18.

92. Anthony Downs, "Up and Down with Ecology—The 'Issue Attention Cycle,'" *Public Interest* 28 (1972): 38–50.

93. A Kaiser Commonwealth Survey conducted two months after the Pennsylvania election, for example, showed 33 percent of respondents supporting the play-or-pay approach, 30 percent the single-payer approach, and 27 percent the tax-credit approach. Thomas, *Health Care in America*, 140.

Chapter 2

1. The pathbreaking neoclassical work of the 1960s was Kenneth J. Arrow's "Uncertainty and the Welfare Economics of Medical Care," *American Economic Review* 53 (December 1963): 941–73. Only a minuscule portion of the formal literature on health economics predates Arrow's classic article. The first U.S. conference on the subject appeared in 1962, the first international conference in 1973, and the first widely adopted textbook in 1979. Victor R. Fuchs, *The Future of Health Policy* (Cambridge: Harvard University Press, 1993), 27–40.

2. Theodore R. Marmor, "Entrepreneurship in Public Management: Wilbur Cohen and Robert Ball," in *Leadership and Innovation: Entrepreneurs in Gov-*

ernment, ed. Jameson W. Doig and Erwin C. Hargrove (Baltimore: Johns Hopkins University Press, 1990), 235.

3. Margaret Weir, *Politics and Jobs: The Boundaries of Employment Policy in the United States* (Princeton: Princeton University Press, 1992), 58–59.

4. Steven E. Rhoads, "Economists and Policy Analysis," in *New Strategic Perspectives on Social Policy*, ed. John E. Tropman, Milan J. Dluhy, and Roger M. Lind (New York: Pergamon Press, 1981), 131–32.

5. See Lawrence D. Brown, *Politics and Health Care Organizations: HMOs as Federal Policy* (Washington, D.C.: Brookings, 1983). Most notable among these attempts was the HMO Act of 1973, the subject of Brown's account, and the National Health Planning and Resource Development Act of 1974, examined at length by James A. Morone in *The Democratic Wish: Popular Participation and the Limits of American Government* (New York: Basic Books, 1990), 271–321.

6. William Glaser, "The Competition Vogue and its Outcome," *The Lancet* 341 (27 Mar. 1993): 806.

7. For a nontechnical analysis of the economistic worldview, see Stephen E. Rhoads, *The Economist's View of the World: Government, Markets, and Public Policy* (Cambridge: Cambridge University Press, 1985).

8. See Brown, *Politics and Health Care Organizations*, 13–17. The term is his.

9. On the beliefs and values of neoconservatives, see Peter Steinfels's now-outdated *The Neoconservatives* (New York: Touchstone, 1979). For a neoconservative's analysis of neoconservatism, see Irving Kristol, "What is a Neo-Conservative?" *Newsweek*, 19 Jan. 1976, 87.

10. See for example Aaron Wildavsky, "Doing Better and Feeling Worse: The Political Pathology of Health Policy," *Daedalus* 106 (winter 1977): 105–23; Leon R. Kass, "Regarding the End of Medicine and the Pursuit of Health," *Public Interest* 40 (summer 1975): 11–43; and Nathan Glazer, "Paradoxes of Health Care," *Public Interest* 22 (winter 1971): 62–77.

11. Ivan Illich, *Medical Nemesis: The Expropriation of Health* (New York: Pantheon, 1976). For a cogent analysis of the doubts about the efficacy of medical care that surfaced in the 1970s, see Paul Starr, *The Social Transformation of American Medicine: The Rise of a Sovereign Profession and the Making of a Vast Industry* (New York: Basic Books, 1982), 408–11.

12. Theodore R. Marmor, *Understanding Health Care Reform* (New Haven: Yale University Press, 1994), 140.

13. Weir, *Politics and Jobs*, 100–103.

14. Martin S. Feldstein, *Hospital Costs and Health Insurance* (Cambridge: Harvard University Press, 1981), and *Economic Analysis for Health Service Efficiency: Econometric Studies of the British National Health Service* (Chicago: Markham, 1968); Milton Friedman, *Capitalism and Freedom* (Chicago: University of Chicago Press, 1962); Milton Friedman and Simon Kuznets, *Income from Independent Professional Practice* (New York: National Bureau of Economic Research, 1945).

15. Friedman, *Capitalism and Freedom*, 149–59

16. On the "oligopsonistic" power of the Blues, see Mark Pauly, "Competition in Health Insurance Markets," *Law and Contemporary Problems* 51 (spring 1988): 237–71.

17. The seminal explanation of the distortionary effects of third-party insurance is Arrow, "Uncertainty and the Welfare Economics of Medical Care."

18. See Theodore R. Marmor, Richard Boyer, and Julie Greenberg, "Medical Care and Procompetitive Reform," in *Political Analysis and American Medical Care*, ed. Theodore R. Marmor (New York: Cambridge University Press, 1983), 239–61.

19. Martin S. Feldstein, "The Welfare Loss of Excess Health Insurance," *Journal of Political Economy* 81 (March/April 1973): 251–80. For a sympathetic review of the literature on the tax treatment of health insurance, see Stephen A. Woodbury and Wei-Jang Huang, *The Tax Treatment of Fringe Benefits* (Kalamazoo, Mich.: W. E. Upjohn Institute for Employment Research, 1991).

20. This consequence of insurance is termed "moral hazard," the incentive for people with insurance to take greater risks than they would otherwise, knowing their losses will be covered. With health insurance, however, the problem is compounded, for it is widely recognized that moral hazard applies to both consumers and suppliers of health services.

21. Paul B. Ginsburg, "The Competition Debate Five Years Later," *Journal of Health Economics* 3 (1984): 307–11.

22. Or so the proponents of cost-sharing argue. The empirical evidence is irrefutable on the first point: cost-sharing influences individual decisions to seek care. It is on the second point—that these individual effects hold at the aggregate level—that health policy researchers have failed to find confirming evidence. For a comprehensive bibliography of the English-language literature on cost-sharing, see Vandha Bhatia, et al., *User Charges in Health Care: A Bibliography* (Ontario: Premier's Council on Health, Well-being and Social Justice, June 1994). For a sympathetic review of the U.S. literature on cost-sharing, see Michael A. Morrissey, *Price Sensitivity In Health Care: Implications for Health Policy* (Washington, D.C.: The NFIB Foundation, 1992).

23. Clark C. Havighurst, *Deregulating the Health Care Industry* (Cambridge, Mass.: Ballinger, 1982).

24. For a list of these cases, see Thomas L. Greany, "Competitive Reform in Health Care: The Vulnerable Revolution," *Yale Journal on Regulation* 5 (1988): 179–213.

25. Paul M. Ellwood, Jr., "Program for Survival: A Proposed Course of Action for the Health Insurance Industry" (address before the Health Insurance Council, Denver, Colo., 5 Oct. 1967).

26. Harold Luft, "How Do Health Maintenance Organizations Achieve Their 'Savings'?" *New England Journal of Medicine* 298 (June 1978): 1336–43.

27. The RAND study estimated that the annual expenditures of study participants enrolled in Seattle's Group Health Cooperative were 28 percent lower than the expenditures of participants in fee-for-service plans. Willard G. Manning, et al., "A Controlled Trial of the Effect of Prepaid Group Practice on Use of Services," *New England Journal of Medicine* 310 (7 June 1984): 1505–10.

28. Starr, *Social Transformation of American Medicine*, 396.

29. Paul M. Ellwood, Jr., et al., "Health Maintenance Strategy," *Medical Care* 9 (May–June 1971): 291.

30. Scott Fleming, Deputy Assistant Secretary for Health Policy Development, "Structured Competition within the Private Sector" (HEW memorandum, May 1973).

31. Joseph A. Califano, Jr., *Governing America* (New York: Simon & Schuster, 1981), 95.

32. Alain C. Enthoven to Joseph A. Califano, "Consumer Choice Health Plan: An Approach to National Health Insurance Based on Regulated Competition in the Private Sector," 22 Sept. 1977.

33. For more on these initiatives and their fates, see Thomas R. Oliver, "Health Care Market Reform in Congress: The Uncertain Path from Proposal to Policy," *Political Science Quarterly* 106 (1991): 453–77.

34. Enthoven, "Consumer Choice Health Plan," 5.

35. For a critique of the plan by an advocate of the cost-sharing approach, see Lawrence Seidman, "Consumer Choice Health Plan and the Patient Cost-Sharing Strategy: Can they be Reconciled?" in *A New Approach to the Economics of Health Care*, ed. Mancur Olson (Washington, D.C.: American Enterprise Institute, 1981), 450–66.

36. See for example Henry Aaron, "Orange Light for the Competitive Model," *Journal of Economics* 2 (1983): 281–84; and Bruce C. Vladek, "The Market vs. Regulation in Health Care," *Milbank Memorial Fund Quarterly* 59 (1981): 209–23.

37. See Joseph P. Newhouse, "Is Competition the Answer?" *Journal of Health Economics* 1 (1981): 109–16, and "Rate Adjusters for Medicare under Capitation," *Health Care Financing Review*, annual supplement (1986): 45–56.

38. Starr, *Social Transformation of American Medicine*, 415.

39. Marmor, Boyer, and Greenberg, "Medical Care and Procompetitive Reform," 248–49.

40. Alain Enthoven, *Theory and Practice of Managed Competition* (New York: North-Holland, 1988), 82.

41. Alain Enthoven, phone interview by author, 21 Dec. 1994.

42. Alain Enthoven and Richard Kronick, "A Consumer Choice Health Plan for the 1990s," parts I and II, *New England Journal of Medicine* 320 (5 and 12 Jan. 1989): 29–37, 94–101.

43. Ibid., 32, 29.

44. Alain C. Enthoven, *Health Plan: The Only Practical Solution to the Soaring Cost of Medical Care* (Reading, Mass.: Addison-Wesley, 1980), 115–17.

45. Alain Enthoven, phone interview by author, 21 Dec. 1994.

46. Mary Jane England, interview by author, 18 Aug. 1993.

47. Quoted in Linda A. Bergthold, *Purchasing Power in Health: Business, the State, and Health Care Politics* (New Brunswick, N.J.: Rutgers University Press, 1990), 43.

48. Ibid., 43.

49. Ibid., 45.

50. Mary Jane England, interview by author, 18 Aug. 1993. The 1984 figure is from Bergthold, *Purchasing Power in Health*, 43.

51. Mary Jane England, interview by author, 18 Aug. 1993.

52. Carol Cronin and Karen Milgate, *A Vision of the Future Health Care Delivery System: Organized Systems of Care* (Washington, D.C.: WBGH, 1993), v.

53. Lynn Etheredge, "A Pro-Competitive Regulatory Structure for the American Health System" (discussion paper for Jackson Hole Conference, Jackson Hole, Wyoming, February 1991).

54. Lynn Etheredge, interview by author, 6 Aug. 1993.

55. Alain Enthoven, "A Route to Universal Health Insurance and Comprehensive Market Reform through Small Employment Group Market Reform" (discussion paper for Jackson Hole Conference, Jackson Hole, Wyoming, February 1991).

56. The "outcomes movement" has been around for quite some time. It received a big boost from studies indicating that a large share of health spending—perhaps 30 percent—goes to care for which the risk exceeds the benefit. Outcomes researchers argue that because of this high level of "inappropriate" care, health spending can be reduced without resorting to rationing. See, for example, David M. Eddy, "Connecting Values and Costs: Whom Do We Ask, and What Do We Ask Them?" *Journal of the American Medical Association* 264 (3 Oct. 1990): 1737–39; and John E. Wenneberg, "Outcomes Research, Cost Containment, and the Fear of Health Care Rationing," *New England Journal of Medicine* 323 (25 Oct. 1990): 1202–4. For an appropriately skeptical view, see Marmor, *Understanding Health Care Reform*, 86–106.

57. Greany, "Competitive Reform in Health Care," 183.

58. Starr, *Social Transformation of American Medicine*, 27.

59. Louis Harris and Associates, Inc., *Trade-Offs and Choices: Health Policy Options of the 1990s* (New York: Metropolitan Life Insurance Company, 1991), 66.

60. Lynn Etheredge, interview by author, 6 Aug. 1993.

61. These were the American Group Practice Association, which was represented by Kermit Knudsen, and the American College of Physicians, which was represented by its executive vice president, John Ball. It was not until February 1992 that other representatives of provider groups—specifically James Todd and John Crosby of the AMA and James Bentley of the American Hospital Association—came to Jackson Hole.

62. On AMA hegemony, see the classic study by James G. Burrow, *AMA: Voice of American Medicine* (Baltimore: Johns Hopkins, 1963). On AMA decline, see Morone, *Democratic Wish*, 253–321; and Sherwin Yih-Wen Chen, "Policies in Decline: The American Medical Association and National Health Insurance, 1945-Present" (senior thesis, Harvard College, 1994).

63. For evidence that biased selection not only exists but is a problem of considerable magnitude, see Joseph P. Newhouse, "Patients at Risk: Health Reform and Risk Adjustment," *Health Affairs* 13 (spring 1994): 132–46.

64. However, many large firms that self-insure purchase stop-loss insurance to cover catastrophic costs. In 1992, for example, 80 percent of firms with more than one thousand employees self-insured and 64 percent of those that self-insured purchased stop-loss coverage. Of firms with fewer than one thousand workers, on the other hand, the comparable figures were 50 percent and 96 percent, respectively. Foster Higgins, *1992 Health Care Benefits Survey* (Princeton, N.J.: Foster Higgins, 1992), 19.

65. Here I am speaking principally of the PPO, which is the fastest growing variety of health plan. Ninety-three percent of PPOs reimburse hospitals on a

discounted basis and 83.5 percent make per diem payments (the total exceeds 100 percent because plans were asked to identify all the approaches they used). By contrast, less than 1 percent of conventional insurers pay "discounted usual and customary charges," while none make per diem payments. Prospective Payment Assessment Commission, *Optional Hospital Payment Rates*, Congressional Report C-92–03 (Washington, D.C.: ProPAC, March 1992), 71.

66. Lawrence D. Brown, "The Managerial Imperative and Organizational Innovation in Health Services," in *The U.S. Health Care System: A Look to the 1990s*, ed. Eli Ginzberg (Totowa, N.J.: Rowman and Allenheld, 1985), 35.

67. For a representative view, see Bernard R. Tresnowski, "Building a Foundation for Universal Access," *Inquiry* 29 (summer 1992): 269–73.

68. This conflict came to a head in mid-1992 when Cigna left the Health Insurance Association of America, a politically powerful trade organization that generally reflects the position of small-claims insurers. Cigna was followed by Aetna, Metropolitan Life, Travelers, and, most recently, Prudential.

69. Paul Ellwood and Lynn Etheredge, "The 21st Century American Health System: Overview and Accountable Health Partnerships" (Jackson Hole Group, 3 Sept. 1991), 1.

70. Lynn Etheredge, interview by author, 6 Aug. 1993.

71. Ellwood and Etheredge, "21st Century American Health System," 2–3.

72. Alain Enthoven, "The 21st Century American Health System: Market Reform and Universal Coverage" (Jackson Hole Group, 4 Sept. 1991); Paul Ellwood, "The 21st Century American Health System: Uniform Effective Health Benefits" (Jackson Hole Group, 30 Aug. 1991); Lynn Etheredge, "The 21st Century American Health System: The Public-Private Health Partnership and the National Health Board" (Jackson Hole Group, 4 Sept. 1991).

73. Indeed, the proposal itself was not published until 1992, well after it had gained national prominence, and then only in a fairly obscure journal. Paul M. Ellwood, Alain C. Enthoven, and Lynn Etheredge, "The Jackson Hole Initiatives for a Twenty-First Century American Health Care System," *Health Economics* 1 (1992): 149–68.

74. Lynn Etheredge, interview by author, 6 Aug. 1993.

75. The newspaper's attacks on alternative reform designs, particularly the single-payer option, could be harsh. One editorial, for example, ridiculed the Canadian model, claiming that "the rationing [Canada] imposes means that, for instance, women must wait months for a simple pap smear." "Ringing: The Health Care Alarm," *New York Times*, 8 Nov. 1991, A26. The editorial provoked an angry response from the Canadian ambassador to the United States, D. H. Burney, who correctly pointed out that the assertion was totally false. Letter to the Editor, *New York Times*, 21 Nov. 1991, A26.

76. Michael Weinstein, phone interview by author, 8 Sept. 1993.

77. Ibid.

78. Jack Rosenthal, phone interview by author, 3 Apr. 1995.

79. "The Wrong Medicine," *New York Times*, 26 May 1991, E10; "The Right Medicine," *New York Times*, 27 May 1991, A18; "And Here's How to Fix It," *New York Times*, 22 July 1991, A14.

80. There has been a good deal of speculation about the relationship between Weinstein and Enthoven. A number of journalists have written that Enthoven was one of Weinstein's professors or even his dissertation adviser. Neither assertion is true. Weinsten and Enthoven had remarkably similar backgrounds (both received their undergraduate degrees in economics from Stanford and their doctorates in economics from MIT), and they shared a common outlook based on their training in economics. But the two did not speak or meet before 1991.

81. Michael Weinstein, phone interview by author, 8 Sept. 1993.

82. Rima Cohen, interview by author, 12 Aug. 1993.

83. Lynn Etheredge, interview by author, 6 Aug. 1993.

84. "Ringing: The Health Care Alarm," *New York Times*, 8 Nov. 1991, A26; "Is It Health Care Reform: A Test," *New York Times*, 17 Nov. 1991, sec. 4, p. 16.

85. See the discussions in Kenneth Shepsle, "The Changing Textbook Congress," in *Can the Government Govern?* ed. John E. Chubb and Paul E. Peterson (Washington, D.C.: Brookings, 1989), 248; Jill Quadagno, *The Transformation of Old Age Security: Class and Politics in the American Welfare State* (Chicago: University of Chicago Press, 1988); and Nelson W. Polsby, *Congress and the Presidency* (Englewood Cliffs, N.J.: Prentice-Hall, 1986).

86. Shepsle, "Changing Textbook Congress," 253–56.

87. This point is explored by Thomas Byrne Edsall and Mary D. Edsall in *Chain Reaction: The Impact of Race, Rights, and Taxes on American Politics* (New York: W. W. Norton, 1991), 5.

88. For a cogent discussion of the sectional split in the Democratic party and how it has changed, see David W. Rohde, *Parties and Leaders in the Postreform House* (Chicago: University of Chicago Press, 1991), 45–65.

89. *Congressional Quarterly* (*CQ*) has constructed an index of the split between northern and southern Democrats: the "conservative coalition support score." *CQ* defines a "conservative coalition" as a voting alliance of Republicans and southern Democrats against northern Democrats in Congress. Such alliances have occurred with decreasing frequency over the last two decades but with increasing success. In 1991, for instance, a conservative coalition appeared on 11 percent of votes and was successful 91 percent of the time. In 1970, by contrast, a conservative coalition appeared twice as often—on 22 percent of votes—but was victorious only 66 percent of the time. In 1991 about 70 percent of southern Democrats voted with a conservative coalition when one formed. *Congressional Quarterly* (28 Dec. 1991): 3793–97. Analyzing voting patterns over a longer time-period, David Rohde documents a considerable increase in Democratic unity since the early 1970s. In 1971 and 1972, for example, the average southern Democrat toed the party line *less than half the time* on votes dividing majority parties. From then on, southern support for Democratic positions on partisan votes increased steadily, peaking at 76 percent in 1987 and 1988. Rohde, *Parties and Leaders in the Postreform House*, 55–56.

90. Ronald Pollack and Phyllis Torda make this case for play-or-pay in "The Pragmatic Road toward National Health Insurance," *American Prospect* 6 (summer 1991): 93–101.

91. Atul Gawande, phone interview by author, 1 Sept. 1993.

92. Anand Raman, phone interview by author, 2 Sept. 1993.

93. Lynn Etheredge, interview by author, 6 Aug. 1993.

94. Employee Benefit Research Institute, *Sources of Health Insurance and Characteristics of the Uninsured: Analysis of the March 1992 Current Population Survey*, SR-16, EBRI Issue Brief Number 133 (Washington, D.C.: EBRI, January 1993), 1.

95. Kenneth E. Thorpe, "Expanding Employment-Based Health Insurance: Is Small Group Reform the Answer?" *Inquiry* 29 (Summer 1992): 128.

96. Paul Starr, "Design of Health Insurance Purchasing Cooperatives," *Health Affairs*, supplement (1993): 61.

97. One might predict that this would open the door to adverse selection, since firms with low expected costs might purchase insurance outside of the HIPC to get a lower rate. There is no question that adverse selection would have been serious under the CDF proposal, but it would have been mitigated somewhat by the fact that tax subsidies were contingent on participation.

98. H.R. 5936, "The Managed Competition Act of 1992," introduced by Representative Jim Cooper (twenty-one cosponsors).

99. S.R. 3299, "The Managed Competition Act of 1992," introduced by Senator David Boren (one cosponsor).

100. Another small and little-noted difference between the Jackson Hole proposal and the CDF bill is that the CDF proposal would have taxed *employers* for contributions exceeding the cost of the lowest-priced plan, rather than making those contributions part of workers' taxable income.

101. "Administration to Come Forward Shortly with System Reform Proposal, Darman Says," *BNA Pension and Benefits Report*, 22 Apr. 1992, 717. The Heritage proposal is presented in Stuart M. Butler, "A Tax Reform Strategy to Deal with the Uninsured," *Journal of the American Medical Association* 265 (15 May 1991): 2541–44.

102. "The President's Comprehensive Health Care Reform Program" (Washington, D.C.: White House, 6 Feb. 1992). For descriptions of the plan, see Congressional Research Service, *The President's Health Care Reform Proposal*, CRS Report for Congress 92–285 EPW (Washington, D.C.: Congressional Research Service, 5 Mar. 1992); and White House, *Cost Containment in the President's Comprehensive Health Reform Program* (Washington, D.C.: White House, 7 May 1992).

103. Initially, Bush's health policy advisers had hoped to finance the proposal in part by capping the tax exclusion of employer-provided health insurance. But the proposed measure, a cornerstone of the Jackson Hole model, provoked such an avalanche of protest from health insurers and congressional Republicans that Darman postponed the printing of the 1992 federal budget to strike it from the text.

104. For one, they would have been completely unregulated and therefore susceptible to abuse. For another, they would have been plagued by the problem of adverse selection, since small business participation was entirely voluntary.

105. Mary Beth Fiske, interview by author, 17 Aug. 1993.

106. Robin Toner, "Hillary Clinton's Potent Brain Trust on Health Reform," *New York Times*, 28 Feb. 1993, C1.

107. David U. Himmelstein, Sidney Wolfe, and Steffie Woolhandler, "Mangled Competition," *American Prospect* 13 (spring 1993): 120, 116.

108. Morone, *Democratic Wish*, 270.

109. Alain Enthoven, phone interview by author, 21 Dec. 1994.

Chapter 3

1. Although the Progressive campaign was the first political movement in support of publicly sponsored health insurance, it is worth emphasizing two key distinctions between the Progressive Era and later reform periods. First, the Progressive campaign was waged entirely at the *state* level (most notably in California and New York). Second, the main concern of Progressive reformers was not lack of access to medical care but poverty caused by sickness.

2. Ronald L. Numbers, *Almost Persuaded: American Physicians and Compulsory Health Insurance, 1912–1920* (Baltimore: Johns Hopkins University Press, 1978), 97.

3. Theodore R. Marmor, *The Politics of Medicare* (Chicago: Aldine, 1973), 9.

4. Still, this was only a fifth of the population, and most did not have insurance for physician services. Paul Starr, *The Social Transformation of American Medicine: The Rise of a Sovereign Profession and the Making of a Vast Industry* (New York: Basic Books, 1982), 311.

5. Marmor, *Politics of Medicare*, 41.

6. Ibid., 61–78.

7. Quoted in James A. Morone, *The Democratic Wish: Popular Participation and the Limits of American Government* (New York: Basic Books, 1990), 263.

8. The former two figures are from ibid., 266; the latter two, from Congressional Budget Office, *Trends in Health Spending: An Update* (Washington, D.C.: CBO, June 1993), 76.

9. Lawrence D. Brown, *Politics and Health Care Organizations: HMOs as Federal Policy* (Washington, D.C.: Brookings, 1983), 13.

10. Robert R. Alford, *Health Care Politics and Interest Group Barriers to Reform* (Chicago: University of Chicago Press, 1975).

11. Richard M. Nixon, "Special Message to the Congress Proposing a National Health Strategy," *The Public Papers of the Presidents of the United States, 1971* (Washington, D.C.: Government Printing Office, 1972), 170–86.

12. Richard M. Nixon, "Special Message to the Congress Proposing a Comprehensive Health Insurance Plan," *The Public Papers of the Presidents of the United States, 1974* (Washington, D.C.: Government Printing Office, 1975), 132–40.

13. Starr, *Social Transformation of American Medicine*, 405.

14. Ibid., 411–13.

15. Mark A. Peterson, "Congress in the 1990s: From Iron Triangles to Policy Networks," in *The Politics of Health Care Reform: Lessons from the Past, Prospects for the Future*, ed. James A Monroe and Gary S. Belkin (Durham, N.C.: Duke University Press, 1994), 105.

16. For more on the beliefs of the reformers who were in the executive branch from the New Deal until the passage of Medicare, see Daniel S. Hirshfield, *The*

Lost Reform: The Campaign for Compulsory Health Insurance in the United States from 1932 to 1943 (Cambridge: Harvard University Press, 1970); Marmor, *Politics of Medicare*, and "Entrepreneurship in Public Management: Wilbur Cohen and Robert Ball," in *Leadership and Innovation: Entrepreneurs in Government*, ed. Jameson W. Doig and Erwin C. Hargrove (Baltimore: Johns Hopkins University Press, 1990); and Monte M. Poen, *Harry S. Truman versus the Medical Lobby: The Genesis of Medicare* (Columbia: University of Missouri Press, 1979).

17. Noting in his special message to Congress that national health care spending represented only 4 percent of national output, Truman argued that America could "afford to spend more for health." Harry S. Truman, "Special Message to Congress Recommending a Comprehensive Health Program," *The Public Papers of the Presidents of the United States, 1945* (Washington, D.C.: Government Printing Office, 1946), 475–91.

18. Real health care spending per capita grew by 3.8 percent from 1970 to 1980 and by 4.4 percent from 1980 to 1990, according to Joseph P. Newhouse, "Medical Care Costs: How Much Welfare Loss?" *Journal of Economic Perspectives* 6 (summer 1992): 3–21.

19. Per capita in 1990 the U.S. spent roughly 45 percent more than Canada, almost three-quarters more than Germany, more than twice as much as Japan, and nearly three times as much as the United Kingdom. George J. Schieber, Jean-Pierre Poullier, and Leslie M. Greenwald, "U.S. Health Expenditure Performance: An International Comparison and Data Update," *Health Care Financing Review* 13 (summer 1992): 5.

20. Although there are a few scattered references to the term in the health policy literature before the late 1980s, *single payer* appears to have gained currency as a reform label after David Himmelstein and Steffie Woolhandler advocated establishing a "single payer for health services" in "A National Health Program for the United States: A Physicians' Proposal," *New England Journal of Medicine* 320 (1989): 102–8. Using the Nexis computerized database's news library, I could find only twenty references to the term prior to 1990, compared with 115 in 1991 and 636 in 1992.

21. The literature on foreign health care systems is extensive and growing. For a good survey of the terrain, see Organization for Economic Cooperation and Development, *The Reform of Health Care: A Comparative Analysis of Seven OECD Countries* (Paris: OECD, 1992); and Joseph White, "An International Perspective on American Reform," *Domestic Affairs* 2 (winter 1993–94): 195–244. On comparative expenditures, see Schieber, Poullier, and Greenwald, "U.S. Health Expenditure Performance."

22. Thus in some countries, such as Germany and the Netherlands, only people whose incomes fall below a set threshold are required to join the publicly sponsored plan.

23. Schieber, Poullier, and Greenwald, "U.S. Health Expenditure Performance," 4.

24. Monoposony—the counterpart of monopoly—obtains when there is only one buyer of a particular good or service. The term does not apply perfectly to the Canadian system. There are actually numerous provincial systems purchasing care, and doctors and hospitals have themselves organized into cohesive bargain-

ing units at the provincial level, leading to a market structure closer to bilateral monopoly (one buyer, one seller). Nonetheless, the term captures the general notion that the ability of the Canadian system and other foreign systems to contain costs is related to their concentrated purchasing power.

25. Theodore R. Marmor, Jerry L. Mashaw, and Philip L. Harvey, *America's Misunderstood Welfare State: Persistent Myths, Enduring Realities* (New York: Basic Books, 1990): 199. See also Theodore R. Marmor and Jerry L. Mashaw, "Canada's Health Insurance and Ours: The Real Lessons, the Big Choices," *American Prospect* 3 (fall 1990): 18–29.

26. John K. Iglehart, "Health Policy Report: Canada's Health System," part I, *New England Journal of Medicine* 315 (17 July 1986): 204–5.

27. H.R. 1300, "Universal Health Care Act of 1991," introduced by Representative Marty Russo (seventy cosponsors).

28. Peterson, "Congress in the 1990s," 38.

29. Indeed, at one point Princeton health economist Uwe Reinhardt asked David Nexon, Kennedy's principal health policy adviser, if the senator was going to footnote Richard Nixon's employment-based national health plan in Health America. Mark A. Peterson, "Momentum toward Health Care Reform in the U.S. Senate," *Journal of Health Politics, Policy, and Law* 17 (fall 1992): 560.

30. The entire data series—from 1958, when the Gallup poll first asked about public trust in government, to 1992—is reprinted in Robert J. Blendon and Ulrike S. Szalay, "The Politics of Health Care Reform: The Public's Perspective," in *Reforming the System: Containing Health Care Costs in an Era of Universal Coverage*, ed. Robert J. Blendon and Tracey Stelzer Hyams (New York: Faulkner & Gray, 1992), 57.

31. See Louis Hartz, *The Liberal Tradition in America* (New York: Harcourt Brace Jovanovich, 1955); and Anthony King, "Ideas, Institutions, and the Policies of Governments: A Comparative Analysis," parts I and II, *British Journal of Political Science* 3, no. 3 (1973): 291–313, and 3, no. 4 (1973): 409–23. James A. Morone's *Democratic Wish* offers one of the more nuanced analyses of American political culture. He posits that antistatist sentiments coexist with a "democratic wish" for direct communal democracy and social solidarity. This wish, Morone argues, can serve as a powerful symbol for reformers wishing to extend state power. Interestingly enough, Morone applies this theory to American medical politics.

32. Reprinted in Starr, *Social Transformation of American Medicine*, 285. The Library of Congress could not find the quote in any of Lenin's writings (ibid., 285).

33. Daniel Levine, *Poverty and Society: The Growth of the American Welfare State in International Comparison* (New Brunswick: Rutgers University Press, 1988), 56–62.

34. See for example Ellen M. Immergut, "Institutions, Veto Points, and Policy Results: A Comparative Analysis of Health Care," *Journal of Public Policy* 10 (October–December 1990): 391–416; and David Wilsford, *Doctors and the State: The Politics of Health Care in France and the United States* (Durham, N.C.: Duke University Press, 1991).

35. Iglehart, "Canada's Health Care System," 204, 206.

36. S.R. 1446, "Health USA Act of 1991," introduced by Senator J. Robert Kerrey (one cosponsor). A full description of the plan is provided by E. Richard Brown, "Health USA: A National Health Program for the United States," *Journal of the American Medical Association* 267 (22–29 January 1992): 552–58. For the political rationale behind the plan, see Robert Kerrey, "Why America Will Adopt Comprehensive Health Care Reform," *American Prospect* 6 (summer 1991): 81–91.

37. S.R. 2153, "The American Health Security Plan," introduced by Senator Tom Daschle (two cosponsors).

38. See the survey evidence presented in Robert J. Blendon and Karen Donelan, "The Public and the Future of U.S. Health Care System Reform," in *System in Crisis: The Case for Health Care Reform*, ed. Robert J. Blendon and Jennifer N. Edwards (New York: Faulkner & Gray, 1991), 189. Since the polls Blendon and Donelan cite did not ask respondents to weigh additional taxes against new benefits or lower private payments, their results should be interpreted with caution. For more on the public's willingness to pay for national health insurance, see the conflicting accounts offered by Robert J. Blendon, et al., "The Beliefs and Values Shaping Today's Health Reform Debate," *Health Affairs* 1 (spring 1994): 274–84, on the one hand; and Lawrence R. Jacobs and Robert Y. Shapiro, "Public Opinion's Tilt against Private Enterprise," *Health Affairs* 1 (spring 1994): 285–98, on the other.

39. This is partly due to the insuperable difficulty of predicting patient costs in advance. Since current risk-adjustment technologies are highly imperfect (and will undoubtedly remain so), the economic cost of treating patients and the capitated, risk-adjusted payments made by purchasing cooperatives will rarely coincide. See Joseph P. Newhouse, "An Iconoclastic View of Health Cost Containment," *Health Affairs* supplement (1993): 167. On a more fundamental level, the whole concept of economic cost is extremely slippery in this context. For example, the higher medical spending of the United States relative to Canada is largely accounted for by greater administrative costs, higher physician incomes, larger hospitals staffs, and extra amenities for insured patients. Are all these *necessary* components of the cost of American medical care? The advocate of competition might argue, "Yes, if that is what consumers want." But then one is back to the insoluble problem of engendering market pricing.

40. For more on the Proposition 13 campaign and its aftermath, see David O. Sears and Jack Citrin, *Tax Revolt: Something for Nothing in California*, 2d ed. (Cambridge: Harvard University Press, 1985).

41. Linda A. Bergthold, *Purchasing Power in Health: Business, the State, and Health Care Politics* (New Brunswick, N.J.: Rutgers University Press, 1990), 69–89.

42. Ibid., 180.

43. Foster Higgins, *1992 Health Care Benefits Survey* (Princeton, N.J.: Foster Higgins, 1992), 8.

44. Zelman, phone interview by author, 2 Sept. 1993.

45. Linda Bergthold, phone interview by author, 6 Dec. 1994.

46. John Garamendi, "California Health Care in the 21st Century: A Vision for Reform" (Office of the Insurance Commissioner, State of California, Sacra-

mento, February 1992). See also Garamendi, "Taking California Health Insurance into the 21st Century," *Journal of American Health Policy*, May–June 1992, 10a-13a.

47. Garamendi, "California Health Care in the 21st Century," 5.

48. Walter Zelman, interview by author, 20 Oct. 1994.

49. The itinerary of the trip is contained in Marc Associates to Walter Zelman, facsimile, 20 Mar. 1992, Walter Zelman Papers, Records of the White House Health Care Interdepartmental Working Group, National Archives, College Park, Md.

50. Senator Bingaman ended up introducing three managed-competition bills in the 102d Congress: S. 2675, "Health Insurance Purchasing Cooperatives Act" (one cosponsor); S. 3165, "Health Insurance Purchasing Cooperatives Act" (three cosponsors); and S. 3300, "21st Century Health Care Act" (no cosponsors). The last of these bills, the most comprehensive of the three, would have essentially created Garamendi-style single sponsors in every state.

51. Walter Zelman, interview by author, 20 Oct. 1994.

52. "California's Medical Model," *New York Times*, 17 Feb. 1992, A16.

53. Michael M. Weinstein, "Is it Jackson Hole–Compatible?" *New York Times*, 22 June 1992, A16.

54. Starr, *Social Transformation of American Medicine*.

55. Paul Starr, phone interview by author, 15 Feb. 1995. The essays include Paul Starr, "The Undelivered Health System," *Public Interest* 42 (winter 1976): 66–85; and "Controlling Medical Costs Through Countervailing Power," *Working Papers for a New Society* 5 (summer 1977): 10–11, 97–98.

56. Starr himself was highly critical of the pay-or-play approach, and his approach to reform was quite different. Nonetheless, several aspects of the Starr proposal were similar in philosophy to play-or-pay. First, Starr focused heavily on the need to recognize public-sector fiscal constraints—a belief that was shared by advocates of play-or-pay. This focus led him to design a plan funded through employer and employee contributions rather than taxes. Second, the plan was designed to accommodate private-sector interests in much the same way as Health America—giving them a little and asking for their cooperation in return. Finally, Starr was willing, in the interest of compromise, to have the HIPCs be mandatory for only small and mid-sized firms. Under play-or-pay it is presumably these same firms that will choose the "pay" alternative. Thus the HIPCs in Starr's approach replace the public plan in play-or-pay.

57. Paul Starr, *The Logic of Health Care Reform: Transforming American Medicine for the Better* (Knoxville: Whittle Direct Books, 1992).

58. Testimony of Paul Starr before the Committee on Finance, U.S. Senate, 6 May 1992.

59. Paul Starr, phone interview by author, 15 Feb. 1995; Walter Zelman, interview by author, 20 Oct. 1994.

60. S. 1720 "Health Care for All Americans Act," introduced by Senator Edward Kennedy, 6 Sept. 1979. The proposal is remarkably similar to Kerrey's Health USA, with one critical exception. Rather than be administered by state governments, the Kennedy proposal would have established five national consortia of insurers, each representing a segment of the insurance industry (the Blues,

commercial indemnity carriers, staff-model HMOs, independent practice associations, and self-insurance plans). The consortia would have overseen private insurers and distributed risk-adjusted capitated payments to the plans. Despite the considerable overlap between Kennedy's 1979 proposal and the Kerrey, Garamendi, and Starr proposals, none of the latter-day proponents of regulated competition within a budget has described the Kennedy proposal as an important antecedent of the liberal synthesis. For that reason, as well as in the interest of brevity, I omitted it from my analysis.

61. Paul Starr, *The Logic of Health Care Reform: Why and How the President's Plan Will Work*, rev. and exp. ed. (New York: Penguin, 1994), xvi.

62. Linda Bergthold, phone interview by author, 6 Dec. 1994.

Chapter 4

1. "Presidential Debate in Richmond, Virginia: October 15, 1992," *Weekly Compilation of Presidential Documents* 28 (26 Oct. 1992): 1953–55.

2. The most widely cited figure is 1 percent of total spending in 1984. Roger Reynolds, John A. Rizzo, and Martin L. Gonzalez, "The Cost of Medical Professional Liability," *Journal of the American Medical Association* 257 (22–29 May 1987): 2776–81.

3. Henry J. Kaiser Family Foundation Poll (Menlo Park, Calif.: Henry J. Kaiser Family Foundation, 28 Oct. 1992). Reprinted in Robert J. Blendon, et al., "The Implications of the 1992 Presidential Election for Health Care Reform," *Journal of the American Medical Association* 268 (16 Dec. 1992): 3371–75.

4. Blendon, et al., "Implications of the 1992 Presidential Election," 3372.

5. Adam Pertman, "Democrats Scored with Most Groups, Exit Polls Report," *Boston Globe*, 4 Nov. 1992, 24.

6. The National Leadership Coalition for Health Care Reform grew out of an earlier group, mainly comprised of providers, called the National Leadership Coalition for Health Care. Participants in the new coalition included Bethlehem Steel, Chrysler, Dayton Hudson, General Electric, Georgia Pacific, International Paper, Lockheed, Meredith Corporation, Northern Telecom, Pacific Gas & Electric, Safeway, Southern California Edison, Time Warner, Westinghouse, Xerox, and the major unions. See Cathie Jo Martin, "Together Again: Business, Government, and the Quest for Cost Containment" (paper prepared for delivery at the Annual Meeting of the American Political Science Association, Chicago, 1992).

7. The meeting was also attended by Theodore Marmor, who argued in support of Canadian-style national health insurance. According to Marmor, Clinton specifically rejected a Canadian-style proposal at this meeting because he did not think it was politically feasible. See Tom Hamburger, Ted Marmor, and Jon Meacham, "What the Death of Health Reform Teaches Us about the Press," *Washington Monthly*, November 1994, 35.

8. Ron Pollack, phone interview by author, 3 Nov. 1994.

9. Bill Clinton for President Committee, "Bill Clinton's American Health Care Plan: National Health Insurance Reform to Cut Costs and Cover Every-

body" (Little Rock, January 1992). See also Michael Duffy and Dick Thompson, "Behind Closed Doors," *Time*, 20 Sept. 1993, 60–63. A journalistic account dramatizing behind-the-scenes interchanges (and including a number of serious factual errors), this article contains some interesting statements by Clinton's campaign advisers about the process by which Clinton developed his proposal during the campaign.

10. Bruce Fried, phone interview by author, 27 Oct. 1993.

11. Robert Pear, "Two in Bush Cabinet Attack Democrats on Health Care," *New York Times*, 29 Jan. 1992, A12. See also Mark A. Peterson, "Momentum toward Health Care Reform in the U.S. Senate," *Journal of Health Politics, Policy, and Laws* 17 (fall 1992): 565.

12. David Nexon, interview by author, 12 Aug. 1993

13. This and similar points about Clinton's philosophy were emphasized by Atul Gawande, phone interview by author, 1 Sept. 1993 and 25 Oct. 1993; Ira Magaziner, interview by author, 21 Oct. 1994; Kenneth Thorpe, phone interview by author, 28 Oct. 1994; and Joshua Wiener, interview by author, 19 Oct. 1994.

14. Walter Zelman, phone interview by author, 2 Sept. 1993, and interview by author, 20 Oct. 1994.

15. Theodore Marmor, conversation with author, 3 May 1995. Ron Pollack also recalled the governor's interest in the approach, which he says was evident as early as late January. Pollack, phone interview by author, 3 Nov. 1994.

16. Atul Gawande, phone interview by author, 1 Sept. 1993.

17. Ibid.

18. Bill Clinton and Al Gore, *Putting People First: How We Can All Change America* (New York: Times Books, 1992), 107–11.

19. Clinton and Gore, *Putting People First*, 110.

20. Ira Magaziner, interview by author, 21 Oct. 1994; Joshua Wiener, interview by author, 19 Oct. 1994.

21. Bill Clinton, "The Clinton Health Care Plan," *New England Journal of Medicine* 327 (10 Sept. 1992): 804–7.

22. Alain Enthoven, "Commentary: Measuring the Candidates on Health Care," *New England Journal of Medicine* 327 (10 Sept. 1992): 807–9.

23. Uwe Reinhardt, "Commentary: Politics and the Health Care System," *New England Journal of Medicine* 327 (10 Sept. 1992): 809–11.

24. Bill Clinton, "A New Covenant," speech before the Democratic National Convention, New York, 16 July 1992.

25. Atul Gawande, phone interview by author, 1 Sept. 1993.

26. Jack Ebeler, phone interview by author, 27 Oct. 1993.

27. Judith Feder, "The Proposal Won't Save Money," *New York Times*, 25 Jan. 1992, A23.

28. Since the group was so large, it is difficult to identify the exact distribution of opinion. Nonetheless, Wiener's claim that "there wasn't a single person in the Washington-based group that you could have identified as a major proponent of managed competition in July or early August 1993" is probably correct. Joshua Wiener, interview by author, 19 Oct. 1994. The only possible exception was Kenneth Thorpe, who by mid-1992 was advocating that cost-control measures

rely on both competition and a national health care budget. Kenneth E. Thorpe, "The Best of Both Worlds: Merging Competition and Regulation," *Journal of American Health Policy*, July–August 1992, 20–24; and phone interview by author, 28 Oct. 1994.

29. See Jeremy Rosner, "A Progressive Plan for Affordable Universal Health Care," in *Mandate for Change*, ed. Will Marshall and Martin Schram (New York: Berkeley Books, 1993), 107–28.

30. Ira Magaziner, interview by author, 21 Oct. 1994.

31. For a critical review of these ventures see Jacob Weisberg, "Dies Ira," *New Republic*, 24 Jan. 1994, 18–24. For a more positive account, see Steven Pearlstein, "The Many Crusades of Ira Magaziner," *Washington Post*, 18 Apr. 1993, W12.

32. Ira Magaziner, interview by author, 21 Oct. 1994; Starr, phone interview by author, 15 Feb. 1995.

33. Since his days as a student leader, Magaziner has compiled a long record of tackling complex problems, formulating equally complex solutions, and, in several high-profile cases, seeing his proposed solutions ignored, repudiated, or politically defeated. The most notable of these cases was the political defeat in 1984 of the Greenhouse Compact, an ambitious proposal to revitalize Rhode Island's economy by establishing a state commission to fund high-technology research and assist specific firms and industries. Magaziner was able to attract support for the proposal among Rhode Island elites, but voters overwhelmingly rejected it in a statewide referendum. See Howard Kurtz, "A 'New Idea' Fizzles on Launch: Skeptical Rhode Islanders Wouldn't Go for 'Industrial Policy,' " *Washington Post*, 15 July 1984, B5; Pearlstein, "Many Crusades of Ira Magaziner"; and Weisberg, "Dies Ira," 20–21.

34. Although Magaziner knew of the Garamendi proposal, he spoke with Zelman only after his mid-July conversation with Starr. Walter Zelman, interview by author, 20 Oct. 1994.

35. Bruce Fried, phone interview by author, 27 Oct. 1993.

36. In July a full 71 percent of voters believed that Clinton would do a better job than President Bush in responding to the problem of providing affordable health care to all Americans; only 14 percent of voters believed that Bush would do a better job than Clinton. By late August, the share of voters naming Clinton had fallen to 55 percent, with Bush's share up to 27 percent. Perot's return to the presidential race skewed the results of the two final polls—the first of which was conducted in early October and showed Bush with a 20 percent share of voters, Clinton with a 62 percent share, and Perot with an 8 percent share; and the second of which was conducted in late October and showed Bush with an 18 percent share, Clinton with a 52 percent share, and Perot with a 16 percent share. Henry J. Kaiser Family Foundation Polls (Menlo Park, Calif.: Henry J. Kaiser Family Foundation, July–October 1992).

37. Atul Gawande, phone interview by author, 1 Sept. 1993.

38. Atul Gawande, phone interview by author, 1 Sept. 1993.

39. Jack Ebeler, phone interview by author, 27 Oct. 1993. My account of the meeting is based in part on Ebeler's contemporaneous notes and in part on inter-

views with the key participants, including Atul Gawande, phone interview by author, 1 Sept. 1993 and 25 Oct. 1993; Ira Magaziner, interview by author, 21 Oct. 1994; Paul Starr, phone interview by author, 15 Feb. 1995; Kenneth Thorpe, phone interview by author, 28 Oct. 1994; and Walter Zelman, phone interview by author, 2 Sept. 1993, and interview by author, 20 Oct. 1994.

40. Atul Gawande, phone interview by author, 1 Sept. 1993.

41. On democratic ritual and symbolic participation, see Robert A. Dahl, *Who Governs? Democracy and Power in an American City* (New Haven: Yale University Press, 1961), especially 112–14; Murray Edelman, *The Symbolic Uses of Politics* (Chicago: University of Chicago Press, 1985); and Robert R. Alford and Roger Friedland, "Political Participation in Public Policy," *Annual Review of Sociology* 1 (1975): 429–79.

42. Jack Ebeler, phone interview by author, 27 Oct. 1993; Kenneth Thorpe, phone interview by author, 28 Oct. 1994; Joshua Wiener, interview by author, 19 Oct. 1994.

43. Atul Gawande, phone interview by author, 1 Sept. 1993.

44. Ron Pollack, phone interview by author, 3 Nov. 1994.

45. Bill Clinton, speech delivered at Merck Pharmaceuticals, Rahway, N.J., 24 Sept. 1992.

46. Clinton/Gore National Campaign, "Controlling Costs and Guaranteeing Care for All: The Clinton/Gore Health Care Plan" (Little Rock, September 1992).

47. The most relevant literature on potential job losses comes from research on the effects of increases in the minimum wage. Although the early minimum wage literature estimated a 1 to 3 percent job loss for every 10 percent increase in the minimum wage, the most recent research suggests that few if any jobs are lost to increases in the minimum wage. In fact, some of the more recent cross-sectional studies indicate that increases in the minimum wage may have a salutary effect on employment, although these findings are the subject of considerable debate.

48. David Nexon, interview by author, 12 Aug. 1993.

49. Medicare—often called the "third rail" of American politics because touching it can mean instant political death for an elected official—was conspicuously absent from Clinton's campaign statements about health care reform. The September 24 press release, for example, only mentioned Medicare to vow that under Clinton's proposal "Medicare payments to providers . . . [would] be subject to budgetary limits." Within the campaign, however, the fate of Medicare was a key subject of debate. The campaign's estimates of the costs of the proposal depended to a significant extent on savings in Medicare. Moreover, there was some talk of wooing Medicare beneficiaries into the purchasing cooperatives with long-term care or prescription drug coverage.

50. "Clinton Waffles on Health," *New York Times*, 27 Sept. 1992, A16.

51. Atul Gawande, phone interview by author, 1 Sept. 1993; Paul Starr, phone interview by author, 15 Feb. 1995; Kenneth Thorpe, phone interview by author, 28 Oct. 1994.

52. John Garamendi, "Clinton Offers a Managed Health-Care Plan," letter to the editor, *New York Times*, 8 Oct. 1992, A20.

53. Clinton/Gore National Campaign, press release (Little Rock, 8 Oct. 1992).

54. "The Bush-Clinton Health Reform," *New York Times*, 10 Oct. 1992, A20.

55. Gary C. Jacobson and Michael A. Dimock, "Checking Out: The Effects of Bank Overdrafts on the 1992 House Elections," *American Journal of Political Science* 38 (1994): 601–24.

56. However, Carter had enjoyed significantly larger Democratic majorities than Clinton when he took office. That this did him little good warns against treating the size of party margins and the condition of party control as overriding determinants of presidential success. For other important factors that affect the president's ability to enact domestic legislation, see Mark A. Peterson, *Legislating Together: The White House and Capitol Hill from Eisenhower to Reagan* (Cambridge: Harvard University Press, 1990). On the surprising inconsequentiality of divided versus unified party control for the passage of major domestic legislation, see David R. Mayhew, *Divided We Govern: Party Control, Lawmaking, and Investigations, 1946–90* (New Haven: Yale University Press, 1991).

Chapter 5

1. Morris Fiorina presents some survey data that comfirm this impression in his *Divided Government*, 2d ed. (Needham Heights, Mass.: Allyn & Bacon, 1996). He shows that in the past three decades the "center" has collapsed as public views of the power of the federal government have polarized. In 1965, "when Lyndon Johnson and the 89th Congress were adopting 'Great Society' initiatives, a plurality of the electorate expressed satisfaction with the level of activity of the federal government, and a significant minority favored additional activity. In contrast, when Bill Clinton and the 103rd Congress were trying to pass a National Health Care plan, only a tiny minority were satisfied with the federal government as is, while large and equal-sized pluralities wanted to go in opposite directions" (ibid., 174).

2. Hugh Heclo, "Clinton's Health Reform in Historical Perspective," in *The Problem That Won't Go Away: Re-forming U.S. Health Care Financing*, ed. Henry J. Aaron (Washington, D.C.: Brookings, 1996), 15–33. Heclo—with the benefit of hindsight, it must be said—accurately diagnoses many of the key strategic difficulties the president faced. But he does so at the cost of making the president's decision to pursue comprehensive health care reform almost completely unintelligible. In contrast, I have sought to show why the president (and so many others) believed his proposal would pass *despite* the obstacles before him and why he was willing to take the risk that it would not. Heclo notes with disdain that "by the time 1992 drew to an end, comprehensive health reform had come to be defined, and explicitly promised, as a purely presidential initiative that would be fully worked out, presented to Congress in the first one hundred days, and passed in the first year of the new administration" (ibid., 30). The question that this book illuminates—and which Heclo fails to address—is *Why?*

3. Atul Gawande, phone interview by author,17 May 1995.

4. See for example Dana Priest, "Mixed Signals on Health Care: Transition Team Leaders Tend toward Different Approaches," *Washington Post*, 23 Nov. 1992, A19.

5. Lynn Etheredge, phone interview by author, 17 May 1995.

6. The budgetary options were later described in Julie Kosterlitz, "O.K. Bill, It's Time to Pick Your Remedy," *National Journal*, 23 Jan. 1993, 200.

7. "Health Reform Technical Work Group on Market Restructuring and Cost Containment," report prepared for the presidential transition office's health policy group, 19 Jan. 1993, Walter Zelman Papers, Records of the White House Health Care Interdepartmental Working Group, National Archives, College Park, Md.

8. Atul Gawande, phone interview by author, 17 May 1995.

9. On the Kennedy task forces, see Arthur M. Schlesinger, Jr., *A Thousand Days: John F. Kennedy in the White House* (New York: Fawcett World Library, 1967), 148–54.

10. Paul Starr, *The Logic of Health Care Reform: Why and How the President's Plan Will Work*, rev. and exp. ed. (New York: Penguin, 1994), xxiv.

11. Paul Starr to Ira Magaziner, 16 Dec. 1992, Ira Magaziner Papers, Records of the White House Health Care Interdepartmental Working Group, National Archives, College Park, Md.

12. Ira Magaziner, interview by author, 21 Oct. 1994. It seems clear, however, that Magaziner knew with a fair degree of certainty that he would head the policy development process even before January.

13. On the Johnson task forces, see Norman C. Thomas and Harold L. Wolman, "The Presidency and the Task Force Device," *Public Administration Review* 29 (1969): 459–71.

14. See Jason Matthew Solomon, "Fighting for Health Security: An Analysis of the Critical Decisions Presidents Make When Pursuing Legislative Initiatives," senior thesis, Harvard College, March 1995, 72–73.

15. Ibid., 72.

16. Starr, *Logic of Health Care Reform*, xxix.

17. The memory of the tollgate meetings remained vivid for many of the working group participants, including Linda Bergthold, phone interview by author, 6 Dec. 1994; Joshua Wiener, interview by author, 19 Oct. 1994; and Walter Zelman, interview by author, 20 Oct. 1994.

18. For example, the working group effort did not initially "include separate groups on mental health services, the Indian Health Service, or academic health centers." Starr, *Logic of Health Care Reform*, xxx.

19. Linda Bergthold, phone interview by author, 6 Dec. 1994.

20. Not all members of Congress were equally involved, however. Senate Democrats sent more staff than House Democrats, while conservative Democrats evinced relatively little interest in the process. And, of course, no congressional Republicans contributed staff (though some Republican governors did). Rima Cohen, interview by author, 12 Aug. 1993; Mary Beth Fiske, interview by author, 17 Aug. 1993; House Staff Member 1, interview by author, 17 Aug. 1993; House Staff Member 2, interview by author, 10 Aug. 1993; House Staff Member 3, interview by author, 10 Aug. 1993; David Nexon, interview by author, 12 Aug. 1993; Shiela Nix, interview by author, 10 Aug. 1993; Senate Staff Member, interview by author, 11 Aug. 1993; Mendi Sossaman, interview by author, 29 July 1993.

21. Linda Bergthold, phone interview by author, 6 Dec. 1994.

22. See Starr, *Logic of Health Care Reform*, xxx.

23. Ibid., xxxi.

24. Paul Starr to Ira Magaziner, memoranda, 21, 22, 23 Apr. and 17, 26, 28 May 1993, Paul Starr Papers, Records of the White House Health Care Interdepartmental Working Group, National Archives, College Park, Md.

25. Starr to Magaziner, 17 May 1993, Starr Papers.

26. Starr to Magaziner, 23 Apr. 1993, Starr Papers.

27. On the virtually insuperable difficulties with the tax cap, see Joseph White, *Competing Solutions: American Health Care Proposals and International Experience* (Washington, D.C.: Brookings, 1995), 292–308.

28. Adam Clymer, "Official Virtually Rules Out Taxing of Health Benefits," *New York Times*, 6 Apr. 1993, A20; Alain Enthoven to Ira Magaziner, 10 May 1993, Magaziner Papers.

29. Atul Gawande and Walter Zelman to Bob Boorstin and Stan Greenberg, memorandum, 19 Mar. 1993, Magaziner Papers.

30. Thomas L. Friedman, "New Tax on Goods is Weighed to Pay for Health Care," *New York Times*, 15 Apr. 1993, A1. This was merely one of the countless articles on taxes that appeared not just on April 15, but throughout the development of the proposal. The possibility of new taxes fixated the press: between April and August, more than twice as many stories (7 percent) focused on the value-added tax or a possible payroll tax than focused on the uninsured (3 percent). "Newspaper Coverage of Health Reform, April 1–July 31, 1993: A Content Analysis," *Columbia Journalism Review*, supplement, November/December 1993. Virtually none of these stories compared the magnitude of the new taxes under consideration to the total cost of medical care in the United States or mentioned that these taxes would offset current private payments.

31. Ira Magaziner, interview by author, 21 Oct. 1994.

32. The final CBO analysis of the CDF bill is contained in Congressional Budget Office, *Estimates of Health Care Proposals from the 102nd Congress* (Washington, D.C.: CBO, July 1993), 47–57.

33. Paul Starr to Ira Magaziner, memorandum, 3 Feb. 1993, Starr Papers.

34. The division of opinion and time constraints are described in Paul Starr to Ira Magaziner, memorandum, 7 Feb. 1993, Starr Papers.

35. The division between the health policy team and the economic advisers is mentioned in Bob Woodward, *The Agenda: Inside the Clinton White House* (New York: Simon & Schuster, 1994), 197–200; and Paul Starr, "What Happened to Health Care Reform?" *American Prospect* 20 (winter 1995): 24. The same split plagued Carter's attempt to forward a reform proposal, and Ford's before him.

36. Paul Starr to Ira Magaziner, memorandum, 22 Mar. 1993, Starr Papers; Paul Starr, working paper, "Why Not Medicare-for-all? Here's Why," 25 Mar. 1993, Starr Papers, 3. Similar themes are sounded in a response by Starr to a policy proposal submitted to the White House by the health policy expert Karen Davis, a critic of managed competition. Paul Starr, working paper, "Karen Davis' 'Alternative Model,' " 22 Mar. 1993, Starr Papers.

37. James A. Morone, "Nativism, Hollow Corporations, and Managed Competition: Why the Clinton Health Care Reform Failed," *Journal of Health Politics, Policy, and Law* 20 (summer 1995): 396.

38. The first-year records of Kennedy, Johnson, Nixon (both terms), and Carter offer striking evidence of the decline in presidential legislative success. An average of 72 percent of the legislative items introduced by these presidents between January and April of the first year were enacted. For items introduced between April and July, the success rate dropped to 39 percent. And for items introduced between July and the end of the year, the success rate was only 25 percent. According to Paul Light, "This pattern does not seem to reflect an effort to present the 'easier' items first." Paul Charles Light, *The President's Agenda* (Baltimore: Johns Hopkins University Press, 1982), 45.

39. On the potential risks of the strategy, see Joe White, "Guest Observer: Put Reconciliation on a Fast Track, but Not Health Care," *Roll Call*, 4 Mar. 1993.

40. Solomon, "Fighting for Health Security," 56–57; Starr, "What Happened to Health Care Reform?" 21.

41. William W. Lammers, "Policy Achievements in the First Year: Carter, Reagan, and Clinton" (paper prepared for the annual meeting of the American Political Science Association, New York, September 1994), 29.

42. Starr, "What Happened to Health Reform?" 21.

43. Richard E. Neustadt, *Presidential Power and the Modern Presidents: The Politics of Leadership from Roosevelt to Reagan* (New York: Free Press, 1991), 34.

44. Solomon, "Fighting for Health Security," 61, 69n.

45. Trudy Lieberman, "The Selling of 'Clinton Lite,' " *Columbia Journalism Review*, March 1994, 20–22. Indeed, between January 1, 1993, and September 30, 1994, Cooper received more from health and insurance political action committees and large donors than any other member of Congress—some $668,000. Citizen Action, "Unhealthy Money: The 1994 Elections and Contributions from the Health and Insurance Industries," part XIII, Research Report by Citizens Fund, Washington, D.C., November 1994, 4.

46. Congressional Budget Office, *Estimates of Health Care Proposals*, 15.

47. Paul Starr and Walter A. Zelman, "A Bridge to Compromise: Competition under a Budget," *Health Affairs* supplement (1993): 7–23.

48. Starr, "What Happened to Health Reform?" 24.

49. Walter Zelman to Ira Magaziner, memorandum, 16 Jan. 1993, Magaziner Papers.

50. Paul Starr, phone interview by author, 15 Feb. 1995.

51. Paul Ellwood to Ira Magaziner, facsimile, 14 Feb. 1993, Magaziner Papers; Alain Enthoven to Ira Magaziner, 26 Feb. 1993, Magaziner Papers; Paul Ellwood to Ira Magaziner, 18 Mar. 1993, Magaziner Papers; Alain Enthoven to Magaziner, 10 May 1993, Magaziner Papers. The hyperbolic phrase is from Alain C. Enthoven and Sara J. Singer, "A Single-Payer System in Jackson Hole Clothing," *Health Affairs* 13 (spring 1994): 81–95.

52. Paul Ellwood to Ira Magaziner, 18 Mar. 1993, Magaziner Papers.

53. Robert Patricelli to Ira Magaziner, 10 May 1993, Magaziner Papers.

54. Starr, "What Happened to Health Care Reform?" 24–25.

55. David Vogel, "Why Businessmen Distrust Their State: The Political Consciousness of American Corporate Executives," *British Journal of Political Science* 8 (1978): 45.

56. Walter Zelman to Bob Boorstin, memorandum, 10 Mar. 1993, Zelman Papers.

57. On this point, see the lively and perceptive analysis offered in James A. Morone, "The Ironic Flaw in Health Care Competition: The Politics of Markets," in *Competitive Approaches to Health Care Reform*, ed. Richard J. Arnould, Robert F. Rich, and William D. White (Washington, D.C.: The Urban Institute, 1993), 207–22.

58. Starr, working paper, "A Conundrum," n.d., Starr Papers.

59. Memorandum, "Talking about Health Care," n.d., Zelman Papers.

60. See Theda Skocpol, "The Rise and Resounding Demise of the Clinton Health Security Plan," in *The Problem That Won't Go Away: Reforming U.S. Health Care Financing*, ed. Henry J. Aaron (Washington, D.C.: Brookings, 1996), 42.

61. Robert J. Blendon, et al., "A Survey of American Attitudes toward Health Care Reform," survey conducted by the Program on Public Opinion and Health Care, Harvard School of Public Health and Mattila & Kiley, Inc., for the Robert Wood Johnson Foundation, June 1993, 18.

62. "Talking about Health Care," Zelman Papers.

63. See Robert J. Blendon, Tracey Stelzer Hyams, and John M. Benson, "Bridging the Gap between Expert and Public Views on Health Care Reform," *Journal of the American Medical Association* 269 (19 May 1993): 2573–78.

64. "Talking about Health Care," Zelman Papers.

65. Skocpol, "Rise and Resounding Demise of the Clinton Health Security Plan," 41.

66. See Samuel Kernell, *Going Public: New Strategies of Presidential Leadership*, 2d ed. (Washington, D.C.: Congressional Quarterly Press, 1993), 196–99. Of course, deference is not the same as favoritism. Presidents from Thomas Jefferson on have complained bitterly about the harsh treatment they receive at the hands of the press (which, according to Jefferson, presented "only a caricature of disaffected minds"). The evidence suggests, however, that press coverage of the president remains quite favorable on balance. What has changed is not the valence of media coverage (although there may well be sharper cycles of critical coverage today), but the need for presidents and their staff to structure presidential actions and public appeals around journalistic routines and standards of newsworthiness. Timothy E. Cook and Lyn Ragsdale, "The President and the Press: Negotiating Newsworthiness at the White House," in *The Presidency and the Political System*, 4th ed., ed. Michael Nelson (Washthington, D.C.: CQ Press, 1995), 297–330.

67. "Newspaper Coverage of Health Reform, April 1–July 31, 1993"; "Newspaper Coverage of Health Reform, September 1–November 30, 1993: A Content Analysis" (a joint project by the Kaiser Family Foundation, Times Mirror Center for the People & the Press, and *Columbia Journalism Review*, n.d.).

68. Julie Kosterlitz, interview by author, 18 Oct. 1994.

69. On public confusion, see Robert J. Blendon, et al., "How Much Does the Public Know about Health Reform?" *Journal of American Health Policy*, January–February 1994, 26–31. On public cynicism, see Joseph N. Capella, Kathleen Hall Jamieson, "Public Cynicism and News Coverage in Campaigns and Policy Debates: Three Field Experiments" (paper prepared for the annual meeting of the American Political Science Association, New York, September 1994).

70. "Clinton's Health Plan: Transcript of President's Address to Congress on Health Care," *New York Times*, 23 Sept. 1993, A24.

71. Bert A. Rockman, "The Clinton Presidency and Health Care Reform," *Journal of Health Politics, Policy, and Law* 20 (summer 1995): 401.

72. Starr reports that the morning after the speech "Stanley Greenberg . . . crowed that overnight surveys showed [the proposal] winning two-thirds approval." Starr, "What Happened to Health Care Reform?" 20.

73. Robert Pear, "GOP Promises Help on Medical Care," *New York Times*, 16 Sept. 1993, A21.

74. Adam Clymer, "The Clinton Plan is Alive on Arrival," *New York Times*, 3 Oct. 1993, E3. Cited in Skocpol, "Rise and Resounding Demise of the Clinton Health Security Plan," 34.

75. Blendon, et al., "How Much Does the Public Know about Health Reform?" 26–31.

76. Starr, "What Happened to Health Care Reform?" 25.

77. Theda Skocpol, *Boomerang: Clinton's Health Security Effort and the Turn against Government* (New York: Norton, 1996), 90.

78. James Fallows, "A Triumph of Misinformation," *Atlantic Monthly*, January 1995, 37.

79. The Annenberg Public Policy Center, "The Role of Advertising in the Health Care Debate, Part Three: The Effect of 'Harry and Louise' on the Press, the Public and the Political Process" (Philadelphia, August 1994), 2.

80. Darrel M. West and Diane J. Heith, "Harry and Louise Go to Washington: Political Advertising and Health Care Reform" (paper prepared for the annual meeting of the American Political Science Association, New York, September 1994), 8.

81. "Newspaper Coverage of Health Reform, September 1–November 30, 1993," 8, 10–11.

82. The complete text of the "Working Group Draft" of the proposal, dated September 7, is contained in *The President's Health Security Plan: The Complete Draft and Final Reports of the White House Domestic Policy Council* (New York: Times Books, 1993).

83. Dana Priest, "Health Groups Launch Ad Blitzes Criticizing Increased Federal Role," *Washington Post*, 25 Jan. 1994, A8.

84. "Newspaper Coverage of Health Reform, September 1–November 30, 1993," 4.

85. Starr, "What Happened to Health Care Reform?" 23.

86. Adam Clymer, "Polls Say People Expect Delay on the Health Plan," *New York Times*, 17 Nov. 1993, A22.

87. The percentage of Americans who believed the press was doing a good job or better covering health reform fell from 72 percent in September to 63 percent

in December and to 54 percent in January 1994. "Newspaper Coverage of Health Reform, September 1–November 30, 1993," 5.

88. The explanation I have offered for the decline in public support for the Clinton plan holds quite well for another dramatic reversal in public opinion on health policy: the passage and subsequent repeal of the Medicare Catastrophic Coverage Act. Between the passage of the MCCA in 1988 and its repeal in 1989, the percentage of elderly Americans who supported the bill dropped an astounding fifty percentage points. The reason: a poorly crafted, poorly understood, and poorly explained bill ran into a well-financed interest group campaign. The tenor of media coverage of the catastrophic bill tracked the decline in elderly support so perfectly, one study concluded, "that the press could represent all the formative influences on public opinion." David P. Fan and Lois Norem, "The Media and the Fate of the Medicare Catastrophic Extension Act," *Journal of Health Politics, Policy, and Law* 17 (spring 1992): 56.

89. "Text of President Clinton's Health Care Reform Package, 'The Health Security Act,'" *BNA's Health Care Policy Report*, special supplement (1 Nov. 1993).

90. Robert Pear, "Clinton's Health Plan: The Overview," *New York Times*, 28 Oct. 1993, A1.

91. The proponents of the managed-competition approach, from Alain Enthoven to the CDF members, never truly acknowledged the amount of regulation that would be required to make managed competition work.

Conclusion

1. Theodore J. Lowi, *The End of Liberalism: The Second Republic of the United States*, 2d ed. (New York: Norton, 1979).

2. Robert Salisbury, "The Paradox of Interest Groups in Washington—More Groups, Less Clout," in *The New American Political System*, 2d ed., ed. Anthony King (Washington, D.C.: American Enterprise Institute, 1990), 203–29.

3. Mark A. Peterson, "Congress in the 1990s: The Change from Iron Triangles to Policy Networks," in *The Politics of Health Care Reform: Lessons from the Past, Prospects for the Future*, ed. James A. Morone and Gary S. Belkin (Durham: Duke University Press, 1994), 123. For an explanation of why citizen groups have proliferated, see Jack L. Walker, *Mobilizing Interest Groups in America: Patrons, Professions, and Social Movements* (Ann Arbor: University of Michigan Press, 1991).

4. See for example Jeff Frieden, "Sectoral Conflicts in U.S. Foreign Economic Policy, 1914–1940," in *The State and American Foreign Economic Policy*, ed. G. John Ikenberry, David A. Lake, and Michael Mastanduno (Ithaca: Cornell University Press, 1988); Thomas Ferguson, "From Normalcy to the New Deal: Industrial Structure, Party Competition, and American Public Policy in the Great Depression," *International Organization* 38 (winter 1984): 41–94; and James Kurth, "The Political Consequences of the Product Cycle: Industrial History and Political Outcomes," *International Organization* 33 (winter 1979): 1–34.

5. This is one of the core arguments of the state-centric and new institutionalist literature that has become so central to contemporary sociological and political

theory. Some of the most important works in this genre are Theda Skocpol, *Protecting Soldiers and Mothers: The Political Origins of Social Policy in the United States* (Cambridge: Harvard University Press, 1992); Peter Hall, *Governing the Economy: The Politics of State Intervention in Britain and France* (New York: Oxford University Press, 1986); Peter Evans, Dietrich Rueschemeyer, and Theda Skocpol, eds., *Bringing the State Back In* (Cambridge: Cambridge University Press, 1985); and James G. March and Johan P. Olsen, "The New Institutionalism: Organizational Factors in Political Life," *American Political Science Review* 78 (1984): 734–49.

6. Thomas R. Oliver, "Health Care Market Reform in Congress: The Uncertain Path from Proposal to Policy, " *Political Science Quarterly* 106 (1991): 466–68.

7. See Peter Alexis Gourevitch's analysis of support coalitions in *Politics in Hard Times: Comparative Responses to International Economic Crises* (Ithaca: Cornell University Press, 1986), 238–40.

8. Lynn Etheredge, interview by author, 6 Aug. 1993.

9. The *locus classicus* of transactional analysis is Raymond Bauer, Ithiel de Sola Pool, and Lewis Anthony Dexter, *American Business and Public Policy* (New York: Atherton, 1963).

10. See Giandomenico Majone, *Evidence, Argument, and Persuasion in the Policy Process* (New Haven: Yale University Press, 1989).

11. Deborah A. Stone, "Causal Stories and the Formation of Policy Agendas," *Political Science Quarterly* 104 (1989): 281–300. By causal stories Stone understands "stories that describe harms and difficulties, attribute them to actions of other individuals or organizations, and thereby claim the right to invoke government power to stop the harm"(ibid., 282). Although Stone has identified a critical aspect of agenda setting, I do not think that she satisfactorily answers the question of why a problem (once it has been perceived as a problem and whatever the classification of its cause) is considered amenable to government action.

12. Jack L. Walker, "The Diffusion of Knowledge, Policy Communities and Agenda Setting: The Relationship of Knowledge and Power," in *New Strategic Perspectives on Social Policy*, ed. John E. Tropman, Milan J. Dluhy, and Roger M. Lind (New York: Pergamon Policy Studies, 1981), 75–96. The concept of policy communities obviously owes its inspiration to Thomas S. Kuhn's famous description of scientific communities. See his *The Structure of Scientific Revolutions*, 2d ed. (Chicago: University of Chicago Press, 1970). On the partisan and ideological fragmentation of networks of national elites, see John P. Heinz, Edward O. Laumann, Robert H. Salsibury, and Robert L. Nelson, "Inner Circles or Hollow Cores? Elite Networks in National Policy Systems," *Journal of Politics* 52 (May 1990): 356–90.

13. John W. Kingdon, *Agendas, Alternatives, and Public Policies* (New York: HarperCollins, 1984), 126.

14. Ibid., 133.

15. See James A. Morone, *The Democratic Wish: Popular Participation and the Limits of American Government* (New York: Basic Books, 1990).

16. Rashi Fein, "Economists and Health Reform," *PS: Political Science & Politics* 27 (June 1994): 193.

17. Kingdon, *Agendas, Alternatives, and Public Policies*, 134–38; and Nelson W. Polsby, *Political Innovation in America: The Politics of Policy Initiation* (New Haven: Yale University Press, 1984), 147.

18. Rima Cohen, interview by author, 12 Aug. 1993.

19. Mary Beth Fiske, interview by author, 17 Aug. 1993.

20. Polsby, *Political Innovation in America*, 158.

21. Of course, analysis can be influential, but only insofar as it is "adaptable to political rhetoric and position taking." Martha Derthick and Paul J. Quirk, *The Politics of Deregulation* (Washington, D.C.: Brookings, 1985), 238.

22. Walker, "Diffusion of Knowledge," 91.

23. See Bryan D. Jones, ed., *Leadership and Politics: New Perspectives in Political Science* (Lawrence: University of Kansas Press, 1989), especially Jones's introduction, 3–14.

24. Richard E. Neustadt, foreword to *Leadership and Innovation: Entrepreneurs in Government*, ed. Jameson W. Doig and Erwin C. Hargrove (Baltimore: Johns Hopkins University Press, 1990), ix.

25. Mark A. Peterson, "Leading Our Way to Health: Entrepreneurship and Leadership in the Health Care Reform Debate," Center for American Political Studies Occasional Paper 92-6, Harvard University, August 1992, 21.

26. Michael D. Cohen, James G. March, and Johan P. Olsen, "A Garbage Can Model of Organizational Choice," *Administrative Science Quarterly* 17 (March 1972): 1–25.

27. Kingdon, *Agendas, Alternatives, and Public Policies*, 129. For an entertaining account of the rise of policy entrepreneurship in the post-Watergate Congress, see Burdett Loomis, *The New American Politician: Ambition, Entrepreneurship, and the Changing Face of Political Life* (New York: Basic Books, 1988).

28. William H. Riker, *The Art of Political Manipulation* (New Haven: Yale University Press, 1986), 34.

29. Frank R. Baumgartner, *Conflict and Rhetoric in French Policymaking* (Pittsburgh: University of Pittsburgh Press, 1989).

30. Frank R. Baumgartner and Bryan D. Jones, *Agendas and Instability in American Politics* (Chicago: University of Chicago Press, 1993), 36.

31. I am indebted to Mark Peterson for clarifying these two types of entrepreneurship, which he calls "policy" and "politics" entrepreneurship, respectively. See "Leading Our Way to Health," 21.

32. Riker, *Art of Political Manipulation*, 34.

33. Lynn Etheredge, interview by author, 6 Aug. 1993.

34. Edmund Faltermayer, "Let's Really Cure the Health System," *Fortune*, 23 Mar. 1992, 46.

35. Kingdon, *Agendas, Alternative, and Public Policies*, 61–64.

36. Fay Lomax Cook, et al., "Media and Agenda Setting: Effects on the Public, Interest Group Leaders, Policy Makers, and Policy," *Public Opinion Quarterly* 47 (1983): 28.

37. Kingdon, *Agendas, Alternatives, and Public Policies*, 62.

38. This is one of the interesting findings of Kingdon, *Agendas, Alternatives, and Public Policies*, 63.

39. See, for instance, Cook, "Media and Agenda Setting," 31–32; Samuel Kernell, *Going Public: New Strategies of Presidential Leadership*, 2d ed. (Washington, D.C.: Congressional Quarterly Press, 1993), 53–88, 231–34; Timothy Cook, *Making Laws and Making News: Media Strategies in the U.S. House of Representatives* (Washington, D.C.: Brookings, 1989); Barbara Sinclair, *The Transformation of the U.S. Senate* (Baltimore: Johns Hopkins University Press, 1989); Stephen Hess, *The Government/Press Connection: Press Officers and their Offices* (Washington, D.C.: Brookings, 1984); and Roderick Hart, *The Sound of Leadership: Presidential Communication in the Modern Age* (Chicago: University of Chicago Press, 1987).

40. Baumgartner and Jones, *Agendas and Instability in American Politics*, 109.

41. Stephen D. Reese and Lucig H. Danielian, "Intermediate Influence and the Drug Issue: Converging on Cocaine," in *Agenda Setting: Readings on Media, Public Opinion, and Policymaking*, ed. David L. Protess and Maxwell McCombs (Hillsdale, N.J.: Lawrence Erlbaum Associates, 1991), 237–50.

42. On "pack journalism," see Timothy Crouse, *The Boys on the Bus* (New York: Ballantine, 1973); and Bernard Roshco, *Newsmaking* (Chicago: University of Chicago Press, 1975). On the agenda-setting power of elite newspapers, see Marjorie Randon Hershey, "The Constructed Explanation: Interpreting Election Results in the 1984 Presidential Race," *Journal of Politics* 54 (1992): 965–66.

43. Senate Staff Member, . . . interview by author, 11 Aug., 1993.

44. Atul Gawande, phone interview by author, 1 Sept. 1993.

45. David Nexon, interview by author, 12 Aug. 1993.

46. Shiela Nix, interview by author, 10 Aug. 1993.

47. House Staff Member 3, interview by author, 10 Aug. 1993.

48. Kingdon, *Agendas, Alternatives, and Public Policies*, 70. For a contrasting view, see Lawrence R. Jacobs, *The Health of Nations: Public Opinion and the Making of American and British Health Policy* (Ithaca: Cornell University Press, 1993).

49. Hugh Heclo touches on some of these points in "Issue Networks and the Executive Establishment," *The New American Political System*, ed. Anthony King (Washington, D.C.: American Enterprise Institute, 1978), 87–124.

50. I. M. Rubinow, "Public and Private Interests in Social Insurance," *American Labor Legislation Review* 21 (1931): 185.

51. Alice M. Rivlin, "Agreed: Here Comes National Health Insurance," *New York Times Magazine*, 21 July 1974, 8, 35, 46–50, 54.

52. Sven Steinmo and Jon Watts, "It's the Institutions, Stupid! Why Comprehensive National Health Insurance Always Fails in America," *Journal of Health Politics, Policy, and Law* 20 (summer 1995): 368.

53. On the centralization of congressional power, see for example Roger H. Davidson, "The New Centralization on Capitol Hill," *Review of Politics* 50 (1988): 345–64; Lawrence C. Dodd and Bruce I. Oppenheimer, *Consolidating Power in the House: The Rise of a New Oligarchy*, 4th ed., ed. Dodd and Oppenheimer (Washington, D.C.: CQ Press, 1989), 39–64; Gary W. Cox and Mathew D. McCubbins, *Legislative Leviathan* (Berkeley: University of California Press, 1993); Keith Krehbiel, *Information and Legislative Organization* (Ann

Arbor: University of Michigan Press, 1991; and David W. Rohde, *Parties and Leaders in the Postreform House* (Chicago: University of Chicago Press, 1991).

54. On "veto points," see Ellen M. Immergut, "Institutions, Veto Points, and Policy Results: A Comparative Analysis of Health Care," *Journal of Public Policy* 10 (October–December 1990): 391–416.

55. The term is Theda Skocpol's, but I use it somewhat more broadly here. As Skocpol employs the term, institutional *fit* is the degree to which the structure of organized groups meshes with the opportunities for political access and leverage that are afforded by government institutions. This is one important aspect of institutional fit, but not the only one. Another important aspect, as I suggest here, is the fit between political institutions and the *strategies* of political actors. Skocpol, *Protecting Soldiers and Mothers*, 54–57.

56. In the Senate, Majority Leader George Mitchell sponsored the Clinton bill. It originally had thirty Senate cosponsors (all but one of whom were Democrats) but later lost a cosponsor. In the House, the bill had 103 cosponsors, all Democrats.

57. David W. Brady and Kara M. Buckley, "Health Care Reform in the 103rd Congress: A Predictable Failure," *Journal of Health Politics, Policy, and Law* 20 (summer 1995): 447–54.

58. William Kristol, "Defeating President Clinton's Health Care Proposal" (Project for the Republican Future, Washington, D.C., 2 Dec. 1993, typescript), 1.

59. Quoted in James A. Morone, "Nativism, Hollow Corporations, and Managed Competition: Why the Clinton Health Care Reform Failed," *Journal of Health Politics, Policy, and Law* 20 (summer 1995): 392.

60. Brady and Buckley, "Health Reform in the 103rd Congress," 449n.

61. Of course, whether legislators will be punished by their constituents for their action (or inaction) on an issue depends not only on whether their constituents care about that issue, but also on whether their constituents assign credit (or blame) specifically to them. The ability of constituents to do the latter hinges upon what R. Douglas Arnold calls the "traceability" of congressional action, as well as upon the presence of electoral challengers who might draw attention to an incumbent's pleasing or displeasing action (or inaction). R. Douglas Arnold, *The Logic of Congressional Action* (New Haven: Yale University Press, 1990).

62. The phrase is used by David R. Mayhew to describe congressional "position taking," in *Congress: The Electoral Connection* (New Haven, Conn.: Yale University Press, 1974), 62.

63. Theda Skocpol, "The Rise and Resounding Demise of the Clinton Health Security Plan," in *The Problem That Won't Go Away: Reforming U.S. Health Care Financing*, ed. Henry J. Aaron (Washington, D.C.: Brookings, 1996), 51–52.

64. Linda Bergthold, phone interview by author, 6 Dec. 1994.

65. Majone, *Evidence, Argumentation, and Persuasion*, 33.

66. A good recent example of political science hand-wringing over government capacity is John E. Chubb and Paul E. Peterson, eds., *Can the Government Govern?* (Washington, D.C.: Brookings, 1989).

67. Baumgartner and Jones, *Agendas and Instability in American Politics*, 235.

68. Polsby, *Political Innovation in America*, 161.

69. David Vogel, "Representing Diffuse Interests in Environmental Policy-making," in *Do Institutions Matter*, ed. R. Kent Weaver and Bert A. Rockman (Washington, D.C.: Brookings, 1993), 237–71.

70. Peter Marris and Martin Rein, *Dilemmas of Social Reform* (Chicago: Aldine, 1973), 7.

71. Morone, *The Democratic Wish*, 23–24.

72. On American administrative capacity (or incapacity, as the case may be), see Terry M. Moe, "The Politics of Bureaucratic Structure," in *Can the Government Govern*, ed. John E. Chubb and Paul E. Peterson (Washington, D.C.: Brookings, 1989), 267–329.

Appendix A

1. The lawsuit was brought by two small groups of conservative physicians—the American Association of Physicians and Surgeons and the American Council for Health Care Reform—along with the National Legal Policy Center. They charged that the secrecy of the task force violated federal open-meeting laws. The White House was not forced to release the records by the lawsuit, but chose to waive the protections provided the records of incumbent presidents in the hope of settling the case.

employer-sponsored health insurance
(*cont.*)
financed health insurance vs., 52, 85,
91–92, 96. *See also* business; employer
mandate; health insurance; managed-
care plans
Energy and Commerce Committee, House,
196n.57; Subcommittee on Health and
the Environment, 196n.57
England, Mary Jane, 54, 55, 70
Enthoven, Alain, 4, 42, 47, 50, 51–53, 56–
63, 65, 70, 71, 73, 74, 75, 76, 91, 92,
98, 105, 156, 158, 161, 205n.80
entrepreneurs, policy, 160–62, 170. *See
also* leadership
Etheredge, Lynn, 53–54, 55, 56–63, 67,
70, 76, 109, 119, 120, 155, 163

Fair Deal, 80, 181
Fallows, James, 145
Families USA, 102
Feder, Judy, 103, 106, 109, 112–13, 119
federal deficit (U.S.): Clinton presidency
and, 117, 126, 130, 173; public health
care spending and, 27, 85, 126,
196n.48. *See also* budget
Federal Employees Health Benefits Program (FEHBP), 47, 98
federal government: business mistrust of,
136; fragmentation of, 172–73, 180;
health bureaucracy in, 79–80; health
care reform issues and, 17–18, 20; history of health care policies of, 77–81;
impact of ideas on, 155–60; influence
of leadership on, 160–62; influence of
vested interests on, 153–55; pro-competitive regulation and, 55; public distrust
of, 43–44, 86, 117, 216n.1; structural
limits of, 180–82. *See also* Congress
fee-for-service health insurance plans, 52,
87, 88, 96, 113, 128, 149, 162
FEHBP. *See* Federal Employees Health
Benefits Program
Feldstein, Martin, 44, 45
filibusters: of Clinton legislation, 130–31;
regional malapportionment of Senate
and, 181; as a barrier to passage of Clinton's reform proposal, 116, 117, 130,
173, 174
Finance Committee, Senate, 40; Subcommittee on Medicare and Long-Term
care, 196n.57

fixed-contribution approach, 51, 52,
57, 62, 97, 114. *See also* managed
competition
Fleming, Scott, 47
Florio, Jim, 113
focusing events, 31, 164, 170
foreign health care systems, 83–84,
208n.19, 208n.21, 208n.22
Fortune, 163
Frankel, Max, 64
Fried, Bruce, 103, 108, 109
Friedman, Milton, 44, 46

"gang of five," in health insurance industry, 53, 59
Garamendi, John, 91, 97, 104, 115
Garamendi plan, 90–95, 104, 108, 111,
113, 166
Gawande, Atul, 69, 104, 106, 108, 109–
11, 112, 115, 119, 167
Gephardt, Richard, 149
Germany, health care system of: all-payer
system in, 83; origins of, 86; rationale
of, 83, 208n.22
global budgeting: Clinton plan and, 109,
111, 114, 115, 132, 139, 150, 167–68,
174; explained, 84; in foreign health
care systems, 83–84; liberal synthesis
and, 88–89, 92, 96, 165–66
Goldbeck, Willis, 54
Gore, Al, 144
government. *See* federal government
Gramm, Phil, 38
Great Society, 44, 181
Greenberg, Stan, 102, 104, 138

Harper's, 16
"Harry and Louise" advertisements. *See*
Health Insurance Association of
America
Havighurst, Clark, 46
Health Affairs, 121
Health Alliances. *See* health insurance pur-
chasing cooperatives
Health America, 23–24, 101
Health Care Financing Administration,
27
health care reform: Bush's proposal for,
71–72; Clinton's presidential campaign
and, 100–116; Clinton's proposal for,
113–15, 124–29, 149–51, 167–68; Clin-
ton's task force for, 122–29; congres-